MEN ARE NOT

COST-EFFECTIVE

Male Crime in America

JUNE STEPHENSON, Ph.D.

HarperPerennial

A Division of HarperCollinsPublishers

Dedicated to the victims of crime

This is a revised edition of a book published by Diemer, Smith Publishing Company in 1991. It is reprinted here by arrangement with Diemer, Smith Publishing Company.

MEN ARE NOT COST-EFFECTIVE. Copyright © 1991, 1995 by June Stephenson. All rights reserved. Printed in the United States of America. No part of this book may be used or reproduced in any manner whatsoever without written permission except in the case of brief quotations embodied in critical articles and reviews. For information address HarperCollins Publishers, Inc., 10 East 53rd Street, New York, NY 10022.

HarperCollins books may be purchased for educational, business, or sales promotional use. For information, please write: Special Markets Department, HarperCollins Publishers, Inc., 10 East 53rd Street, New York, NY 10022.

First HarperPerennial edition published 1995.

Designed by Alma Hochhauser Orenstein

Library of Congress Cataloging-in-Publication Data

Stephenson, June.
   Men are not cost-effective / June Stephenson. — 1st ed.
      p. cm.
   Originally published: Napa, Calif. : Diemer, Smith Pub. Co., c 1991
   ISBN 0-06-095098-6
   1. Crime—United States. 2. Men—United States—Social conditions. 3. Violent crimes—United States. I. Title.
HV6791.S84 1995
364.3'73'0973—dc20   94-46397

95 96 97 98 99 ❖/RRD 10 9 8 7 6 5 4 3 2

ACKNOWLEDGMENTS

I gratefully acknowledge suggestions, proofreading, and encouragement from friends Katherine Smith, Margaret Paul, Evelyn Smith, Maureen Daly, June and Paul Charry, and Nancy Sellers. Thanks to my research assistant, Nancy Brennan, and to Garry Carter for his computer assistance. I extend loving appreciation to my husband for his great patience and consistent faith in my work.

I also gratefully acknowledge permission to reprint from:

Russell Mokhiber, *Corporate Crime and Violence: Big Business Power and the Abuse of the Public Trust* (San Francisco: Sierra Books, 1989).

Excerpts from Gina Allen, Annie Laurie Gaylor, Sol Gordon, Lester Kirkendall, and Cleo Kocol, "Pornography: A Humanist Issue," *The Humanist* (July/August 1985).

The information in the first sixteen chapters of this book is based primarily on crime reports from newspapers. Attribution has been given in the text to the various publications for the multitude of short quotes. I hope news publishers will accept attribution in lieu of permission in this case. If, however, there are quotations for which a fee is warranted, I am willing to pay the reasonable amount.

June Stephenson

CONTENTS

INTRODUCTION

Who's Causing All This Crime?

It's no secret that the police in this country are understaffed and overworked. In many cities there is a "forget it" approach toward certain categories of theft or fraud if the amounts stolen are minimal or suspects cannot be identified. Because of the high volume of crime, often the most a police department can do is a quick write-up, not an investigation.

In large cities, police are taking longer and longer to respond to calls for help for property crimes. They simply have too many calls for help, and property crimes are considered lesser crimes. The criminal justice system is overloaded and, because of this, criminals are profiting. When convicted, criminals rarely serve out their terms because of prison overcrowding.

Though the FBI reported in May 1994 that crime overall went down 3 percent in 1993, the murder rate went up 3 percent. The California attorney general's office reported that crime was down in major offenses by 2.7 percent, except for homicide, which went up 4.5 percent in the state and as much as 10 percent in San Francisco. Seventy percent of victims knew their killers, and 62 percent of these killers used guns.

It is the changing style of violence that engenders fear in this country. Aggravated assault is down—which may simply mean that instead of beating up someone, the offender simply pulls out a gun and shoots.

Parole officers whose caseloads are impossibly high cannot see all of their parolees. If they did, their time would be limited to a few minutes per parolee per month. Even if a parolee is arrested for a parole violation, he seldom spends much time in prison. Three months or less is the usual sentence for the majority of parolees who are rearrested, according to a series of articles published in February 1993 in the *Los Angeles Times* on the criminal justice system in Los Angeles County. As Germane Di Maggio, the Los Angeles area state parole administrator, said, "You'd have to just about commit murder to get a year on a parole violation."

The more crime there is, the less punishment and the more plea bargaining, because the courts are overloaded. Often, crimes that come into the police station as felonies, for which years in prison should be served, end up after plea bargaining in court as misdemeanors with a few months in prison.

But who do the police investigate if the identities of the perpetrators of a crime are unknown? Almost always they would be investigating young men. Thirty-one percent of the people arrested and sent to prison are men between the ages of eighteen and twenty-four, and another 45 percent are men aged twenty-five to forty-four. Ninety-four percent of prisoners are males. Whether it is robbery, burglary, arson, white-collar crime, crime against children, crime against women, drug dealing, drunk driving, murder, crime in government, treason, or gang violence, crime is a masculine statement. Criminologist Marvin Wolfgang from the University of Pennsylvania says that violent crime rises anytime there is an unusually high proportion of the population of young men between the ages of fifteen to twenty-four.

Ten years ago there were approximately 200,000 people in prison in this country. Today there are approximately one million behind bars, a number exceeded only during the Hitler and Stalin periods, at a combined annual cost for federal, state, and local budgets of $61 billion. The United States incarcerates more people than any other country, including South Africa and the Soviet Union, according to the Sentencing Project, a nonprofit organization studying sentencing and offering alternatives to incarceration. If one includes those who are on parole or probation, the number rises to 3.4 million, almost all of whom are men.

For many, crime is a full-time job. In Florida's Dade County alone, there are 1,800 career criminals known to the police, and in New York City there are over 57,000 career criminals known to the police. In virtually all cases, career criminals are male. Some police officers do nothing more than keep track of career criminals in their cities. One such criminal in Albuquerque, New Mexico, committed eighty armed robberies. As the police say, crime is an action of choice. Deliberately and calculatingly, career criminals rob, abduct, and rape. It is not only for the pursuit of excitement but because, for these men, crime does pay.

When a Rand Corporation study revealed that 10 percent of the criminals in California committed 60 percent of all violent crime, a career criminal division was set up to prosecute chronic offenders. The problem is that there are too many to prosecute. When Peter German, who heads the division, was interviewed for the *Los Angeles Times* articles, he lamented that because of the overload "we take only the biggest armed robbers and a handful of burglars. . . . The reality is, we're missing the guys who are preying on this community." He went on to say that of the ninety or so burglary and robbery cases that come before the courts in Los Angeles County, more than half involve repeat offenders. There are not enough attorneys to prosecute.

First-Time Offenders Arrested for Violent Crimes, 1991	
Offenders	Percentage
Male	93%
Female	7%
White	53%
Black	43%
Other races	4%
Median age	23

Prisons

There were three times as many prisoners in the United States in 1993 as there were in 1980, according to a report by the Justice Department issued June 1, 1994. Approximately one half of the new prisoners were incarcerated because of the "war on drugs," which mandates lengthy prison terms for drug offenses.

In addition nearly 50,000 entered prison in 1992 for sexual assault, aggravated assault, robbery, and burglary. In 1992 California had the largest prison population (119,951). The next highest state prison populations were Texas (71,103) and New York (64,569).

The state of California may need twenty new prisons by the year 2000, since the California Department of Corrections estimates the prison population may grow more than 63 percent in the next five years. During the eight years of Governor Deukmejian's terms in California, prison costs rose 160 percent. California outpaced all other states in growth in state and federal prison population in the 1980s, the number increasing by 263 percent. The national average in the 1980s was a 113 percent increase.

In ten years, prison population has doubled and yet violent crime rises. The excessive financial burden on states for correctional activities necessitates lower spending on education, libraries, and health care.

In virtually every part of the country, prisoners fill state and federal correctional facilities beyond 100 percent capacity. Michigan leads the other states with nineteen new prisons under construction and another seven in the planning stage.

Parole

Probation officers have so many parolees to monitor that they often have to cut their caseloads and leave many without supervision. In Los Angeles County as of February 1993, 3,300 probation officers were monitoring 90,000 adult ex-convicts. In addition there were 21,000 juveniles on probation with limited numbers of officers and reduced budgets. With the paucity of parole officers that exists, communities must virtually surrender to the criminals.

Probation's heavy caseloads arise out of huge prison populations. Probation is cheaper than jails, costing about $5,000 a year per person compared to $20,000 to $40,000 for prison incarceration. Studying a "matched sample" of criminals who had committed similar crimes, with one group given probation and one group sent to prison, the Rand Corporation found that those sent to prison had a higher recidivism rate than those on probation.

There is a fear in many communities that overcrowded state prisons mean that criminals must be released before they have served their time in order to make room for the new criminals. But releasing nonviolent prisoners early does not mean they will necessarily commit new crimes. A study of groups of prisoners released early compared with groups that served their full time revealed that whether or not they served their full sentence made an insignificant difference in whether or not they committed a new crime.

In the "get tough" policies of keeping prisoners incarcerated for the full length of their sentences, several states are looking at the costs of eliminating the parole system altogether. Although politically popular, eliminating paroles would be prohibitively expensive. In Texas, it was estimated by the parole board chairman James Grabber that it would cost taxpayers $6.5 billion a year to retain inmates who could otherwise be paroled. Also, as inmates grow older they require more medical attention, and so they are increasingly costly.

Private Prisons

With prisons as a growth industry, private investors are moving into the business of building prisons. Many states are under court order to end prison overcrowding, yet these states do not have enough money to build prisons. The enterprising developer fills this need even as justice systems around the country argue about the advisability of privately owned prisons, which are built to incarcerate prisoners for a profit. Four private prisons were opened in Texas in the summer of 1989, one is under construction in New Mexico, and one is in operation in Kentucky.

The question of whether to privatize prisons seems to come down to whether private prisons can do a good job and do it cheaper than public prisons. When Samuel Brake, a former project director at the American Bar Association, examined one private prison in Chattanooga, Tennessee, he reported that in more than half the categories he checked, the prison was better than a public prison and in no case was it worse. The reason that private prisons can operate less expensively is because they don't have to endure the red tape. Yet opponents say it is the red tape that ensures prisoners' rights.

A comparison of costs is pertinent. The following chart comes from the Center for Studies in Criminology and Law at the University of Florida.

Private v. Public Prison Costs Per Day		
	Government	Private
Beattyville, Ky.	$32.00	$26.89
St. Mary's, Ky.	28.00	26.89
Grants, N.M.	80.00	69.75
Winnfield, La.	29.50	26.00
Cleveland, Tx.	42.53	35.25
Venus, Tx.	42.53	35.25
Kyle, Tx.	42.53	34.79

Throughout the United States, spending for prison construction is the top state priority for the sixth year in a row. According to the Justice Department, prison inmate population in 1988 had grown 7.4 percent over that of the previous year, a growth rate mostly related to illegal drug activities.

One prison cell costs $100,000 without considering the interest to be paid on bonds raised for prison construction. Keeping a person in prison for a year costs from $20,000 to $24,000; maximum-security prisons cost from $30,000 to $35,000. Approximately 50,000 new prisoners are added to the total prison population each year. In California, $1 million a day is spent on interest for prison bonds.

In 1989 it was noted by then U.S. Department of Justice Acting Director Joseph Bessette that nearly 63 percent of inmates released from state prisons are rearrested for a serious crime in three years. Rapists who are released are ten times more likely than other offenders to be arrested again for the same offense, and former murderers are about five times more likely than others to be charged once again with a killing. Reconvictions, known as *recidivism*, are higher for men than for women, often because women have children they do not want to be separated from.

Of the first-timers in state prisons, 73 percent of the males are charged with committing violent crimes, compared with 7 percent of the females. Of those who had prior violent crime convictions, 98 percent of the males are returned to jail for committing another violent crime after being released, compared with 2 percent of the females.

Of those in federal prison, 84 percent were male, 16 percent female.

Persons Arrested in the United States, 1991		
	Male	Female
Forcible rape	99%	1%
Weapons (carrying, etc.)	93%	7%
Burglary	91%	9%
Robbery	91%	9%
Other sex offenses	93%	7%
Motor vehicle theft	90%	10%
Drunkenness	90%	10%
Vandalism	89%	11%
Stolen property (possession)	88%	12%
Driving intoxicated	87%	13%
Vagrancy	89%	11%
Murder, manslaughter	90%	10%
Aggravated assault	86%	14%
Arson	87%	13%
Drug abuse violations	84%	16%
Other assaults	84%	16%
Offenses against family	82%	18%
Liquor laws	81%	19%
Gambling	87%	13%
Disorderly conduct	80%	20%
Curfew loitering	73%	27%
Larceny-Theft	68%	32%
Forgery	65%	35%
Embezzlement	61%	39%
Fraud	57%	43%
Runaways (juveniles)	43%	57%
Prostitution	31%	69%

U.S. Department of Justice Bureau of Statistics

Do higher incarceration rates mean lower crime rates? There seems to be little connection. For instance, in Louisiana the average prison sentence for armed robbery is about seventeen years, which is just about twice the national average. Even so, Louisiana has one of the highest rates in this country for armed robbery.

Characteristics of State Prison Inmates: 1991	
Male	94%
Female	5%
White	49%
Black	47%
Hispanic	14%
Other races	4%
Never married	55%
Married	18%
Widowed	2%
Divorced	19%
Separated	6%
Less than 12 yrs. of school	41%
12 yrs. or more of school	59%
Pre-arrest employed	69%
Under 18	1%
18–24	21%
25–34	46%
35–44	23%
45–54	7%
55–64	2%
65 & older	1%

While it is questionable whether incarceration deters crime, there is little question that incarceration does not rehabilitate. What incarceration does is get criminals off the street for a period of time. When they are returned to society many return to crime. In the meantime, the get-tough policy of imposing longer sentences has come to mean that more prisoners are released early because of prison overcrowding. From 1965 to 1985, though judges quadrupled prison sentences, the actual time prisoners served remained about the same. In California it is estimated that roughly two-thirds of the bulging prison population are repeat offenders. It appears that putting people in prison may do other things, but it does not decrease the crime rate.

In the United States over the past four years $25 billion has been spent on prison construction. California in 1993 had twenty-six prisons, which employed 31,000 people and cost $2.7 billion. The state had 113,000 inmates (in 1977 there were 19,000), 88 percent above capacity. As more than 60 percent of California's inmates are nonviolent, according to the National Council on Crime and Delinquency in San Francisco, these criminals could possibly serve their time under alternative sentencing programs, thereby curtailing expense and alleviating prison overcrowding.

Are there programs to rehabilitate in prison? Very few. And political conservatives object to what exists, referring to rehab programs as "coddling." Many prisoners who did not graduate from high school are given the opportunity to earn their high school equivalency certificate, which is aimed at helping them find employment when they are released. Some inmates with long sentences enroll in correspondence courses from universities and earn college degrees. There is a lower rate of recidivism for prisoners who have taken college courses in prison.

Other so-called "coddling" refers to conjugal visits, which opponents refer to as "sex at taxpayers' expense." Yet prisoners who are allowed to maintain contact with their families are able to leave prison more ready to be accepted back into society and less ready to commit crimes that sent them to prison in the first place. And rewards for good behavior, such as conjugal visits, serve to make prisons more manageable.

Those who criticize what is done for prisoners are apt to forget that most will be returned to society. In the anticrime fervor, politicians respond to the fears of their constituents. "Lock 'em up and throw away the key" is the public outcry, supported by prison guards' unions and crime victims' organizations. If inmates' rights are taken away by politicians, they will probably be restored by the courts protecting inmates' constitutional rights.

How prisoners emerge will depend on whether they were warehoused and brutalized and returned to the dangerous world they came from unchanged or whether they were treated as human beings and offered opportunities to improve themselves. If not the latter, in a few years there will be millions of angry, uneducated, unskilled professional convicts—men ready to cause more disturbance and mayhem in this country than we can imagine.

Alternative Punishment

With prison overcrowding, largely as a result of the huge number of drug offenses and mandatory sentences that make it impossible to parole many prisoners, other methods of punishment to relieve overcrowding and cut costs have evolved. In 1989 there were 1,247,000 drug arrests in the United States, compared to 471,000 in 1980, as reported by the Washington, D.C., Sentencing Project. Of all inmates in federal prison now, over 50 percent are drug offenders, but that figure will be 75 percent by 1995. Prisons cannot be built fast enough, especially now with the Three Strikes laws that have been passed in several states. As a consequence, other means of punishment will become more important for handling convicted criminals.

Some new programs for nonviolent criminals include electronically monitored home detention, in use in California, Kentucky, Florida, Oregon, Delaware, and Utah. These programs allow the prisoner to go to work or look for jobs during a period that is often as long as a prison sentence would be. An ankle bracelet lets the authorities know where the prisoner is at all times. The cost for these new programs is approximately $1,700 per year, compared with approximately $20,000 a year for prison detention. House arrests, with or without electronic equipment, have proved successful. In several counties in California—San Diego, Contra Costa, Santa Clara, San Mateo, and San Francisco—criminals under house arrest are rearrested at a rate of less than 10 percent, whereas criminals who serve out their time in jail are rearrested at a rate of 66 percent.

A University of California study recorded that nonviolent prisoners who worked in community service for the time they would have been in prison were no more likely to return to prison than those who had actually been imprisoned. The two-year study of 930 federal prisoners showed that 35 percent of felons return to prison after release whether or not they have actually been incarcerated. As Malcolm Feeley, at Boalt Hall School of Law at Berkeley, director of the Guggenheim criminal justice program said, the results of this study should lay to rest the charge that community service is too easy on nonviolent criminals. Community service, he said, would alleviate overcrowding in prison and reduce prison costs. The monthly cost to supervise a community service felon is $97.66 compared with $1,415 for imprisonment.

Boot Camps

Boot camps, so-called because of their military approach to incarceration, are referred to as "shock incarcerations." Boot camp is an alternative given to young, nonviolent offenders. Generally their options are to go to jail and serve a full sentence or go to boot camp, and serve sixty to ninety days. If the men survive the rigorous training they are released into probation for years.

In boot camp inmates learn discipline, teamwork, and can increase their self-esteem. By January 1993, 21,000 men had been through these camps, but it is too early to assess their value. They do, to a small degree, decrease prison overcrowding. About one-fourth drop out of the program and elect to finish their sentence in prison.

Twenty-seven states and the federal government now send some first-time offenders to boot camps, where prisoners rise at five each morning and endure a vigorous regime of soldier-like training, in which they are often subjected to verbal abuse. This kind of incarceration is relatively inexpensive for the state compared with traditional incarceration, but the rate of recidivism is only slightly less than for the traditionally incarcerated prisoner. In Georgia, for instance, 34 percent of released boot camp prisoners were picked up for subsequent crimes, compared with a re-arrest rate of 38 percent of ex-convicts from traditional prisons.

In states where these camps are male only, as in Virginia, a federal magistrate ruled that the camp was unconstitutional because it gives men an opportunity for a shorter sentence than women would receive for an identical crime, such as possessing cocaine with intent to sell. All but 8 percent of the twenty-eight states' camps exclude women.

The Three Strikes Law

In this country's great fear of violent crime, politicians rush to seek solutions and to ease public anxiety. One remedy, which has been adopted by some states, is the Three Strikes legislation. Adapting baseball terminology—"three strikes and you're out," the law will put people in prison for twenty-five years to life, without possibility of parole, after a third conviction if previous convictions were for felony crimes.

The Three Strikes law in California, signed into law May 7, 1994, will necessitate building twenty more prisons by the year 2000 for 109,000 more inmates. This does not take into consideration the $2 billion additional annual cost of operating the prisons. The first two offenses must be "violent" or "serious" to qualify, but the third need not be violent—it could be petty theft. Fearful that legislators might weaken the Three Strikes law, voters approved an initiative on November 8, 1994, that restates the law, limiting plea bargaining and curtailing judges' rights to sentence convicted criminals to probation, indirectly guaranteeing that thousands of felons will spend 80 percent of their sentence in prison. In California, laws evolving from initiatives cannot be changed by legislators. The Three Strikes law prompted a witness in San Francisco to refuse to testify against a man who had broken into her car because that felony would have been the man's third and would have put him in jail for at least twenty-five years.

Steven Gordon, thirty-five, who became a drug addict after years of being the ordinary citizen, playing high school varsity football then working for six years in a food processing plant in Vacaville, was arrested for robbing a bicyclist of his wallet, which contained $100. At that point in his life Gordon became eligible for California's Three Strikes sentencing because he had previously been convicted of stealing $200 from Kentucky Fried Chicken and of grabbing a woman's purse. No weapons were used in his crimes.

The public defender argued that Gordon had never served time in state prison and, except for knocking down the bicyclist from whom he robbed the wallet, he had not been violent. The governor's press secretary (speaking for Governor Wilson, who supports the Three Strikes law), however, said that Gordon is a repeat criminal with little chance of reforming. Chances are the press secretary is right if treatment for drug addicts remains as limited as it is.

A man who robbed $154 from a sandwich shop in Seattle, Washington, was sentenced to life in prison June 20, 1994, under that state's Three Strikes law. There were no injuries in that robbery. Larry Fisher, thirty-five, had been convicted twice previously, once for stealing $390 from his grandfather in 1988, and once for stealing $100 in 1986 from a pizza parlor.

The United States Supreme Court ruled on May 23, 1994, that defendants in federal trials will not have the right to question old convictions that would count as strikes, i.e., even if he may have new evidence, a defendant cannot question a ruling in a previous sentence. The reason for this decision was "ease of administration." Opponents of this decision claim a defendant may be sentenced to life in prison because of previous convictions that were possibly unconstitutional.

The Three Strikes law may put thousands of check-bouncers or petty thieves and others in jail for life at great taxpayer expense. As men age, their health needs increase. Geriatric prisoners cost about $60,000 a year. When men need operations many are treated at private hospitals and then returned to prison. There are now sections of prisons that are more like convalescent homes filled with wheelchairs and walkers. All medicines, operations, and nursing care are provided by the state. In the years to come these "old men's wards" will multiply with the implementation of the Three Strikes law.

States will be better served by releasing low-risk men— except for sex-offenders and those convicted of violent crimes such as murder—as they approach their elder years and become expensive inmates, rather than housing them for life. After a man turns forty-five he is less likely to be a threat to society. Persons in their forties and fifties, according to the Correctional Health Care Studies, are less violent, less impetuous. The FBI statistics on aging predict the odds on who will return to prison, with those eighteen to twenty-four years old having a 22 percent chance of return and those over fifty years old, only 2 percent.

Because prisons can't be built fast enough to take care of the new wave of "lifers," violent younger prisoners will be released to make room for those aging men who, by the Three Strikes law, cannot be released.

In Seattle, Washington, in May 1994, Paul Rivers stole a bag of money with $337 from an operator of an espresso stand. Because he had two robbery convictions behind him, this third conviction put him in prison for life. Paul Rivers is twenty-nine years old. If he lives to be seventy-five his incarceration will cost the state of Washington $1,150,000 plus medical expenses (it costs $25,000 a year to house a prisoner in Washington state).

There is an effort to change the Three Strikes laws. Two Strikes would apply to child molesters, and, for others, only the most violent criminals would be candidates for Three Strikes.

Blacks in Prison

The perception is that most prisoners in this country are black, but that is not the case. Most prisoners are white. But within the total black population, a larger percentage is imprisoned than is imprisoned within the white population. Blacks comprise only about 12 percent of the nation's population and make up 46 percent of the total prison population. In 1990, according to the Sentencing Project in Washington, D.C., 23 percent of black men between twenty and twenty-nine were under court supervision. That percentage represents 607,000 men. During 1986, 436,000 black men of all ages were enrolled in college.

Whites commit crimes and blacks commit crimes, but according to a report written by criminologist Donald Taft in 1956 and not disputed today: "Negroes are more likely to be suspected of crime than are whites. They are also more likely to be arrested. If the perpetrator of a crime is known to be a Negro, the police may arrest all Negroes who were near the scene—a procedure they would rarely dare to follow with whites. After arrest, Negroes are less likely to secure bail, and so are more liable to be counted in jail statistics. They are more liable than whites to be indicted and less likely to have their cases nol prossed [abandoned] or otherwise dismissed. If tried, Negroes are more likely to be convicted. If convicted, they are less likely to be given probation. For this reason they are more likely to be included in the count of prisoners. Negroes are also more liable than whites to be kept in prison for the full terms of their commitments and correspondingly less likely to be paroled."

The total cost of incarcerating one million prisoners in this

country is about $16 billion annually, according to the Sentenc-
ing Project. The cost of incarcerating approximately 450,000
blacks is $7 billion a year. The Sentencing Project also states
that though there has not been a great increase in the crime
rate over the past ten years there has been a great increase in
the rate of incarceration, especially for blacks. This is the result
of harsher sentencing and the drug war. "Although the crime
rate has dropped by 3.5 percent since 1980, the prison population has doubled in that period." In Michigan, for example,
drug arrests for blacks have tripled since 1985, though the
overall rise in drug arrests only doubled.

The National Center of Institutions and Alternatives
reported in November 1990 that one-third of black males
between twenty and twenty-nine years of age in California are
under the criminal justice system—that is, either in jail, on probation, or on parole. Though the report says 80 percent of drug
usage occurs in white communities, 80 percent of drug busts
occur in black communities. As Steven Whitman of Northwestern University's Center for Urban Affairs and Policy Research
says, "Incredibly, blacks in the United States go to prison more
often than blacks in South Africa." A public health expert in
Atlanta, Georgia, says that for all races, "poverty is a more
important factor than race. If you control socioeconomic status,
the homicide rate is the same for blacks and whites."

States with large nonwhite populations have large prison
populations, even those with low crime rates. Social scientist
William Nagel, who studied this prison phenomenon, noted,
"There is no significant correlation between a state's racial
composition and its crime rate, but there is a very great positive relationship between its racial composition and its incarceration rate."

Reverend Floyd Rose, a former president of the Toledo
chapter of the NAACP, expressed concern for blacks. Quoted
by Robert Staples in his book, *Black Scholar*, Rose says, "When
they get to high school age, they are not in school, and they are

not in jobs—they are on the streets. By the year 2000, it is estimated that 70 percent of all black men will be in jail, dead or on drugs, or in the throes of alcoholism."

Women in Prison

With the increase in drug offenses, the population of women in prison is rising. Only about one-fourth were employed at the time of their arrest. Most women are imprisoned for nonviolent crimes, most are black, and more than 80 percent are mothers of small children. Although blacks in the country make up about 12 percent of the population, black females represent 43 percent of the women in the nation's federal prisons, according to the U.S. Bureau of Justice Statistics. The Bureau notes that "most black women are incarcerated because of relatively minor crimes committed to make ends meet, such as check forgery or petty theft."

Prison statistics changed from 1981, when 4.2 percent of prisoners in this country were female, to 1991, when 6 percent were female, an increase attributed to rising drug offenses. If incarceration is not for actual drug use, it is generally for theft and prostitution to support addiction. The warden at the women's prison in New York's Rikers Island estimates that 95 percent of the women there are imprisoned as the result of drug offenses.

While more than 80 percent of women prisoners are mothers with custody of their children, only 60 percent of male prisoners are fathers. Of those women who are mothers, few get child support from the fathers. The difference in attitude about women and men prisoners, as explained by Allyn Sielaff, New York City's Corrections Commissioner, is that when a woman is imprisoned her husband, boyfriend, or brothers "drop her like a hot potato," whereas sisters, wives, and girlfriends frequently visit the men on visiting days. Also, for many young men, as Kristen Bachler, executive director of The Delinquency Prevention Commission in San Francisco, explains, going to prison is a rite of passage. Quoting from her *San Francisco Chronicle* column of May 29, 1991, "This is not the case for young women. When a woman is arrested she finds she has crossed one of the invisible barriers that define society's attitudes toward women." Another difference is that women inmates are much less violent than their male counterparts.

White Americans are incarcerated at a rate of 114 per 100,000 people, according to Linda Rocawich, in her article "Lock 'em Up," published in *The Progressive* of August 1987. Blacks are incarcerated at a rate of 700 per 100,000 people. If we separate out the women from these figures, women, including whites and minorities, were incarcerated at a rate of 10 per 100,000 in 1977. This figure has been rising since 1977 because of harsher sentencing. Women are going to prison, not so much because they are committing more crimes, but because judges are giving them equal treatment with men. Women are going to prison for crimes for which they used to receive probation.

Nicole Hahn Rafter, a prison historian at Northwestern University, was quoted in *The Progressive* of August 1987 as saying, "Women serve time for relatively minor crimes such as larceny, welfare fraud, prostitution, receiving stolen property and shoplifting. Drug or alcohol abuse is often a complicating factor." The American Correctional Association reports that women's violent crimes are most often murders of husbands or boyfriends who inflicted long-term physical abuse on them. "The nature of their crimes," reports New York state researchers in their issue of *Battered Women and Criminal Justice*, "and the existence of a very low recidivism rate for those who have committed murder and manslaughter provide substantial evidence that these women and others like them are not a danger to society. The wisdom of imprisoning them at all is certainly questionable."

The attitude about women in prison is different than the attitude about men in prison. Women experience great negativism because, as women, they are expected to uphold the virtue of the community. The standards of "womanhood" stereotypically rule against prison for women. When a woman prisoner is released she is often ostracized from her previous friends.

For women who are arrested for nonviolent acts, such as property crimes, prison serves little purpose and punishment, an advisement made by the American Correctional Association. Society could be better served by placing these women in the community under supervision, greatly reducing the tax burden.

One new prison opening in Chowchilla, California, will house 2,000 women and will provide dormitories with four beds in a room with a toilet and shower connecting to a central corridor. Warden Teena Farmon said that since "female inmates have been shown to be less prone to violence than male inmates, the women can live in groups." The design of the prison was conceived so that the women can communicate with each other and with the officers. The warden believes that if inmates are allowed to communicate they are less likely to cause trouble.

The Death Penalty

Currently there are about 2,800 prisoners on death row across the country, and the number is growing by 200 to 250 a year. Of these, 1.5 percent are female.

Expenses for keeping prisoners on death row and for the several appeals that come to court on their behalf amount to approximately $4.5 million per death row inmate, with each appeal costing approximately $1 million and requiring about a year of preparation. As a comparison, it costs from $600,000 to $900,000 to keep an inmate in prison for life, depending on the state where the prison is located.

"Special circumstances" that call for the death penalty are: multiple murder, murder of a police officer, murder during a felony, murder involving torture, or murder while lying in wait. Seven countries, including the United States, permit the execution of children. Nine children under eighteen years of age have been executed since 1985. There are now thirty juveniles on death row.

Prisoners Under Sentence of Death, 1991
(TOTAL 2,482)

Characteristics	Numbers of Inmates
White	1,464
Black	1,018
7 years education or less	173
8 years education	181
9–11 years education	810
12 years education	783
More than 12 years	222
Education unknown	313
Never married	1,073
Married	663
Divorced	746

According to a 1988 study by the American Academy of Child and Adolescent Psychology, of the 7,000 prisoners executed in this century, 139 were proven innocent after their death.

Since the United States Supreme Court permitted states to resume the death penalty, Arkansas was the first state to execute two people on the same day, May 11, 1994.

In 1990, 39 percent of death row inmates were black; 52 percent were white. In 1991, 41 percent were black and 59 percent were white. California taxpayers could save $91 million each year if the death penalty were abolished. There are currently 328 men and 2 women death row inmates in California. The number who could afford private counsel for an appeal is two.

The expense of death penalty cases are the result of the automatic state review, post-conviction hearings, and petitions to the Supreme Court that are routine in capital cases. In New York it was estimated that the average capital trial and first stage of appeals costs taxpayers $2 million. In addition there is the added cost of maintaining a person in maximum security, clemency hearings, and then the execution itself.

Many judges and others in law enforcement oppose the death penalty on the grounds that it takes too much time and too much money away from other areas of law enforcement. And though the execution of a criminal is said to give some final relief to victims' families, there are those who say prolonged appeals cause greater anxiety to the family, by diverting attention from the family and concentrating it on the criminal. Also, although it may be agreed that some crimes deserve the death penalty, most agree that it does not deter crime.

With the passage of the Crime Bill in September 1994, the number of federal offenses for which the death penalty will apply increased from twenty-three to sixty, including genocide, murder of a foreign official, murder for hire, murder by prisoners serving life sentences, murder in the course of kidnapping, hostage taking in the aid of racketeering, and murders committed during "carjacking" or drive-by shootings.

Racial Justice Provisions legislation discussed by some members of Congress specify that a death penalty cannot be used if the defendant can prove that the state where he is being prosecuted has imposed the death penalty more frequently on persons of one race than another and that this frequency cannot be explained by nonracial factors. A February 1990 General Accounting Office report released information that reviewed twenty-eight studies on racial bias since the mid-1970s. In this information, 82 percent of the studies showed that people who murdered whites were more likely to receive the death penalty than those who murdered blacks. In Alabama, blacks have been convicted by all-white juries. In Georgia, a poor black man was represented by a Ku Klux Klan Grand Wizard. In

Florida a judge called witnesses for the defendant "niggers" and referred to the defendant as a "colored boy."

This "racial justice" measure is supported by the American Bar Association, the ACLU, and the NAACP. It is opposed by the U.S. Department of Justice, twenty-three state attorneys general, and others in law enforcement. Opponents of the Racial Justice Provisions claim that it is a sneak attack to end the death penalty. Yet one U.S. senator, Carol Mosley-Braun, referred to the death penalty as the last vestige of apartheid in this country, race being a primary factor, she said, as to whether a person is sentenced to death.

In April 1991, the U. S. Supreme Court ruled that appeals in death penalty cases will be limited. Those on death row who have challenged their convictions in the federal court and had their challenge rejected cannot challenge their convictions a second time through habeas corpus petitions in the federal courts. If new evidence is discovered between the first time a federal court challenge is rejected and the time when another appeal would be made, it would be too late. The argument is that defense attorneys should have discovered the evidence sooner and therefore will not be permitted to present the evidence for a second challenge.

Of the death row inmates who were paroled as a result of the *Furman* v. *Georgia* Supreme Court decision of 1972, which temporarily ruled the death penalty unconstitutional, 80 percent remain free. According to a criminal justice professor at Sam Houston State University, James Marquart, "Murderers very rarely do it again." Recidivism for death row inmates is considerably lower than for other parolees.

A Note from the Author

My interest in this subject began when I realized that in my daily perusal of the newspaper and watching nightly TV news

I noticed that almost all crimes reported were committed by men. While this is probably understood to be true, it has never been brought to the attention of the public, and I think that it should be. We must begin to study this phenomenon. I did not determine right away just how I might do this, but I did begin to clip newspaper articles about crime.

I read a paper almost daily. When I am in Northern California I generally read the *San Francisco Chronicle*, and when I am in Southern California I generally read the *Los Angeles Times*. At the time I conceived this book, some days I did not read a paper and some days, though I read a paper, I did no clipping. Nevertheless, without much effort, it was not long before I had amassed two large boxes of clippings.

Many of the crimes reported here are crimes committed in California. Being the largest state, California does have the highest crime rate, but the crimes cited here are representative of crimes in other states. Out-of-state crimes were also reported in the two California newspapers.

For the most part, the crimes I clipped articles on are those for which men were arrested, indicted, or convicted. Though some of these crimes happened several years ago, new information about them appeared during the time I was clipping articles, and that information is included.

Over time, my interest developed into a study, my intention becoming threefold: to learn to what extent crime is a male phenomenon; to learn *if* crime is almost exclusively male, why that might be so; and to learn what could be done to change a situation in which so many of us live in constant fear and in which so many young men waste their lives in prison.

Surely to the relief of many readers, there are no footnotes in this book. Most statistics are quoted from the National Data Book, a yearly government publication that includes statistics from all government departments. For sources of other information, attribution can be found in the text.

CHAPTER 1

THEY START YOUNG

Just Having Fun, or "Boys will be boys!"

In August 1990 approximately forty youths scaled the wall of an amphitheater in Mountain View, California, and randomly attacked and injured more than thirty people attending a rap concert. Who were these rampaging youths? They were young men, in their late teens and early twenties. When a plain-clothes policeman tried to stop the assault, he was severely beaten by ten of them.

There were no arrests, because by the time uniformed officers arrived, the young men had blended into the crowd. Since no one was singled out for a beating, it was not believed to be a gang action. Lt. Gary Smith of the Mountain View police described the attack in the *San Francisco Chronicle*: "This was very random—basically a bunch of young guys out trying to raise heck. Whoever got in their way they pushed, whoever resisted got hit. These guys just wanted to flex some muscle."

This random attack was similar to one that occurred in the Westwood district of Los Angeles. From 400 to 600 teenage boys rampaged through town, beating up moviegoers and shoppers before police arrived to restore order.

In a "boys will be boys" episode, four boys, aged four to thirteen, killed a retarded child in a Florida playground. When one of the boys started teasing six-year-old Torrence Davis, the other three joined in. Torrence died a day later from a crushed liver, believed to have been caused by a kick from one of his attackers.

Then there is the seemingly less harmful prank of driving around, usually in the middle of the night, and knocking down rural mailboxes with a baseball bat. On one occasion this led to the death of a young man, sixteen-year-old Terence Murphy, who had joined a group of his friends for "mailboxing" or, as others call it, playing "mailbox baseball." In Contra Costa County, California, when an attack on Anthony Fanucchi's mailbox was attempted, he was waiting for the teenagers with a .38-caliber revolver. At 3:30 A.M. on a Saturday night in August 1990, angry because his mailbox had been destroyed several times before, Fanucchi shot into an occupied vehicle. Seven hours later he was arrested.

A "just having fun" episode in New York's Central Park became a highly publicized crime that acquired the name of "wilding." When the rampage ended in the rape and near murder of a jogger, "just having fun" resulted in jail terms for three of the teenagers.

This was all the result of the April 19, 1989, evening when a gang of thirty boys ran through Central Park attacking people. The woman jogger was left in a coma because her skull had been broken in three places, her cheekbone crushed, and her brain damaged. After the "wilding," one of the assailants admitted in a videotaped confession that he had raped the woman. His attorneys claimed that the youth was being prosecuted because he was black and the woman was white. The prosecution claimed that the crime was racist.

A month after that incident, another so-called wilding

occurred. This time about forty youths from Brooklyn got off a train in Manhattan and began attacking people. As the youths ran through the tree-lined streets of Greenwich Village they grabbed at women's breasts and groins and terrorized other pedestrians with straight razors and at least one ice pick. They ripped chains from people's necks. When police rounded up the boys they found that two were only twelve years old. Witnesses identified twelve of the teens, who were then charged with riot and robbery. Police said there seemed to be no racial motive because the victims were black, white, and Hispanic men and women.

Nothing in the newspapers stated specifically that the youths were male. But when reference is made to grabbing breasts and groins or crotches the reader assumes the attackers are male. When the word *youth* is used in a news report, it refers to males. If girls are included, it will be stated. Otherwise, youthful crime is male crime. When a news report refers to *juveniles* involved in carjackings, it is also assumed the reference is to young males.

Shootings on school grounds hardly faze students anymore. According to Police Chief Isaac Fulwood in Washington, D.C., known as the murder capital of the world, the continual violence on TV, the lack of moral upbringing, and easy access to guns is at fault. He says there is no remorse after a shooting by a youngster—"not the first tear. There's no sense that there's anything wrong."

With the sale of guns in California alone numbering 5,000 a month, the injuries and killings will only increase. Fifteen-year-old Cordell Robb might have been looking for something to do when he walked into a Lora High School drama class in Anaheim in 1989 with a shotgun and a pistol and ordered the teacher to leave the room. Because it was a drama class, the thirty-five students at first thought the action was a joke, until one of the students was shot. Eventually the police negotiated with Robb to surrender.

In another case, seventeen-year-old Dustin Pierce armed himself with a shotgun, a .357 Magnum, and an automatic pistol and held eleven students hostage in a world history class in McKee, Kentucky. He burst into the classroom, shot at the ceiling, and demanded that the teacher and two rows of students leave. Though the remaining students were frightened, they remained calm. Dustin talked with the class, sometimes leaving his guns on the teacher's desk. Eventually the police negotiated with him to let the hostages go and give himself up. His real need, as he explained to a friend, was that he wanted to see the father he had not seen since his parents' divorce thirteen years earlier. The police assured Dustin they would contact his father, who then flew from Florida to Kentucky to be with his son. The father-son reunion was warm and held the promise of a continuing relationship. Dustin pleaded guilty to kidnapping and wanton endangerment and was required to undergo psychiatric evaluation.

In Anderson, Indiana, police arrested a sixteen-year-old boy, charging him with planting two bombs that exploded on two consecutive days at his high school. One pipe bomb exploded in a hallway outside the auditorium, and on the next day another bomb exploded in the wrestling room. Damage was estimated at $8,000. The teenager, who had no arrest record and had never been in trouble before, was charged with two counts of arson and two counts of making an explosive device.

Looking for action, two young men beat up Rep. Gerry Studds on a Washington, D.C., street in June 1990. Beaten and mugged, Studds survived the attack, and arrests were quickly made of Thomas Carter, eighteen, and James Byrne, nineteen. They indicated to the police that it was "something to do at the time."

Just how juveniles should be treated in the courts is a matter of concern for those who see them committing more and more violent crimes. When a male juvenile was sentenced to only five years in a juvenile detention facility after he had brutally murdered two people in the subways of New York in the late 1970s, there was a public outcry for juveniles to be tried as adults. This launched a trend toward what became known as "man-sized punishment for man-sized crimes."

In Boston, eight males were accused in the Halloween 1990 rape-murder of twenty-six-year-old Kimberly Rae Harbour. She was beaten, repeatedly raped, and stabbed at least 100 times. Three of her assailants were seventeen, eighteen, and nineteen years old and were charged as adults. But five were legally juveniles, one only fifteen years old.

In California, if a defendant is tried as an adult for first-degree murder, that would mean an automatic life sentence. If tried as a juvenile and convicted of first-degree murder, he could be released on his eighteenth birthday. The prosecution would like all alleged attackers to be charged as adults; the defense would like them charged as juveniles.

In Dade County, Florida, on June 30, 1990, twelve-year-old Carlton Bailey alledgedly killed his friend with a gun taken from his grandmother's house after he broke into her home. The question was whether he should be tried as a juvenile or as an adult. The defense attorney indicated nothing would be gained in locking him up, maintaining that the shooting was an accident. The mother of the victim said Carlton did an adult thing and should pay for it as an adult. The defense attorney, appearing on "60 Minutes," reminded the interviewer that Carlton Bailey's father was a drug dealer who was murdered, and, according to the boy's grandfather, the boy's mother was an addict. The grandfather was trying to raise the boy but seemed to have had no control over him.

A boy of ten was arrested in Santa Clara, California, for raping and sodomizing two boys and two girls, ages four to ten, in his apartment complex. He told the police he learned how to do those things from reading pornography, but the arresting officers believed he was a victim of sexual abuse. His probation officer said that "there's no other way they can learn that behavior." For a while the boy was released to friends, but then he was returned to the detention home for fear of reprisals from neighbors. The prosecutor claimed that the only way she could get the boy into therapy was to get him into the justice system.

Sentencing, whether for adults or for juveniles, is often set at maximum because the offender is expected to serve only about 20 percent of the sentence. Also, many offenders would rather go to jail than receive probation because when jail time is over, they have served their sentence. Probation is held over them, sometimes for years.

In 1994 California spent $4,200 a year to educate a child and $32,000 a year to incarcerate a child in a California Youth Authority detention center.

Juveniles who have been tried as adults in courts have characteristically received lighter sentences than they would have if they were adults being tried as adults. Judges seem to go easy on them because they are juveniles. Yet get-tough policies have an appeal as crimes of rape and murder by juveniles increase.

CHAPTER 2

MURDER

A Few Statistics

In 1993 an American was murdered every twenty-one minutes. Considered the most murderous industrialized nation, the United States has a murder rate eight times higher than Germany, ten times higher than Japan, and four times higher than Canada. While the murder rate in the last five years rose 14 percent, the murder rate of children under the age of fourteen rose 94 percent.

Thirty years ago 90 percent of all murders were solved, compared with 65 percent today, according to FBI statistics. In Los Angeles County only 42 percent of all murders are solved. Though the FBI reported a 3 percent drop in crime overall for 1993 compared with 1992, the rate for murder increased 3 percent—especially, and surprisingly, in rural areas.

Years ago, when .22-caliber guns were in use, there was more chance of surviving a gunshot wound. Then along came .38-caliber guns and .45-caliber guns. Now there are AK-47s, other semiautomatic weapons, and standard military hardware that is much more sophisticated than police weapons.

While many murders are drug related—in drug centers such as Miami, Los Angeles, or Washington, D.C.—this is not the case in Chicago, for instance, where family arguments are the cause of most murders. Of the 23,760 murders in the United States in 1993, which amounts to 65 a day, 13,220 were from handguns. This compares with 13 handgun deaths a day in Australia, 33 in Great Britain, and 6 in Sweden, as reported in the CBS program "Kids Killing Kids." Increased firepower is turning what would be assault into murder.

Circumstances of Murder, 1991

Robberies	10%
Drugs	6%
Sex offenses	1%
Other felonies	4%
Arguments over money	2%
Romantic triangles	2%
Other arguments	28%
Other motives	20%
Unknown	27%

Weapons of Murder, 1991

Handguns	50%
Other guns	13%
Cutting or Stabbing	16%
Blunt objects	5%
Fists, etc.	6%
Strangulation	2%
Arson	1%
Other	7%

Victims of Murder, 1990

White male	9,147
Black male	9,961
White female	3,006
Black female	2,163

Comparison of Male and Female Killers

In 1991, 90 percent of those arrested for murder were men, who tend to murder for more trivial things than women. Women arrested for murder most often have killed their husbands or boyfriends after long-term physical abuse. Managers of prisons estimate that 30 percent of the women in prison are incest victims and that the other 70 percent have been physically, sexually, or emotionally abused. In Cook County Jail in Chicago, studies showed that about 90 percent of the murders by women had not been previously planned. Even though the women who had killed their husbands had been beaten on average for five to six years preceding the murder, the murder was not premeditated.

Teen Killers

Between 1988 and 1992 there was a 300 percent increase in teens who murder compared to a 5.2 percent increase for adults who murder, even as the number of teenagers declines. As of April 1994, 200,000 children carry guns to school, according to U.S. Sen. Herb Kohl, who attempted to legislate a federal law to keep guns 1,000 feet away from any school. The bill was defeated because of the fear that the federal government was intruding on states' rights. Even fourth- and fifth-graders are arming themselves. At least 25 percent of the nation's schools have metal detectors. Since guns usually come from the home, a California law now makes parents responsible for their children's gun violence.

When a juvenile buys a gun he does it based on which style of gun carries the most prestige. The semiautomatic weapon of choice today takes .357-caliber or 9-millimeter bullets and fires fifteen–eighteen rounds a second.

The CBS program "Kids Killing Kids," which aired in April 1994, reported that 14 children a day are killed by other children and 100 children a day are wounded by other children in this country. Studies of why juveniles kill point to family violence—not necessarily violence directed against the child, but violence directed against other members of the household.

Anger does not so much lead to fistfights anymore; it leads to murder. When a seventeen-year-old boy in the Bronx became angry at a group of boys in May 1990 because he felt that one of them had insulted his thirteen-year-old girlfriend, he lured them into a schoolyard, forced them to kneel, and then shot them, execution style, killing two.

Black teens are eleven times more likely to die of gunshot wounds than white teens. For the first time in history, more teenagers, white and black, are dying from gunshots than by natural causes. In 100 hours more teens are killed by guns than soldiers killed in the 100 attack hours of the Gulf War.

When twelve-year-old David Opon refused to smoke crack with a thirteen-year-old bully who had just robbed two other children on the way to school, David was dragged into a garage. After his hands were tied behind his back, he was beaten with a baseball bat, then soaked with gasoline and set on fire. He managed to escape and run for help. His attacker was found guilty on charges of attempted murder, kidnapping, assault, and robbery, and was sentenced under juvenile law. He could remain in juvenile hall until he is twenty-one years old. David will have to have skin graft operations over most of his body throughout his life.

On May 3, 1994, a jury in session less than four hours convicted nineteen-year-old Robert Chan of planning the murder of a classmate after he and other friends ambushed him on New Year's Eve, 1992. Chan claimed he was afraid of the victim, Stuart Tay, saying Tay was going to reveal their plans to rob a computer dealership. Five teens were indicted for the murder of Tay in Orange, California; they forced Tay to drink rubbing alcohol and then taped his mouth and nose shut before burying him in a yard. Both Chan and Tay were honor students from stable homes. Chan was sentenced to life in prison without possibility of parole.

Sometimes when an aggressive boy attempts to overpower and bully a smaller youth, the more aggressive boy ends up dead. That was the case in Ventura County, California, when a popular junior high school sports star accosted another boy, punching him and challenging him to a fight. Little did the bigger boy know the smaller boy had a knife, which he used to defend himself, killing his tormentor. The judge on May 2, 1994, sentenced the juvenile to four years in detention, believing he had not intended to murder. The prosecution had sought a sentence for the fourteen-year-old to remain in detention until he was twenty-five.

On September 4, 1990, five juveniles were arrested in Fresno, California, for eleven related shootings that resulted in one death and two critical injuries. These boys ranged in age from fourteen to seventeen.

In Rochester, Minnesota, a teenage boy faces a possible life term in prison for allegedly killing his parents, his eleven-year-old brother, and his thirteen-year-old sister with an ax in March 1994. Also in Rochester, two teenagers were spotted driving the car of a General Motors Corporation executive. They were subsequently arrested for the murder of Glenn Tarr and his wife, Wanda, whose bullet-riddled bodies were found in a park a day after their home had been robbed.

In Union, Kentucky, on May 26, 1994, seventeen-year-old honor student Clay Shrout surrendered to police in his trigonometry class after he was charged with killing his parents and two sisters before going to school.

In what is known as the Bensonhurst case, thirty white men chased a black teenager out of their white neighborhood in August 1989. During the chase the sixteen-year-old black boy was shot. Four young men, two eighteen, one nineteen, and one twenty-one, were charged with assault, riot, aggravated harassment, violation of civil rights, and possessing a weapon.

The weapon was a baseball bat. Police said none of those arrested fired the shot that killed the victim. Those arrested were described by a local delicatessen clerk as "good kids."

Maybe it's nothing more than staring that provokes murder in teenagers. In February 1990 a sixteen-year-old Long Beach, California, boy was charged with shooting two deaf brothers, killing one and wounding the other. The problem started when the brothers and the accused stopped at a stop sign at an intersection and began to stare each other down. The deaf brothers were on a motorcycle, the accused in a car of five teenagers. The driver of the car forced the motorcycle off the road and into a parking lot. The deaf boys, who ordinarily communicated in sign language, did not understand what was happening. The boys got out of their car, and one started shooting.

Anyone may be killed by a teenage boy if that boy sees something he wants, like another's jacket. This happened in Chicago in October 1989, when a twenty-four-year-old was shot in the back after four youths demanded his Chicago Bears jacket. In Huntington Park, California, three teenage boys approached Felix Pena as he was walking home and demanded his Dallas Cowboys jacket. When he refused and ran away, they caught up with him, stabbed him in the face and abdomen, then fled. Pena stumbled to a phone and dialed 911 and saved himself from bleeding to death.

Many teenagers who murder have emotional problems that were never alleviated and result in disaster. Such was the case of the twelve-year-old boy who strangled his seven-year-old neighbor and then hid her body behind his bed. It was discovered three days later. The victim's mother said the murderer was a "monster" and condemned the boy's parents for failing to notice his emotional problems.

Other murders by young men seem to be for no apparent reason. A car carrying four young men (sixteen to twenty-six years of age) rear-ended a motorcycle on which sixteen-year-old Jimmie Torrez was a passenger. When the driver of the motorcycle tried to elude the attackers, Torrez fell off. The occupants of the car then stopped and beat Torrez before they shot him several times. He was dead on arrival at the Holy Cross Medical Center in Los Angeles.

Another motorcycle-car tailgating incident, in Costa Mesa, California, in May 1988, resulted in another murder. Dallas Keith Carter, nineteen, and two friends tailgated Javiar Sarabia and his brother, Alex, who were riding their motorcycle home from a family barbecue. Carter and his friends chased the brothers, and there was a scuffle in which Sarabia was knocked to the ground. Carter and his two friends got back into the car and ran over Sarabia several times. The deputy district attorney described the incident as "a night of random assault just for the heck of it. Come hell or high water, whoever got in his way that night was going to pay." Carter was sentenced to twenty-five years to life in prison.

Then there are those unfortunate people who happen to be around when a young man wants to pick a fight—with anyone. That is what happened to eighteen-year-old Malik Smith, who went to a suburban Utah nightclub after a day on the slopes during his annual skiing vacation. At the nightclub he was accosted by a stranger, John Tavo Leota, also eighteen. Leota beat Malik Smith into unconsciousness, and Smith died a day later from brain injuries. After the murderer was arrested, a police sergeant said, "The real tragedy is that the suspect just went around and picked fights and this guy Smith just happened to be the target. It was an unprovoked attack."

In Imperial City, California, witnesses are credited with the arrest of a fourteen-year-old who verified that the boy shot "the doughnut man." The Ayalas were a popular family, for many years selling doughnuts from their van in the Watts housing project. When the fourteen-year-old suspect had an argument with Enrique Ayala, he fatally shot the doughnut man. Police believe witnesses came forth and identified the suspect because the vendors were well liked in the neighborhood.

It doesn't pay, in many cases, to come to the rescue of a person being attacked. When Richard Roybal and four friends were going to a San Francisco beach bar to drink beer, they saw a teenage boy beating a woman in the parking lot near the Cliff House. One of Roybal's friends asked the woman if she was all right. The teenager beating her took out a knife, cut one of Roybal's friends on the hand, and then fatally stabbed Roybal in the stomach. The teenage assailant sped away in a pickup truck.

In Riverside County, California, when a Good Samaritan tried to break up a fight between a car occupant and a man who had run into the car with his bicycle, one of the men in the car jumped out and, with three others, chased the man into a market where they beat him to death with a bat and a pipe. Twenty-year-old Michael Andrade was booked for suspicion of murder on June 7, 1994.

Traveling in groups seems to give boys courage to be killers. In January 1990, the police arrested thirteen teenage boys between the ages of fourteen and seventeen in the killing of fifteen-year-old Alex Calderon in Alameda County, California. It appears there was a "personality conflict" between Calderon and one of the boys, which means they didn't like each other. They were all "party to the crime," as one of the detectives said, even though only one boy fatally stabbed Calderon. Because they all participated one way or another, the detective said they would all be charged with murder.

Not driving fast enough in a car in front of a teenage boy may anger him to the point of murder. On December 3, 1988, Laurence Ellingsen and his wife, Sheri, were on the Nimitz Freeway in Oakland, California. They were on their way home from a family party celebrating their twenty-ninth wedding anniversary when Darryl Poole, nineteen, decided he wanted to make them drive faster because a passenger in his Chevrolet Impala wanted to get to the bathroom. He picked up a rifle in the front seat of his car and fired, killing Laurence Ellingsen, who slumped over the steering wheel. Though the car was going about 65 miles per hour, his wife managed to steer to the side of the road. Poole said he was just firing into the air.

In the age of video cameras, malicious boys will need to be more discreet if they want to escape capture. Danny Ornelas, nineteen, used his car to run down and kill Debbie Ann Killedea in the alley behind her home in Newport Beach, California, on September 1, 1988, as her two small sons watched. But a video camera got inadvertently turned on in his car. The videotape, which was played at Ornela's trial, showed that as Killedea tried to move out of the way, the car moved in her direction and killed her as her children screamed. He was sentenced to the maximum of ten years for gross vehicular manslaughter.

One also has to be careful what one says about another's girlfriend. At a taco stand in Stockton, California, in July 1990, one man referred to another man's girlfriend as "some pretty lady." The man who made the remark was punched. The attacker then left, only to return with fifteen friends and guns. When the shooting began, patrons ran for cover. When it was over two people were dead and twelve were wounded. Eight young men in their early twenties and one juvenile were arrested.

Not all young male murderers come from impoverished homes. A ten-year-old in Stroudsburg, Pennsylvania, comes from a "good" family but is the youngest murderer ever to be tried as an adult because, as the judge said on June 23, 1989, the boy's crime was "deliberate and willful." The defense attorney argued for the case to be tried in juvenile court.

After receiving a slight reprimand while playing at a neighbor's house, this ten-year-old ran home and took the key to his father's ten-rifle gun cabinet from its hiding place under a bedside lamp. He then unlocked the ammunition drawer, loaded the 20-power scope rifle with a single Remington cartridge, opened the window, removed the screen, and allegedly fired a single fatal shot at a seven-year-old girl. This neighbor was riding behind another girl on a snowmobile traveling at about a walking pace. Later the boy lied at first about the cut over his eyebrow, which was determined to be an injury from the gun's scope. He was read his Miranda rights sitting on his mother's lap.

Who would have thought when the Watkins family left Provo, Utah, to see the U.S. Tennis Open in New York that they would bring back their twenty-two-year-old son Brian in a casket. He had been fatally stabbed—because eight teenage boys wanted some money for their evening's entertainment. After cutting open Mr. Watkins's pants and stealing his wallet, they punched Brian's mother. When Brian and his brother Todd ran after the attackers, Brian was stabbed in the chest with a butterfly knife (so-called because of its folding handle). According to police, the teenage attackers went dancing within minutes of the stabbing.

When a driver closed the window on his Mister Softee ice-cream truck because a young man was demanding money, the young man entered from the back of the truck to shoot the driver dead. As the Mister Softee employee staggered out to the pavement on that hot Philadelphia evening, June 15, 1994, witnesses said that teenagers stood around and laughed at him as the music from his truck played on. They made up songs about his dying: "Mister Softee is dead. He didn't give out enough sprinkles." As he was loaded into an ambulance, they composed a rap song on the spot, including the line "They killed Mister Softee." A sixteen-year-old boy was arrested two days later. The victim, Mohammed Jaberipour, father of three, had been on the job only a week, as reported by Dinah Brin of the Associated Press.

Male murderers start young and many show no remorse.

They are said to have no regard for human life and consider murder as a kind of sport. Many psychologists, sociologists, jurists, and criminologists have attempted to find causes for the rising juvenile crime rate. An easy target is the single-parent family, and that parent is overwhelmingly the mother. Without a father figure in the home, there usually is less money and less supervision. But citing the lack of a male role model as a cause does not take into account the thousands of children raised by single mothers who do not get into trouble. Nor does it take into account the number of teen murderers who were raised in average-income, two-parent families.

Other factors must be looked at that may be affecting young men. Although numerous studies indicate that violence in movies does not cause violence, other studies show, for example, that students who watched the most television at age eight were the ones most apt to show aggressive behavior by age nineteen. By age thirty about 25 percent had been convicted of many crimes and were abusive.

Studies have shown that by sixteen a typical child has been exposed to approximately 33,000 murders and over 200,000 acts of other violence in movies and on TV. What becomes the reality for children? Movies are becoming more violent and so is TV; slasher films are presented without qualms, as well as rape, murder, and female mutilation, as shown in *The Silence of the Lambs*. Dr. Joyce Brothers writes, "The greater the level of exposure to TV violence, the more the child is willing to use violence and see it as a solution to conflict."

This violence-viewing starts with Saturday morning cartoons that parade continual acts of destruction. The cartoon victims are never shown to suffer, so there is nothing for the child to empathize with except the victory of the conqueror over the vanquished. Comic books as well will show women in bondage, for example, in full color.

A law signed by President George Bush in December 1990 gave television stations immunity from antitrust laws if they would meet periodically to discuss how to set standards reducing the violence in programming. As the vice president of CBS said, "It is a well-intentioned effort on Congress's part, but this is a problem that is not easily solved." People who keep track of violence on TV maintain that programs are now twice as violent as they were ten years ago. It is claimed by the National Coalition on Television Violence that prime-time television programs presented an average of ten violent acts per hour in 1990. Yet, with any effort to limit violence on TV comes the argument that First Amendment rights of free speech are being violated.

Television is only one of many mediums that influence people, but it is a major time consumer for children. Pre-teens, teens, and young adults listen to rap music, which often has violent lyrics degrading to women. What respect can a young man have for women if he buys into lyrics that, in a sense, give him permission to kill his girlfriend, as in Mötley Crüe's "Girls, Girls, Girls," a song that sold more than two million copies? What did that song say? It's about a man who killed his girlfriend by slicing her, because by killing her he could keep her.

During the week of March 27, 1989, fifty-six people were killed on prime-time shows on the three major networks. During the first part of October 1990, eight new gangster movies opened for fall viewing at movie theaters. These included *State of Grace, GoodFellas, Miller's Crossing,* and, at the end of 1990, *The Godfather Part III* was released. *Marked for Death,* a movie about a hit murder, was the number-one box-office draw for the week of October 22, 1990.

Whatever else may be said, the fact remains that the public has a great appetite for violence in entertainment, and producers feed that appetite.

HOW TO FIND YOUTHS HEADED FOR MURDER, read a headline in the May 11, 1989, *San Francisco Chronicle.* In the article, Dr. Dorothy Otnow-Lewis refers to a seven-year study on youthful violence based on ninety-seven boys incarcerated in a Connecticut reform school. Seventy-nine boys were in for violent crimes including murder, and eighteen for nonviolent crimes.

Otnow-Lewis's conclusion is that a boy's violent behavior does not necessarily mean he will continue to be violent unless several categories of problems exist for him at the same time. If, for instance, the boy has learning problems, or psychological or neurological problems, or if he was brought up in a family where there was a great deal of violence, then he may very well continue to react violently to situations. However, boys who had no learning disabilities or other problems and did not come from a violent family did not continue their previous violent behavior when they were released. Though all but six of the youthful offenders amassed police records as adults, and 77 percent of the violent youthful offenders became violent adult offenders, 61 percent of those who became violent adult offenders had no record for violence when they were juveniles.

"Violence alone," Otnow-Lewis stated at the American Psychiatric Association meeting in San Francisco, "was not a way to pick out those who were likely to stay violent." Boys who had one risk factor, such as low reading ability, and also came from a violent family "committed violent crimes at the rate of nearly four per year." Boys with two risk factors and a violent family background committed an average of almost six violent acts each year. These acts included murder and rape.

There is a clue here for prevention of violent crime among teenage boys. A pilot study would be advisable, with schools and preschools identifying boys who live in violent homes and offering these boys concerted reading skill sessions and family counseling. So much falls on the school, but schools are the principal socializing institution for children; schools are where a youngster can learn to appreciate himself instead of deprecating himself. What happens to the cherubic kindergartner as he goes through school that sees him end up at age fourteen stabbing a schoolmate? This is something that demands study.

Charles Dutton, who gained fame as an actor on Broadway playing the role of Boy Willie in *The Piano Lesson*, was just such a boy. He grew up in a housing project in sight of the Maryland State Penitentiary. The boys in his neighborhood more or less expected that they, too, would end up in that big building. Dutton was sent to reform school at the age of twelve, and at seventeen he was convicted of manslaughter and sentenced to five years. He has said that he didn't care then that he had killed someone. He had no feeling about it. "You can't lead the street life and have an ounce of sympathy," he said on "60 Minutes." "Killing somebody measures the hardening of your feelings. I learned as long as one nigger was killing another, it was fine with the judicial system." Going to prison, he claimed, was a test of his manhood.

After he was paroled, Dutton was rearrested for gun possession. In solitary confinement, a five-by-seven room with no light, no sink, no toilet, only a grate in the floor, he read a book by the light that seeped through the door. When he got out of isolation he knew what he wanted to do. In reading that book he had found something to believe in—acting. The book he had read was a play by Douglas Turner Ward, *Day of Absence*. He put the play on in prison, and when he got out of prison he enrolled in school and studied acting.

The crucial statement Dutton makes is that he never allowed himself to feel remorse until he came to believe his own life had worth. The clue to prevention lies in trying to determine which youngsters are headed for trouble and to build their sense of self-worth before it is too late. So easy to say, even as the juvenile crime rate increases.

When Men Get Angry at Women

About 40 percent of women murdered are murdered by husbands or boyfriends.

FBI REPORT

When a woman marries or moves in with a boyfriend, she increases her chance of being murdered. Short of that, she may end up in the emergency ward as the result of her mate's anger. *The Journal of the American Medical Association* reported in 1990 that about one-third of women who end up in emergency wards are there because of wounds inflicted by their mates.

The estranged wife lies in a pool of her own blood, shot three times by her husband, whose body lies on the asphalt in the parking lot, a single bullet in his head. His wife's rejection had crept through his body like a poison. The poison took possession of all his thoughts and actions to the point where the only way to expel it was to expel his wife and himself from the living.

And so it happens in offices, where an angry husband hunts down his estranged wife. It happens in restaurants where she works as a waitress. It happens in her mother's home where she is caring for her children, and it happens in her new boyfriend's or new husband's bed. It may happen immediately after the breakup, or it may happen a week, a month, or even years later when his whole being accepts the rejection as something he must destroy by destroying her. And in destroying her, it is the final act of possession because then no one else can have her, either. Tragically, these killings often involve other people—other family members or people who just happen to be there when his rage peaks to uncontrollable heights.

Often the law views domestic violence as a family issue, and "family disputes" between men and women are viewed as private affairs. The same violence between men is viewed as assault. Women, too, are known to kill ex-husbands and ex-boyfriends out of rejection, but the numbers of those incidents are barely significant when compared with the numbers of men killing in rejection rage.

Men too often consider women as property. Although women have been able to hold property in their own name in this country since 1850, a *San Francisco Chronicle* article dated August 1, 1994, shows that this view of women as property still prevails: its headline is EXPERTS SAY WIVES-AS-PROPERTY STILL A COMMON U.S. ATTITUDE. In some cultures and some religions fathers and husbands have had the legal right to kill their women. Judge Edward Pincus cited "cultural differences" when he sentenced Don Lu Chen, fifty-one, to probation for killing his forty-year-old ninety-nine-pound wife, Jean Wan Chen, by hitting her on the head eight times with a hammer on September 7, 1987, because he believed she had been unfaithful. The judge noted that the husband, who had emigrated from Canton, China, in 1986, had brought his Chinese customs with him to the United States. The sentence of probation caused an outcry from members of the National Organization for Women. As one chapter president said, "It is not acceptable for a man to kill his wife for any reason."

But acceptability for wife killing, especially in cases of adultery, has been part of history. In the Napoleonic Code, which has influenced our legal system, "crimes of passion," meaning murder, were not only forgiven but were lauded as the only manly thing a husband could do if he learned of or suspected his wife's infidelity.

This notion stems from the English common law of property, which is primarily responsible for the double standard emanating from the eighteenth century, when Dr. Samuel Johnson wrote, "The chastity of women is of the utmost importance as all property depends on it."

As property passed from father to son, fathers needed to know absolutely that sons were their own. The only way to ensure that legitimate sons inherited a man's property was to restrict the wife's sexual activities to husband only, though a husband's sexual activities could be limitless. A wife must be monogamous. Killing an unfaithful wife was justified because unfaithful wives threatened the law of property.

Many men still see their women as property. To love a woman, for many men, is to own her—to possess her. If a man sees his woman in the arms of another man, he senses that his property has been stolen, along with his manhood, and the sense of rejection is, for some, unbearable.

Women, who are the "property" possessed by the men, have different problems. Until World War II women generally did not work outside the home; they were groomed for marriage. They needed to please some man enough for him to want to marry her. In essence, a woman needed someone to give her status in the community and to provide for her. If her husband left her, that rejection meant she did not please him enough and she was a social failure. Many turned their despair in on themselves in a solitary, quiet suicide. In many parts of the world, a woman rejected may not return home, and she has no chance of remarriage. She is "used goods." Not so with husbands.

Today, in this country especially, women are learning to take care of themselves. They earn their own living, rent their own apartments, and raise their children by themselves. This in itself is cause for unspoken anger by many men. The women's movement, and women's newfound ability to be independent, instead of giving men cause to rejoice that their burden is lessened, takes away many a man's sense of control and possession: his status and ego suffer. Therefore, when the woman in a man's life rejects him, that may be too much for him to bear, and so he eliminates her.

When Joan Cooper of San Mateo, California, criticized what often epitomizes manhood for a man—his sexual performance—she was killed by her husband of only four months, thirty-nine-year-old Peter Cooper. Enraged, he bludgeoned his wife to death with a hammer. He was sentenced to fifteen years to life in prison.

The head housekeeper of a first-class motel in the sleepy California tourist town of Carmel had told friends she was having marital problems. One day she accepted a ride to work from a male friend, and as they drove into the parking lot, her husband pulled up behind them and started shooting. The wife and her friend tried to run for cover, but the male friend was shot and killed and the woman critically wounded by shotgun blasts to her chest, abdomen, arms, and legs. The husband, who had been under court order to stay away from his wife, then exchanged the shotgun for a .22-caliber rifle and killed himself. He had purchased the shotgun and twenty-five rounds of ammunition the day before the shooting.

In East Los Angeles an uninvited estranged husband showed up at a birthday party in August 1989 and opened fire on the gathering, killing four people. He fled but was later arrested.

This act was echoed in December 1989, in Spanaway, Washington, when an ex-husband shot his ex-wife, her current husband, and her two daughters. The girls, ages six and fourteen, were the gunman's daughters. All bodies had more than one wound from a shotgun and another gun. When the ex-husband had killed them all, he killed himself. The attack had been planned well in advance; the killer left a suicide note to his parents saying, according to the sheriff's office, that he was sorry for what he had to do.

Another murder-suicide occurred when twenty-three-year-old Kendall Ramsell murdered the sister of his girlfriend and then drove his car over a cliff. He died from multiple injuries incurred when his body hit the rocks in a gully near Leggett, in Northern California. The body of his victim was found in her parents' home in Walnut Creek. Laura Wang was fully clothed and had put up a great struggle in several rooms before she died. She had been stabbed to death with kitchen knives.

A former Vietnamese pilot who came to the United States in 1985 fled the apartment of his girlfriend, with whom he had once lived, after he killed her and a man in Fullerton, California. Identified as Dan Van Nguyen, thirty-five, he was seen running from the apartment by the manager.

In so many of these murders, where an estranged or ex-husband or boyfriend sets out to eliminate his pain by eliminating the woman who no longer wishes to see him, the killer often kills more than the intended victim. David (Moochie) Welch, thirty-one, killed six people on December 8, 1986, the worst mass murder ever committed in Oakland, California.

As they slept in their beds, Welch killed his ex-girlfriend, Dellane Mabrey, seventeen; her two brothers, Sean, twenty-one, and Darnell, twenty-three; her three-year-old daughter, Valencia; family friend Kathy Walker, thirty-four; and Walker's four-year-old son, Duane. Twenty-one-year-old Leslie Morgan, Dellane's new boyfriend, and her two-month-old son fathered by Welch were shot but did not die. Welch, convicted and sentenced to the gas chamber, said he was relieved for the victims' families and for himself that the ordeal was over.

Sometimes a whole city can be terrorized by the antics of a man enraged when things go against him involving a wife or ex-wife. Alfred Hunter, forty-two, a mail handler and former army medic, was placed on probation in May 1989 because he was found guilty of assaulting his twenty-six-year-old ex-wife when he ordered her not to change a TV station. Placed on probation after being sentenced, he went to his ex-wife's home, despite a restraining order not to see her, and shot her in front of their five-year-old son. He then drove to the Boston airport and demanded to be given an airplane.

With no radio contact for three hours on that May night in 1989, he buzzed Boston, occasionally firing on cars when he came close to area roads. The Logan Airport control tower was forced to close down when Hunter fired his AK-47 at the men inside, and night flights were canceled. Possibly bent on suicide, he aimed the Cessna 152 Model II straight at buildings, pulling up moments before he would have crashed. Hunter finally landed at Logan and was arrested. He pleaded not guilty to murder and armed robbery. Although several cars and buildings had been hit by bullets from the AK-47, no injuries occurred during those three frightening hours.

Whether it's over the night sky of Boston or somewhere else, enraged ex-husbands find devious ways to get revenge on ex-wives. A hooded man broke into a children's Bible study graduation ceremony at the Mount Olive Church of God in Christ, in Oakland, California, and shot three, killing two. The attack was almost a satanic mystery, but not for long. Two days later, it was discovered that one of the women shot point-blank in the face was related to the hooded gunman's estranged wife.

The police commander, William Booth, after arresting Anthony Oliver, twenty-seven, and Albert Lewis, Jr., thirty-three, said the shooting was "a family dispute between Lewis and his estranged wife." One of the women killed was Patronella Luke, thirty-five, a gospel soloist who had just returned from touring Europe. She was in the church to attend the ceremony with her five-year-old son and her husband. Albert Lewis was said to have shot her husband, Peter, in the leg and then fatally shot another woman, Mae Lee, seventy-six, as she tried to run away, as children screamed in fright.

When the shooting was over, neighbors in the church area said they had seen two men approach the church earlier. Lewis was accompanied by his half-brother Anthony Oliver, who waited outside, crouching near the church. When Lewis emerged with a shotgun, the two men ran in different directions.

In January 1990, Joseph Charan, thirty-four, killed his wife, Veena, twenty-eight, outside a Baptist church school in San Francisco. Veena Charan had received a restraining order against her husband after he had beaten her and damaged her car. In front of the church school at 8:15 A.M., in the presence of many children, including his nine-year-old son, Joseph Charan began firing his gun at his wife. He chased and killed her at close range. Joseph Charan then reloaded his pistol and killed himself.

If headlines read MURDER-SUICIDE, it appears most often to mean the murder of an estranged wife and the rejected husband's suicide. They are usually small stories in the newspaper, almost hidden away on the back pages, such as this one in the *San Francisco Chronicle*, July 26, 1989:

> A couple found shot to death in an apartment in Pacifica, San Mateo County, were identified as Monique Lamonte, twenty-five, and Anthony Lamonte, twenty-four. Police said Anthony Lamonte entered the apartment and took his wife hostage. Her boyfriend, daughter, and a neighbor fled the apartment. Police said they found a large-caliber revolver on the floor next to Anthony Lamonte's body.

News clippings, short and factual, cannot begin to tell the story of how Monique Lamonte suffered. Nor can news clippings relate the hysterical terror of ex-wives or ex-husbands or witnesses to murder.

Many enraged husbands kill their ex-wives in the presence of their children. In July 1989 Reginald Maynard shot and killed his estranged wife in Oakland and then killed himself— yet their eighteen-month-old daughter was found unharmed lying next to her dead mother's body.

When John Blecha, fifty-four, stabbed his twenty-eight-year-old wife, despite a restraining order to stay away from her, their four young children, ages one through eleven, witnessed the beating and the stabbing. Their mother survived this horrible crime and will be scarred for life. As will the children.

Lovers of women with jealous husbands or jealous ex-boyfriends have justification for fearing for their lives. Shot in bed by Garritt Van Raam, Jr., sixty-one, at 4:00 A.M. in San Francisco were Margaret Kimball, forty-five, and her new lover. Garritt Van Raam then attempted suicide with his .38-caliber revolver. He was found bleeding on the floor of the bedroom and underwent brain surgery.

Many of these incidents of murder cast large shadows before them. Previous brutal incidents indicate the possibility of further violence. Many women had gone to court to get restraining orders, requiring the husbands to stay away from them. For husbands who turn to murder, these restraining orders no doubt further escalated their anger toward their wives.

Some of these murders seem to be calculated for an audience, whether they are worshipers in church, children in school, or employees in a workplace—as when Richard Farley murdered seven people in a defense plant in Sunnyvale, California, after a female employee indicated she was not romantically interested in him.

Farley was armed with two shotguns, one hunting rifle, two revolvers, two semiautomatic pistols, and one thousand bullets when he entered the plant on February 16, 1988. He had been fired from his job two weeks earlier for harassing a female employee. He is quoted as telling the police negotiators before he surrendered that he wanted "to do as much damage to equipment as I could. Some people popped out around corners. I just shot them. Once I had run around and gotten through being upset, it wasn't fun anymore." The female employee he was enamored with escaped with her life, but seven other employees lay dead.

When his trial opened in July 1991, his attorney admitted that Farley killed seven people, but that he didn't intend to do it. He was, the defense attorney argued, so obsessed with the woman that he cracked under the stress. While the defense argued that the murders were not premeditated, the prosecutor argued that Farley had deleted the woman's name from his will a few days before the shooting and rented a motor home that he then filled with the ammunition.

In another case, when Carmen Semidey discovered that her husband was still married to someone else, she left him, taking their six-month-old baby with her. She lived with different friends but was always asked to leave because her husband constituted a threat to their safety. Eventually she turned to living on the streets, maintaining her job at a medical clinic in Santa Fe Springs in Southern California, until a fellow employee, a woman, took her in and gave her money to hire an attorney. Carmen Semidey's husband found out where his wife was living and, according to her friend, made repeated threats to kill his wife. He shot her once and, when she fell, shot her several more times until she was dead.

Most of these murders occur with guns, but some men, as has been mentioned, resort to stabbing. Sometimes the enraged man stabs not only his intended victim but all her children as well. It was only two weeks after George Foreman, thirty-six, and Catherine Chandler, thirty, moved into their apartment in Oakland, with three children, one a three-month-old infant fathered by Foreman, when he fatally stabbed Catherine and critically wounded her nine-year-old son and seven-year-old daughter. Foreman then stabbed himself in the stomach in a try at suicide but survived. Police spoke of a note he'd left saying the woman "was going to put him out and change the baby's name and he couldn't handle that." The infant was unharmed.

Strangulation is not used as often by angry men as guns or stabbing, but one wealthy Venezuelan confessed to strangling his girlfriend when he was vacationing with her in Marin County on June 10, 1989. Upon his return to South America, where he was arrested on suspicion of murder, he told Caracas police that he had thrown his girlfriend's children, four and five years old, off a bridge near the Colombian border on July 17, 1989. He told the police he had been unhappy because his girlfriend wanted to return to her common-law husband, the father of her children.

It is best for women not to argue with men who anger easily. Patti Ahmed, twenty-seven, argued with her thirty-seven-year-old boyfriend, Frank De Young, who then killed her, stuffing her body in a drum that was found along the highway near Napa, California.

Neither an estranged wife nor girlfriend, Wendy Cheek was murdered by Robert Fairbank, thirty-six. Four days before the murder, Fairbank had been released on parole for the rape of a San Francisco woman, for which he had been sentenced to forty years. Wendy Cheek, a twenty-four-year-old San Francisco State University student, was abducted, beaten, stabbed many times with both a knife and a screwdriver, and possibly sexually assaulted, according to an autopsy report. Then Fairbank poured gasoline over her body and set her on fire. A jury convicted him of first-degree murder and voted for the death sentence in April 1989.

Mass Murder

Where is one safe from a mass murderer? Not in a post office, a commuter train, a fast-food restaurant, a college classroom, or an elementary school playground. At anytime and at almost any place, men with semiautomatic weapons may burst upon a peaceful scene and wreak havoc.

On April 13, 1994, in a North Carolina fiber optics company, an ex-employee, Ladislav Antalik, who had resigned over difficulties with coworkers a few weeks earlier, walked into the plant at 8:00 A.M., and opened fire. He killed his former supervisor and another employee, and wounded two more before he killed himself.

In November 1993, a gunman rode a Long Island commuter train, packed with New York City workers returning home. He opened fire with his semiautomatic handgun with high-capacity fifteen-round ammunition clip and trapped ninety people in one car until passengers jumped him and kept him from reloading a third time. By then he had killed six people and wounded seventeen. Colin Ferguson, the killer, a black, was said to have a longtime hatred of whites. All his victims were white.

Mark Hilburn, an Orange County, California, postal employee, entered the post office two days after he had been fired for his constant harassment of a coworker. Hilburn allegedly murdered his best friend and then wounded another person. The trial is set for February 1995.

Some mass murderers try to cover up their crime by eliminating witnesses, as happened in a bowling alley in Las Cruces, New Mexico. According to three survivors, robbers rounded up the patrons in the bowling alley and herded them into the office. They then shot and killed an employee, his two daughters, ages two and seven, and another child, age thirteen, before they set fire to the office, their attempt to cover up their crime spree.

On a pleasant July 1993 afternoon in San Francisco, financial district transactions came to a halt as news of a man in a high-rise office building killing people reached the police. Streets were cordoned off, and SWAT teams entered the building at 101 California Street. The gunman, Gian Ferri, carried two TEC-9 assault pistols and a .45-caliber pistol and 100 rounds of ammunition. He killed eight people.

Since then the relatives of the San Francisco victims have sued the gun manufacturers, alleging the sale of the guns used was abnormal dangerous activity and that the sale was negligent in that the guns are not used for anything except crime. Other such lawsuits in Louisiana and Connecticut in 1989 have failed, but the attorney for this California case believes he can prove when the case goes to trial that the passing of time has shown how much more these guns are used in crime than for any other purpose. Semiautomatic weapons make mass murder a greater possibility than before. When shots come out of the barrel of a gun at 600 bullets a minute, there isn't much time for the intended target or innocent bystanders to run for cover.

Mass murder is a horror, but seems even more horrendous when the targets are children, as they were in Stockton, California, on January 17, 1989. As 450 schoolchildren from the first, second, and third grades were playing on swings or laughing and chasing each other, they suddenly became the targets of a man with an AK-47. Dressed in army combat fatigues, the young man wielded a gun designed to kill people during a war in a schoolyard. Six children died and thirty were injured, at least fifteen of those critically.

One teacher in a classroom thought she was hearing firecrackers and looked out her window. She said she saw the man spraying gunfire back and forth. "He was not talking, he was not yelling, he was very straight-faced. It did not look like he was really angry. It was just matter-of-factly."

Mass chaos ensued, with children running in every direction. Another teacher, who had a daughter in school, said, "There were a dozen students lying on the ground."

The deputy police chief said the gunman, identified as Patrick Purdy, twenty-four, had earlier that morning set his car on fire, apparently as a diversion. He then entered the Cleveland Elementary School with two handguns and the automatic rifle and calmly walked around the school grounds shooting and reloading, shooting and reloading. He killed three children on the grounds and three in the school building. Four were Cambodian and two were Vietnamese. He fired more than 100 rounds. The last one he used to kill himself.

As parents descended on the school it was quickly evident that language was a barrier to communication. Most parents could speak only a little English, and the bilingual aides could not handle the confusion. Injured children had been taken to hospitals, but there was no record of who went where. Parents drove from hospital to hospital searching for their children.

Patrick Purdy had a history of alcoholism and, according to

acquaintances, loved to play "Rambo," wearing camouflage clothes, part of a "wannabe Vietnam vet" syndrome. They also said he hated Asians, that he believed the Vietnamese were taking jobs away from Americans.

Joe Wesbecker also used an AK-47 assault rifle when he killed seven people in Louisville, Kentucky, on September 14, 1990. At first, employees at the Standard Gravure Printing Company did not realize what was happening because they could not hear the sound of gunshots—most were wearing ear protectors to block out the noise of the printing presses.

For twenty minutes Wesbecker canvased the printing plant, going from floor to floor killing anyone he could see. He was armed with a 9-millimeter semiautomatic weapon and an AK-47. By the time he was through, seven were dead. He ended his own life with a pistol. When the doctor arrived on the scene he said it looked like a bloody war zone. Most victims had multiple gunshot wounds, and since the AK-47 shatters bones, the injuries were said to be devastating.

Wesbecker had worked in the printing plant for twenty years but had been on disability and under a doctor's care for emotional problems. Homicide detective Lt. Jeff Moody said that Wesbecker had attempted suicide before and may have been planning this suicide for months. After release from a mental hospital eight months earlier, he started collecting stories about mass killings, according to relatives. These included articles about Patrick Purdy and another mass murderer, Robert Sherrill, who killed fourteen in an Oklahoma post office.

"He has been acting flakey," his twenty-six-year-old son said. Many pointed to the stress of his disability leave and his inability to reconcile himself to changing management style and numerous layoffs, the result of a corporate buyout, as contributing factors.

Two years after their father's death, Wesbecker's sons sued the Eli-Lily Company, claiming his death and murderous rampage were the result of his use of Prozac, a drug produced by Eli-Lily. The sons lost their case against the company on December 12, 1994, when the defense proved that Joe Wesbecker had a grudge against his superior and that that grudge—not Prozac—was responsible for the massacre.

In Escondido, California, postman John Taylor shot his wife twice in the head as she lay in bed and then drove the half-mile to work, where he shot and killed two coworkers.

Dressed in his postal uniform, Taylor arrived at the post office at 7:35 A.M. on August 10, 1989, with a .22-caliber semi-automatic pistol. It was his usual habit to meet his two coworkers for coffee on the loading dock at the start of the workday. These were the two men he killed. After that he went into the building, shooting, injuring one man in the arm. He walked right past some workers, gun in hand. One employee said later, "He didn't have any emotion. He was stern-faced." When Taylor pulled the trigger pointed at his own head he slumped to the floor and spilled the unused ammunition. He had brought 100 rounds and had fired between fifteen and twenty.

Taylor was described as cheerful and probably the best-liked among his coworkers. He had received awards for his performance and was within three years of retirement. One of his close friends told police that John Taylor was "feeling the heat" at the post office. They had had a discussion about how postal employees are always being watched by their managers.

Killing with a semiautomatic weapon and then committing suicide is a pattern for the mass murderer. Such was the case for James Pough, forty-two, in Jacksonville, Florida, on June 18, 1990. His victims were eight customers and employees of the General Motors Acceptance Corporation, the financing department for car loans.

Pough's car had been repossessed five months prior to the shootings. Armed with a .30-caliber semiautomatic rifle and a .38-caliber revolver, he walked in the door of the finance company, shot a customer fatally, then proceeded to pass through the office firing at the rows of employees. When some tried to hide, Pough found and shot them under their desks.

In addition to the eight killed, five were critically injured. As the sheriff described it, Pough walked from the front to the back of the building, firing without stopping. When there seemed to be nobody left, he shot himself, dying on the premises.

Because Pough had pleaded guilty to aggravated assault in 1971, he was prohibited from owning a gun, even though he had somehow managed to register two in his name. In addition to the two illegally purchased guns used in the killings, he also owned a 9-millimeter pistol and a .357 revolver, which the police found later.

In a prostitution-related incident that occurred before the mass murders, the police said Pough had shot and killed two people, and that he had shot and injured two teenagers ten minutes after that. All of these murders occurred in one weekend.

Though there was a restraining order against Pough to stay away from his wife, he was considered by neighbors to be a nice, quiet man. One neighbor said she treated him like a son and he treated her like a mother. Another neighbor said he was "an all right dude. But you better not get him mad."

In San Diego, California, on April 14, 1990, a man unhappy over his father's health care at the Mission Bay Memorial Hospital, entered the emergency room and started shooting. An emergency medical technician and a nurse who had worked at the hospital for ten years were killed. Wounded were a doctor, shot in the abdomen, a nursing supervisor, and a man who had just brought his sick infant to the emergency room. The gunman, whose father had died after emergency surgery for an aneurysm, was arrested later that night.

On September 27, 1990, in Berkeley, California, a deranged man held hostage a café filled with college students. He killed one and wounded nine students and shot into the walls and ceilings of the café in a reign of terror that lasted seven hours.

The gunman, Mehrdad Dashti, thirty, used three pistols to establish control of the thirty-three hostages. The guns he carried into the café in a briefcase included an M-11, a .380-caliber semiautomatic gun referred to as a Cobray; a .44-caliber revolver; and a 9-millimeter Ruger. The Cobray is popular because it emulates an illegal submachine gun and has the same firepower as an AK-47. The police said Dashti had enough ammunition for a small army.

In the course of the seven hours, Dashti ordered the male hostages to stand in a circle around him as a shield. He then ordered all the blond women to take off their pants and ordered the men to sexually molest them, which, according to a witness, they pretended to do. Dashti allowed brunettes to leave, and then released women he had told to remove their pants. Dashti, a college graduate with a degree in science and engineering, hated blondes, saying they wore provocative clothes and tempted men.

At one point he fired shots into the ceiling and told a hostage to go outside and tell police he had shot someone. One of the hostages said Dashti seemed upset when he learned that he had actually killed a person. Whatever Dashti's intentions, it was miraculous he didn't kill more people before police fatally shot him.

Only a short time before this rampage, a gun dealer who had reluctantly sold a gun to Dashti had purposefully crippled the hammer so the weapon would not fire because, as he said to the *San Francisco Chronicle*, "We knew the guy was loony and we told the State Department of Justice about him, but they said there was nothing they could do about it." Dashti brought the defective gun back to the gun dealer and was told it would be sent to the manufacturer. He still owned other guns, however. Though he had been judged by the Alameda County social services officials to be a paranoid schizophrenic, he could purchase a gun as long as he had not been convicted of a felony or had not been declared by a judge to be criminally insane.

Ten days before the café shootings, a painter had gone to Dashti's apartment and was alarmed when he came across an Uzi and two pipe bombs in the closet. The painter told the local grocer, and the grocer, fearful that something was going to get blown up, phoned the FBI and left his number. The FBI never returned his call.

Dashti was insane. He said he "heard voices" and was on record for reporting delusions. It could easily be claimed that every mass murderer is mentally deranged, at least at the time of the rampage. But then one has to ask, why aren't all unstable people mass murderers? What is the particular combination that sparks this violent action? And, why are virtually all mass murderers men?

Rampage killers often have suicidal preoccupations. Whatever the cause, there does seem to be a deadly combination of people with some mental instability and people who stockpile guns, which is a predominantly male activity.

The following is an account of Ramon Salcido's murder of his wife, children, mother-in-law, and others:

Bob Richards, Salcido's father-in-law, a slight, balding man in his late fifties, watched as his wife's casket was lowered into the large open grave. He had served as his wife's pallbearer, along with his three grown sons from a previous marriage, carrying her gray casket from the first funeral car. Longingly, he looked down at her casket for a few minutes, took his handkerchief from his coat pocket, and wiped his eyes. Then he turned and walked firmly down the hill to a second funeral car. There, he and his sons were given the casket of one of his three daughters. The four men carried that casket back up the hill to the same large hole in the earth. After pausing in silence they then returned back down the hill to the same funeral car where the casket of his second daughter was handed over.

A few minutes later they returned to the third funeral car where they picked up two small caskets in turn, and walked them up the hill. These contained his two granddaughters, ages one and four. The casket of their mother, who was Richards's third daughter, was the last of this family group— six females killed by his son-in-law and buried together in the same grave.

On April 14, 1989, Ramon Salcido had also killed a fellow wine company employee in Sonoma County because, as he said when he was arrested, he suspected that his wife was having an affair with him. All who know the situation say that that is absurd. Neighbors said his wife was barely allowed out of the house by Ramon because she was beautiful and he was insanely jealous.

Authorities believe that he went on his killing rampage because an ex-wife, Debra Salcido, whom he may never have divorced, had sent him court papers the day before, requiring him to pay $6,000 in past-due child support. After the murders and until Salcido's arrest, she hid for fear of her own life.

The violence of Ramon Salcido was well thought out and methodical. He tells us now that he killed his two little girls first and dumped them in a garbage fill. He actually slit the throats of all three daughters, but one, the two-year-old, survived. When the surviving daughter was discovered about thirty hours later, she said, "Daddy cut me."

According to his account, he then went to his mother-in-law's house in Cotati and killed her and her two daughters, nine and eleven years old. Then he went to the Grand Cru Winery in nearby Glen Ellen where he worked. There he killed his fellow worker. After that he returned to his home in Boyes Hot Springs and killed his wife.

Art Hoppe, writing in the *San Francisco Chronicle* ten days after the murders, says he can understand Salcido's killing his wife because he suspected her of having an affair with someone else, and he can understand his killing his wife's mother because she sided with her daughter, because, he says, these were crimes of passion.

Stephanie Salter, writing in the *San Francisco Examiner* on April 23, 1990, suggested that Ramon Salcido was not temporarily insane, but a normal male. Brought up to believe that he must be in control of his wife and fearing that he might be losing that control, he became violent. Salter refers to the Marin Abused Women's Services, founded by Hamish Sinclair, who said men must have power over nature and over women.

Sinclair explains that the patriarchal society gives men the right to believe they are superior to women and that they must keep their women subordinate. The law has supported men in this. Salcido, Sinclair states, believed he was losing his grip on his wife and so he followed Hobbes's definition of possession, which is to destroy that possession so that no one else can have it, either.

As is the case with other mass murderers, Salcido is described by an eyewitness, a man who was shot but not killed, as being matter-of-fact. In a tape played to the jury in his trial, September 27, 1990, Salcido is quoted as saying, "I don't feel like I wanted to kill nobody. I wanna have some beers, you know, and forget everything else. But wife's made me feel that way when she start, when she left me at home with my kids and take off." He said he was angry with his wife because she had married him while pregnant with another man's child, though they went on to have two more children together. He was angry with his mother-in-law because she didn't tell him about the child's parentage, and he was angry at the man at work because he thought he was going to be fired. His defense attorney claimed that Salcido was an alcoholic who had consumed three grams of cocaine and three bottles of champagne before going on his rampage. Salcido said on tape that because of money problems, he and his wife had talked about killing their three children.

After a trial of three weeks, at a cost of about $1 million,

Salcido was convicted of first-degree murder for six of the slayings and second-degree murder for the seventh. His mother and two brothers came from Mexico to plead for life in prison without parole rather than the death sentence. His mother told the court through an interpreter that Salcido was a loving son though he had "roughed her up." His brother said Ramon was a good brother, but since he was the oldest he ordered the others around, and he had a quick temper.

About two weeks after the conviction, the same jury returned and recommended, after deliberating for more than three days, that he should die in the gas chamber. He joined 290 other men on death row in California's San Quentin Prison. It is expected that he will appeal as many as four times. Each appeal will cost the state approximately $1 million.

Serial Murder

Serial killing is distinguished from mass murder by the timing of the action. Mass murders either take place all at the same time—for instance, the spraying of bullets from an automatic weapon at a roomful of office workers—or by systematic slaying, of a family, for example, stretched out over the course of a day. Mass murder is a short-term rampage. Serial murders may take place over a period of days, months, or even years, usually with the murderer concentrating on the same type of target—for instance, prostitutes, young college women, handsome men, or gay men.

Criminologist Steve Eggers maintains that almost all serial killers are men who murder for no material gain. However, Dorothy Puente was convicted of murdering elderly men in her boardinghouse and then cashing their Social Security checks. Not that her motive for serial murder is any less horrible, but it does appear more pragmatic. The male serial murderer appears to kill for the thrill of killing. Robert Ressler, a former FBI specialist in serial killings, says that most serial killers become very confident after three or four murders, and he adds that most have an elaborate fantasy life.

Like Jack the Ripper, the serial murderer becomes almost a folk hero. Serial killing is referred to as phallic terrorism, male domination, and a mythic ritualistic art in Jane Caputi's book, *The Age of Sex Crime*. She says that usually something typical of each murder ties them together, though ultimately what ties them together is "the utter vanquishment and annihilation of the enemy." Strong, independent women often represent an attack on men and must be avenged. In a December 1978 *New York Times Magazine* article on sex murderers, "All-American Boy on Trial," Jon Nordheimer writes, "For reasons not understood, notions of virility are expressed through violence."

In California alone at least twenty-five serial killers were arrested from 1900 to 1990. The list follows:

- Joseph Briggen, sentenced to life in prison in 1902 because he killed men to feed to his pigs
- J. P. Watson, known as "Bluebeard" because he killed twenty-five rich widows; sentenced to life in prison in 1920
- Alfred Cline, also a "Bluebeard," who killed as many as eight and probably more wealthy widows after marrying them
- William Cook, sentenced to the gas chamber in 1952 for murdering six people
- The "Zodiac Killer," who wrote cryptograms to the police in the 1960s saying he had killed approximately thirty-five people
- Patrick Kearney, known as the "Trash Bag Killer" because he killed twenty or more people over a ten-year period ending in 1977, leaving their bodies in trash bags along the road
- Charles Manson, convicted with his followers of murdering nine people in 1969

- Edmund Kemper, convicted of killing and dismembering eight people at UC Santa Cruz in 1973
- Juan Corona, convicted of murdering twenty-five migrant workers in 1973
- Vaughn Greenwood, known as the "Skid Row Slasher," who ritualistically slashed nine people in 1976
- Bobby Maxwell, known as the "Skid Row Stabber," sentenced to life in prison without parole; charged with ten murders, convicted of two
- William Bonin, known as the "Freeway Killer" because he left twelve bodies of young men and boys along the freeway in Los Angeles from 1979 to 1980
- David Carpenter, known as the "Trailside Slayer," sentenced to death for killing seven people in Santa Cruz and Marin County on mountain hiking trails
- Brandon Tholmer, who between 1981 and 1983 raped, beat, and strangled to death four elderly women for which he received a life sentence
- Douglas Clark, known as the "Sunset Strip Killer," who on a Chino Hills Ranch in 1983 slashed four people to death and was himself sentenced to death
- Michael Player, known as the "Skid Row Shooter," who went on a five-week shooting rampage killing ten transients in 1986, before he killed himself
- Joseph Danks, who stabbed six people living on the streets in January 1987; adjudged not mentally competent, he was committed to a mental institution
- Louis Craine, convicted of killing four women in Los Angeles, sentenced to death in May 1990
- Angelo Buono, known as the "Hillside Strangler," who with his cousin, Kenneth Bianchi, was sentenced to life without parole for the rapes and murders of ten women from 1977 to 1978
- Lawrence Bittaker, sentenced to death for the torture

killings in 1979 of five teenage girls whose screams he recorded
- Randy Kraft, who sex-tortured sixteen boys and young men and was sentenced to death in November 1989

Joel Achenbach writes in the *Washington Post* of April 14, 1991, that "when police bag a serial killer, he is usually a weak man, cowardly, not terribly savvy and a failure at most everything he's ever done in life. He's a loser. He manages to get away with multiple murders not because he's smart, but because he kills strangers and keeps moving." The intelligent, well-educated serial killers portrayed in the movie *The Silence of the Lambs* and in Bret Easton Ellis's novel *American Psycho* are unrealistic.

Criminologists estimate that at any time in this country there are twenty serial killers at work. They further claim that the serial killer is sexually dysfunctional, does not have a healthy relationship with another person, and is a user of pornography. Bob Ressler says he has yet to see a serial killer who has a good long-term sexual relationship with a woman, or who is a happily married family man. In Steven Eggers's *Serial Murder: An Elusive Phenomenon,* he says that in all the literature on serial murders it should be emphasized that these killers are all men. He further points out that serial killing exemplifies an exaggeration of masculine attitudes such as objectifying women, male aggressiveness, and the desire for immediate satisfaction.

SERIAL MURDER OF PROSTITUTES

Prostitutes are easy targets for serial killers. They are available, ready to get into the cars of potential murderers, and easy victims for men bent on living out their moral outrage at women who sell sex. Not all serial killers of prostitutes are motivated by the same psychological drives. Each man brings to these crimes his own personal history, values, and frustrations.

Having admitted to killing seventeen female prostitutes, Joel Rifkin, thirty-four, was convicted in Mineola, New York, on June 8, 1994. He had been arrested during a routine traffic stop when police found a body in the pickup truck he was driving. Rifkin was sentenced to twenty-seven years to life in prison. His attorney will file an appeal declaring that Rifkin, an adoptee, suffered extreme sensitivity to rejection, which caused him to fly into a murderous rage.

Arthur Shawcross, forty-four, had moved back to Rochester, New York, in 1987, when he was paroled after serving fifteen years for the strangulation death of an eight-year-old Rochester girl. In January 1990, he was charged with killing eight women. He told police where to find several of the bodies. Police believe they can link him to eleven killings in the past two years.

Shawcross approached the prostitutes as a potential customer and then killed them, dumping their bodies in various places. In most cases he killed them by strangulation. In February 1991, he was sentenced to 250 years in prison, twenty-five years to life on each of ten counts of second-degree murder, the terms running consecutively.

In Oakland, Dewain Hall, twenty-five, a paroled convict, married with one child, was arrested in October 1989 and confessed to the murder of two prostitutes whose bodies were found under freeways. He indicated the motive for his killing was that "they didn't act right." He also confessed that he had shot another prostitute because she wouldn't date him.

Quite often, men who kill prostitutes pose as policemen to entice their victim into their cars. But in a few cases they actually are policemen, as in the case of an eighteen-year veteran of the Los Angeles Sheriff's Department, Ricky Ross. He was arrested in February 1989 on suspicion of killing three prostitutes. Ross, forty, is married and the father of three children. Margaret Prescod, the founder of a black coalition against serial murders, said her group had tried to convince the police department that the killer was a man in the police or sheriff's department but was rebuffed.

Ross was with a woman in the area frequented by prostitutes and using cocaine when a policeman noticed him. Alarmed, he sped away, driving erratically. He was apprehended, arrested for being intoxicated, and then released. He was then rearrested on the murder charges when ballistics tests were made on his personal gun—a gun that was not a police issue. The three women he killed were ages twenty-four to thirty-five. One body was found in October, one in November, and one in December 1988.

Convicted of killing four prostitutes by strangulation after sexually assaulting them, Louis Craine, thirty-one, an illiterate, unemployed construction worker, was originally arrested on suspicion of killing eighteen women in Los Angeles, dumping their bodies in various southern Los Angeles communities. These murders were referred to as the "Southside Slayer Killings."

Twenty-two-year-old Ray Shawn Jackson was charged with killing six prostitutes in Kansas City between September 1989 and April 1990. All of the women were strangled. He was also charged with the attack on another woman that might have resulted in murder except that a person passing by interrupted the attack. According to the police, all women were lured to their final destination by Jackson promising to give them cocaine.

Men who kill prostitutes come from many walks of life. They can be construction workers, sheriff's officers, paroled killers, and attorneys. Kenneth Ponte, forty, a lawyer, was charged in New Bedford, Massachusetts, for one of nine murders of prostitutes and drug users. His specific offense is the beating to death of Rochelle Dopieria on April 17, 1988. The investigative department believes three more of the victims were known to him.

The "Green River Slayings," so known because they took place along the Green River in King's County, Washington, have not yet been solved. Between 1982 and 1985 forty-eight women, mostly prostitutes or drifters, were either stabbed or strangled by the so-called Green River Murderer, setting off the biggest manhunt in U.S. history, at a cost of $15 million so far. Many believed that the killer used a police car and equipment, either to attract his prey or to intimidate them. Carlton Smith writes in his book *Search for the Green River Killer* that he believes the murderer is still alive and still committing murders.

Male prostitutes are often just as apt to be the victims of serial killers. Larry Eyler sought out young male prostitutes in Chicago and then tortured and killed them. It is believed he may have killed as many as twenty-three people. Casual about his activities, he carried the ropes and the knife for attack in the trunk of his car and wore boots that carried the blood of his victims. The gruesome case of Larry Eyler is fully told in *Freed to Kill: The Larry Eyler Story*, by Gera-Lind Kolarik with Wayne Klatt. Because of legal entanglements, Eyler was freed from jail, permitting him to go kill again. It was only when a janitor saw him dumping a plastic bag with a body in it that he was arrested again. With all the evidence legally seized this time, he was sentenced to death by lethal injection for kidnapping, murder, and dismemberment of his victims.

SEXUAL ATTACK SERIAL MURDERS

Certainly one of the most notorious serial murderers is Jeffrey Dahmer, who was convicted in Milwaukee of killing and cannibalizing at least seventeen men over a period of ten years. Dahmer lured them to his apartment, gave them beer or other alcohol, took nude photos of them, had sex with them, and when they wanted to leave, killed them. He was caught when one young man ran from his apartment, naked and in handcuffs, to tell police Dahmer was trying to kill him. Sentenced to life imprisonment, Dahmer was murdered by another inmate on November 28, 1994.

Fifty-two-year-old John Wayne Gacy received the death sentence by lethal injection, in Joliet, Illinois, on May 10, 1994, for killing thirty-three boys and men after having sex with them. The victims were male prostitutes or men looking for work in Gacy's construction company. He buried twenty-seven of the bodies in a crawl space under his house.

Gacy was a political precinct captain, a successful business-man in the contracting business, and a man who did charity work and performed as a clown at children's parties. Like many violent, repeat offender criminals, he consciously ignored the murders he had committed and was therefore able to proceed without remorse.

On a Tuesday night in winter 1982, two country cousins in their twenties, Dennis Alt and Christopher Schoenborn, did not return home from a horticulture show at the Amway Grand Plaza Hotel in Grand Rapids, Michigan. The following Thursday their frozen, nude bodies were found in the snow on a rural road. Chris Schoenborn's body had been mutilated with an ice pick bearing the hotel's name. Both young men had been strangled and autopsies revealed the presence of the drug diazepam (Valium) in their bodies. Alt's car keys and Schoen-born's jacket were found in a room in the hotel that had been rented by a man named Randy Kraft, forty-four, a computer programmer from Anaheim, California.

Kraft was not immediately arrested for the murders of Schoenborn and Alt because he had fled the Michigan area. His arrest came in May 1983, when a California highway patrol officer noticed a car driving erratically. He pulled Kraft to the side of the road and then saw the body of a strangled marine in the car. Kraft was subsequently charged with the murder and sexual torture of sixteen white males in their late teens or early twenties. All had drugs or alcohol in their systems and all had been strangled.

Randy Kraft was sentenced to death in California in November 1989, six years after his arrest. He was convicted of the Michigan murders and the sexual murders of fourteen other young men, a twelve-year spree, 1972–1983, of violence, torture, necrophilia, and mutilation. In addition, he has been accused of twenty-one other murders and is believed to have killed as many as sixty-five men, which, as one of the investigators said, "would make him probably the most prolific serial killer in the country." He was executed in May 1994.

In Dennis McDougal's *Angel of Darkness*, the author portrays Kraft as coming from a "spotlessly all-American family, in the 'Leave It to Beaver' mold." Kraft worried about his emerging homosexuality in high school and college. When he let it be known that he was homosexual, at twenty-four, it resulted in his removal from the army air corps. He had a good job as a computer analyst and a live-in lover of eight years. He was considered a compassionate person by his family and friends, and his lover never questioned why he went for so many solitary night rides. He was able to remain undetected for so long because he picked up hitchhikers with no ties to the locality. He dumped their bodies along freeways.

Was he, as sometimes claimed in crimes against homosexual men, trying to kill the homosexual in himself? It does not appear that any of his victims were homosexual. So what was the cause of his murderous anger against straight men? Kraft kept coded entries in a notebook, all of which could be tied to a murder, as in *GR2*, meaning "Grand Rapids, two deaths." There are six entries with the word *Portland*, where six similar murders occurred. Like other serial murderers, Kraft kept pictures and personal belongings in his home of several of his victims. Kraft is said to have come from a so-called perfect family. What was missing in that family relationship?

Charles Ng is accused of twelve murders in Calaveras County, California, and the Bay Area during 1984 and 1985. He escaped to Canada, where he was then arrested on a shoplifting charge and subsequently identified as the alleged serial murderer wanted in California. Because of a Canadian law that prohibits extraditing a person who may face the death penalty in the country requesting extradition, Ng was held in a Canadian prison for more that five years at a cost to the Saskatchawan taxpayers of more than $100,000. Legal costs for fighting extradition cost Canada more than $1.5 million.

Ng's crimes in California came to light when his friend Leonard Lake committed suicide by swallowing a cyanide tablet after his arrest in San Francisco. He had been caught driving a car belonging to a missing person, Paul Cosner. Ng had been in the car with Lake, but Ng escaped. The police then visited a mountain cabin belonging to Lake and discovered the grisly remains of twelve people. They also found forty-five pounds of burned bones, guns, videotapes of sexual torture, and bloody tools. Ng and Lake sexually tortured nearly two dozen women and videotaped them in agony. The remains of men and children were also found.

Aside from the Calaveras County charges against him, Ng was charged with the murders of Donald Giuliette, a San Francisco disc jockey, and his roommate who, on July 11, 1984, were fatally shot in their home.

Even though he was eventually extradited, Ng has spent three years in a Folsom, California, prison waiting for legal problems to be resolved. It is estimated that costs for legal wrangling now amount to approximately $8,000 a day. As the *San Francisco Chronicle* reported on July 20, 1994, "The current delay is over where to hold the trial."

Sex serial murderers usually have specific hate targets beyond simply hating women, such as hating all women who are prostitutes, or blondes, or redheads. Most victims are from powerless socioeconomic groups—blacks, runaways, elderly women, prostitutes, singles. All easy targets. Though the male sex murderer refers to women as castrating, it is men who are the actual castraters. Male sex murderers do not discriminate:

they castrate both their male and female victims. The victims are left desexed.

OCCULT SERIAL MURDERS

On November 10, 1989, after a year-long trial, twenty-nine-year-old devil worshiper Richard Ramirez, a drifter from El Paso, Texas, was convicted of murdering thirteen people, for which he received the death sentence. He was also sentenced to fifty-nine years for numerous rapes and attempted murders. In addition to these crimes, he is suspected of kidnapping and sexually assaulting probably twelve children, aged from six to early teens.

As the death sentence was read, Ramirez shouted at the jury that "Lucifer dwells in us all," and "Big deal! Death always went with the territory," and that he was beyond good and evil. The self-proclaimed satanist had terrorized the Los Angeles area for more than a year. One of his murder victims had a pentagram drawn on her body.

He was captured by a neighborhood mob on a Labor Day weekend in 1985, as he attempted to pull a woman from her car and grab her keys. By that time he had murdered at least thirteen people. One victim had her eyes gouged out. A woman was raped beside the body of her husband, whom Ramirez had killed after he broke into their home. He also beat up the couple's eight-year-old son, but did not harm the couple's two-year-old daughter.

Survivors have said he ordered them to "Swear to Satan." One woke up early on the morning of August 16, 1985, and saw Ramirez in her house. She screamed at him to get out, whereupon, from three feet away, he shot her in the face and then laughed at her when both husband and wife fell backward on the bed. Somehow her husband managed to chase Ramirez away and then drove to the hospital with his wife and their unharmed four-year-old daughter.

Another survivor said she woke up just before dawn and

heard a popping sound, not realizing it was a gunman shooting her husband. Ramirez joked to the woman that he had just knocked him out. He then beat, kicked, and handcuffed her. With blood coming from her nose and mouth he dragged her to a guest bedroom and raped her. He demanded she not scream for help, making her swear on Satan. He blindfolded and gagged her, saying he would kill her and her two small boys.

When the three-year-old woke, the mother begged Ramirez for permission to calm her son down. Naked and handcuffed she lay down with her child until he went back to sleep. When the child woke up again, Ramirez tied him to a chair and put a pillow over his head.

Ramirez left her handcuffed to the bed. She managed to free herself and her boy and asked him to wake up his father. The little boy returned and said, "He's not waking up." Though it was dark outside she persuaded him with promises of candy to go get the neighbors, who freed her.

At the trial she shouted to Ramirez about her husband's death, "What did you get out of killing him? He was such a nice man."

In a remote Sierra Madre home a sixteen-year-old girl awakened in her ransacked bedroom with a terrible headache. Ramirez had severely beaten her with a tire iron, and from the marks on her throat he had tried to strangle her. A bloody print of an Avia shoe on the young woman's comforter linked Ramirez to this crime. This shoe print was also found on the face of a Monterey Park woman who was beaten and strangled two days afterward.

A young mother awoke to see a man with bad teeth screaming at her to give him jewels and money. He dragged her from room to room and then back to the bedroom where he had shot her husband, calling her "bitch." After he raped her, he sodomized her eight-year-old son while she lay helpless.

Ramirez became known as the "Night Stalker." His method was to cut telephone wires and then enter through an unlocked door or window, kill the husband, and attack the wife who was then also usually killed. One man still carries one of Ramirez's bullets in his head.

In his jail cell Ramirez showed two pictures of nude murder victims to the sheriff's deputy who guarded him. The deputy testified that when Ramirez showed him the pictures he said, "People come here and call me a punk and I show them these pictures and say 'There's blood behind the Night Stalker,' and they go away pale." One picture was of the victim who had her eyes gouged out after she was stabbed.

Another sheriff's deputy testified how he had seen Ramirez with self-inflicted cuts in his hand using the blood to write "666" and draw a pentagram on the floor of his cell.

As of December 1994, Ramirez is on death row in San Quentin, where he has been for nine years: he has received nineteen death sentences. The trial for a twentieth murder will probably take another year and then there will probably be another ten years before he actually faces his own death. In his trial for the twentieth murder, relatives of the first nineteen victims will have to testify again, reopening old wounds. The family of the twentieth victim has stated that it wants no part of the trial.

SERIAL MURDERS OF GAY MEN

Sean Flanagan, a male prostitute, was executed by lethal injection in June 1989 in the state of Nevada for the murder of two gay men. He did not try to stop his own execution because he believed if he had not been arrested he would have ended up as another Ted Bundy, but against homosexuals.

In February 1990, David Porter, twenty-six, pleaded guilty in San Francisco to killing one gay man, and is suspected of having killed gay men in several other cities throughout the United States.

SERIAL MURDERS OF WOMEN OTHER THAN PROSTITUTES

Ted Bundy is famous for the number of women he killed, an estimated fifty, and for the number of appeals he made to escape death in the electric chair. Bundy, forty-two, was executed in Florida's electric chair on January 24, 1989.

The subject of five books and a TV miniseries, *The Deliberate Stranger*, Bundy was quick-witted, a law school dropout described as cocky and arrogant. With his arm in a prop sling he lured girls to his Volkswagen and asked them to help him carry his books.

In the early morning of January 15, 1978, Bundy entered the Chi Omega sorority house at Florida State University at Tallahassee, and went from bedroom to bedroom bludgeoning four sleeping women with a three-foot-long tree limb and killing two. At least one of the girls was sexually assaulted.

Shortly after his attack at the Chi Omega house, Bundy broke into the apartment of a twenty-one-year-old student. He broke her jaw and caused other injuries, but she survived. He preferred young women who were pretty and dressed as though they were upper middle class.

Bundy was suspected of killing at least thirty-six women, but as his execution date neared, he revealed the circumstances of thirty additional murders. His actual execution was for the murder of twelve-year-old Kimberly Leach of Lake City, Florida, kidnapped February 9, 1978, from her junior high school and found three months later in a pigsty. Bundy was under three death sentences at the time he was executed, eleven years after his conviction.

In another rampage against women, also in Florida, a serial killer, thirty-seven-year-old Danny Rolling, stalked coeds at Florida State University in Gainesville, committing murders in August 1990. With a surgically sharp blade he mutilated three bodies and, of those, decapitated one, whose body had been slashed open. Police said some of the victim's flesh was missing and pictures of the victims had been taken from the apartments. In one case the victim's decapitated head was placed on a shelf. Except for one young man, all the victims were young, petite brunette women.

An FBI expert on serial murders, John Douglas, said that these serial murders were different from others in that there was no "cooling off" period between killings. He said these were "spree" serial killings. The murderer's "signature"—that is, something he does other than murder—was mutilation. The killer entered the victims' apartments by forcing sliding doors or got in through unlocked doors. All victims died from stab wounds. On April 20, 1994, Rolling was condemned to death for these heinous crimes, having been a suspect since 1991. He was also a suspect in the murder of three in Shreveport, Louisiana, his home town, and also a suspect in the murder of his father. He was linked to the Gainesville murder by DNA tests.

The 1989 TV movie "Two of a Kind: The Case of the Hillside Strangler" chronicled the murders of ten women by Angelo Buono and his cousin, Kenneth Bianchi, in Los Angeles from 1977 to 1978. The women were killed within a five-month period, their bodies dumped in the hills. Bored with simple rape, the murderers used electrical torture on the girls, who were from different backgrounds and of different ethnic groups. Women were the game in this hunt by two men who stumped the Los Angeles Police Department. When Bianchi was arrested for strangling two women in Washington while employed as a security guard, he was connected to the Hillside Strangler murders.

SERIAL FREEWAY MURDERS

Until recently a serial freeway killer was someone who killed his victims and then dumped them near a freeway. Now it means someone who shoots his victims as they drive on the freeway.

Why men sit on hillsides, shoot at, and attempt to murder strangers in passing cars is difficult to understand. But when a Los Angeles County police officer does it, it is even more confounding. In June 1994, Robert Cardona, a twelve-year Los Angeles Police Department officer, was arrested, gun in hand, after two drivers called 911, having been shot at as they exited Interstate 10 in Colton, California. The cartridges found in the area from where the shots were fired were the same as in Cardona's gun.

Driving to Lake Tahoe on July 2, 1990, with his family for a July Fourth holiday, Peter Martinelli, twenty-six, was shot and killed on Interstate 50 by a freeway serial killer. At first the family heard a popping sound that they believed was a tire blowing out. Then the car went out of control and rolled over. The family believed Peter had been killed by the accident. Later, in an autopsy, a bullet fragment was found in his head.

On the same day that Martinelli was killed on I-50, a car driven by a man from Idaho, also going to Tahoe on the same highway with his family, was hit by a bullet, but no one inside was injured.

Around midnight on the night of the shootings, police arrested Kenneth Millikan, thirty, believing he was intoxicated. In his car police found a .38-caliber semiautomatic pistol, in addition to a .41-caliber Magnum. He was released, but on July 16 was arrested on suspicion of murder after a ballistics test on his guns related him to the freeway murders.

On another highway, Interstate 580, east of Oakland, a freeway killer destroyed the life of Raymond August, twenty-eight, on July 27, 1990. August, an airline engineer, was driving home from a dinner date with his fiancée. An honor student in high school, he was well liked. Six hundred people attended his funeral.

The freeway serial murderer of Raymond August was caught because he was followed by Rodney Stokes, a man who only moments before had been shot at but escaped injury.

Stokes said he saw Charles Stevens shoot August and alerted police. Stevens, twenty-one, was also accused of fatally shooting Lori Rochon, thirty-six, of Oakland, on July 6, 1990, as she drove to her night job as a computer technician. Two other drivers reported being shot at several days after Lori Rochon was killed, but they reported no physical injuries.

Charles Stevens is also accused of killing Laquan Sloan, sixteen, on June 8, 1989, in a drive-by shooting, ostensibly because of an unpaid drug debt and Leslie Noyer, twenty-nine, on April 3, 1989. He shot her several times as she sat in a stolen car. All told, Stevens killed four people, two he knew and two strangers on the freeway. And all of these killings occurred when he should have been in jail. Stevens had been jailed for auto theft but was released after serving only sixteen days on a one-year sentence due to overcrowding at Alameda County Santa Ritas Jail. Prisoners not convicted of a violent crime or of drug dealing can be released on a court order. He was freed March 3, 1989, and killed his first victim one month later.

At the arraignment, Stevens's sister yelled to the judge that she and her bother were nonviolent Jehovah's Witnesses. In the quiet area where Stevens lived, neighbors found it hard to believe he might be the freeway killer.

Murder to Get Rid of a Human Obstacle

In mass murder the victims are usually unknown or barely known to the killer. The killer may have set out to kill, but not to kill any specific person. In a more typical form of murder, premeditation is involved. The killer plans how he will get rid of a spouse, a business partner, or someone else who is getting in his way. In the case of spouse murder, it is likely that the killer is having an affair, or there may be insurance money to be gained.

The strangulation death of a well-liked Oakland woman who ran two preschools mystified police until they learned that her husband had been having an affair for a year and a half with a Daly City woman. She said he promised to marry her and had given her a diamond ring. The husband was arrested for murder.

The victim and her husband had just celebrated their twenty-seventh wedding anniversary and were planning a trip to Florida. Her body was discovered by their sixteen-year-old son.

A strange case in Santa Ana, California, came to light when a young woman, Cinnamon Brown, revealed, after spending three years in a youth prison, that her father, David Brown, thirty-eight, a millionaire computer expert, had persuaded her to kill her stepmother when Cinnamon was fourteen. Her stepmother was the mother of a seven-month-old girl at the time Cinnamon shot her. David Brown had convinced Cinnamon that her stepmother was plotting to kill him. Evidence later revealed that he had taken out a $1 million life insurance policy on his wife's life. Because Cinnamon was a juvenile at the time of her crime—her father had advised her that she was too young to stay in prison long—she was sentenced to remain in California Youth Authority prison until she was twenty-five.

After her stepmother's death, Cinnamon's father married her stepmother's sister, Patti Bailey, his sixth marriage to a much younger woman. David Brown was sentenced in September 1990 to life without possibility of parole. In addition to making the arrangements to have his wife killed, he was also convicted of attempting to have the prosecuting attorney murdered. He is in Folsom Prison, under protection because of threats by other inmates against his life. Patti Bailey is also in jail as an accessory to the murder plot. A juvenile at the time of the crime and charged with complicity, Bailey was sentenced to remain in prison until she was twenty-five.

This case was made into a TV miniseries entitled *Love, Lies and Murder*. In it the writers attempted to depict the evil in a father who would use his devoted daughter in a plot to kill his wife, a crime that put his daughter in prison. The sentencing judge referred to David Brown as frightening because he did such a terrible thing to his wife and his own daughter, yet he looked so normal.

In a gruesome case in San Jose, California, a plumber named Bruce Grant, thirty-six, was arrested in August 1989 for the 1982 murder of his friend's wife, Nancy Crew. Grant allegedly cut off her head after she was shot by her husband but was not yet dead. The husband, Mark Crew, thirty-three, was convicted of murdering his wife by shooting her in the back of her head as they were talking.

Though the jury recommended the death penalty, the Santa Clara County Superior Court judge sentenced Grant to life in prison without parole. Mark Crew was convicted of first-degree murder with special circumstances. Crew and his wife, a nurse, had been married only two months. He was convicted of murdering her for her yellow Corvette and her insurance money.

The body of Nancy Crew has never been found. It was related by Crew's best friend, a key witness, that her body and head were dropped from the Dumbarton Bridge in San Mateo County. The parts were put into containers, filled with concrete, and thrown into the water.

In Boston, Massachusetts, Charles Stuart, twenty-nine, took advantage of the high crime rate to camouflage the killing of his wife, Carol, thirty-three, a lawyer eight months pregnant. As they left a childbirth class together, he drove to a designated spot where he was to meet his brother.

The next day the nation was caught up in the story of a young, successful couple who had, as Charles Stuart told it, been robbed by a black gunman who had killed his wife. Stuart himself had been shot but had managed to call police with his car phone.

People were outraged. They called radio stations, demanding, "We've got to find the guy that did this and string him up." The *Boston Herald*'s front page editorial asked, "When will we demand that the random shooting, the gratuitous violence that we too often accept as part of urban life, cease?" The tape of Stuart's car phone call for help were transcribed onto newspaper front pages, "My wife's been shot. I've been shot . . . Oh God . . ."

Charles Stuart's story was that a black man forced them to drive to an inner city neighborhood where he told them before he shot them, "I think you're five-oh," meaning, "I think you're police." As the story turned out, it was Charles Stuart who drove to the inner city neighborhood, and it was he who shot his wife, and then, intending to shoot himself in the foot, accidentally moved as he pulled the trigger and shot himself in the abdomen. After that, he threw a bag to his brother, Matthew, that contained the revolver and some of Carol's things, including her engagement ring, which he reported stolen. Charles told Matthew to take the bag to their parents' house.

Matthew Stuart, twenty-three, instead went to the police with the evidence after his brother singled out an innocent black man as the attacker. When Charles realized he had become the prime suspect, he committed suicide by drowning himself in Boston Harbor. WCVB-TV in Boston said he had admitted committing the crime for $600,000 of insurance policies. It was later learned he had a budding relationship with another woman.

The black community, which had been the target of white fury for the killing of the bright young white woman and her unborn child, in turn became furious that everyone had so automatically accepted the accusation that a black man had committed the crime. As a result of Stuart's accusation, young black men had been routinely pulled into Boston police stations for questioning in the crime. Charles Stuart, it was said, could as easily have sent an innocent black man to death as he did his wife.

The shame that Charles Stuart should have felt became a collective embarrassment for the white community. The people who sought to rectify this injustice were the De Maitis family, the parents and siblings of the dead Carol Stuart. They set up a scholarship fund for children in the inner city neighborhood that had been unjustly implicated in their pregnant daughter's murder. Carol Stuart's baby was delivered by cesarean section after her death, but the infant boy lived for only seventeen days.

Murder for money is age-old. It occurs among spouses, siblings quarreling over their parents' inheritance, and friends. But it is particularly poignant when it occurs between children and parents. The case of the Beverly Hills Menendez brothers, suspected of murdering their mother and their father, startled the community and the nation.

On August 28, 1989, Jose Menendez, forty-five, chief executive of a music and video distribution company, and his wife, Kitty, forty-four, were shot at close range by two shotguns using more than twelve rounds of ammunition. The two sons, Erik, nineteen, and Lyle, twenty-two, heirs to the $14 million estate, claimed they found their parents' bloodied bodies when they returned home that evening. By the time they were arrested, a $400,000 life insurance policy had already been issued to the boys.

After the death of their parents, both brothers underwent psychological therapy from October to December 1989. Because the psychologist had "reason to believe that his own and the safety of others was in jeopardy," the District Court of Appeals judge ruled that the audio tapes made by the psychologist summarizing each session could be used in the trial. The right to privacy did not apply since the brothers had threatened their psychologist.

On one of the tapes the psychologist summarized, "Erik revealed in detail the planning and execution of the crime, including the brothers' fabricated and alibi defense." Later in the tape he explained, "They didn't kill their parents for money but rather out of hatred and out of a desire to be free from their father's domination, messages of inadequacy, and impossible standards."

Previously secret testimony by a woman known as a paramour of the psychologist was also released in the ruling. The woman had given testimony to the police that she had overheard Lyle Menendez explode in anger after he learned that his brother, Lyle, had admitted to the murders. "I can't believe you did this!" Lyle yelled at his brother. "I can't believe you told him. I don't even have a brother now! I could get rid of you for this! Now I hope you know what we are going to do. I hope you realize what we are going to have to do. We've got to kill him and anyone associated with him." The woman then said she heard Erik sob, "I can't stop you [Lyle] from what you have to do, but I can't kill anymore."

The brothers said they didn't kill their parents for money but to escape the domination of their father, even though they did stand to inherit $14 million. Theoretically, this sum has since been dissipated through legal fees and other expenses; the estate also may have been overvalued at the outset. Later the brothers claimed they killed their parents because their parents were going to kill them: Jose and Kitty feared that their children were going to tell the world that they had been sexually abused.

The six-month trial of the Menendez brothers ended in a hung jury in the spring of 1994. The defense successfully convinced enough members of the jury that "the boys" had been sexually abused, especially Erik, over a long period of time by their father. A new trial is scheduled for 1995.

In another case of murder for money, a man suspected his benefactor was going to change her will, so he bludgeoned her to death aboard ship. Robert Frisbee, fifty-eight, was the companion of widow Muriel Barnett, seventy-nine, a member of San Francisco high society. Frisbee was accused of murdering her shortly before their Alaska cruise ship docked on August 19, 1985. He was convicted of premeditated first-degree murder and sentenced to twenty-five years to life.

Frisbee apparently needed to kill Muriel before they returned home, when she planned to change her will and reduce his inheritance to $250,000. She had previously agreed, at his urging, to leave him two-thirds of her vast fortune. Frisbee had been her husband's valet, but when Philip Barnett died he had left Frisbee nothing, though it was alleged that Philip Barnett and Frisbee had had a sexual affair. The San Francisco coroner's office ruled that the victim had been hit at least four times on the forehead by a "rigid, rounded object," such as a liquor bottle.

Sometimes the real or imagined burdens of men become so great they set out to destroy their whole family. Such was the case in Taylor, Michigan, on August 3, 1989, when Laurence De Lisle, twenty-eight, a sales manager at a tire store, confessed to driving his car into the river "to be rid of his present burden"— his wife and four children. Though he intended to kill his entire family, his wife, Suzanne, thirty-two, escaped from the station wagon as it was sinking. Their four children perished.

Before his confession De Lisle claimed a leg cramp made him accidentally jam the accelerator. Friends and relatives said he was heavily in debt and worried about supporting his family on $33,000 a year. The four children, ages ten months, two, four, and eight were buried together after a funeral attended by over 500 residents of the Michigan suburb.

Murder for Hire

At least one man hired a hit man from this ad that ran in *Soldier of Fortune* magazine in February 1985: "Ex-marine, 67–69 vet Ex-DI, weapons specialist-jungle warfare. Pilot. ME High-risk assignments. U.S. or overseas." Robert Black read the ad and hired John Wayne Hearn to kill his wife, Sandra. Black was sentenced to die and is on death row in Texas. Hearn is serving life sentences for three killings, including that of Black's wife. Though the son and mother of the slain woman brought the publishers of *Soldier of Fortune* to trial, there eventually was no conviction against the publication. The publishers contended there was no way they could have interpreted "high-risk," as "gun for hire."

A murder-for-hire case involved a multimillionaire sports agent, Michael Blatt, forty-three, of Stockton, California, and two ex-college football stars, who claim they were hired by Blatt to get rid of a business associate, Lawrence Carnegie. According to the victim's wife, Blatt, believing Carnegie had prevented him from getting the job of general manager of the Seattle Seahawks, had Carnegie killed.

Aside from the tragedy of the murder, the other tragedy was that Blatt could persuade otherwise nice young men to commit murder. James Mackey and Carl Hancock, both twenty-six, pleaded guilty to first-degree murder. They confessed that they lured Carnegie to an empty house, pretending to discuss a real estate deal. Mackey testified that he shot Carnegie with a crossbow and shoved him into the trunk of a rented car. As they were driving they heard noise from the trunk. They stopped and, seeing that Carnegie was still alive, strangled him. The two men then dumped his body in a ravine.

Though Blatt insisted on his innocence, investigations revealed that he wrote checks to the two men, one that would have paid for the crossbow and another to pay for a trip to Mexico for Mackey right after the murder.

In November 1990, the judge declared a mistrial after the jury deliberated for fourteen days and deadlocked on a 9–3 vote favoring conviction. Several jurors did not believe it was fair that Blatt should be headed for a possible death penalty when those he had hired did not receive the death penalty.

Murder to Get Rid of a Witness

After a year-long international search, Enrique Zambrano, forty-five, was captured in Palm Springs, California, a suspect in the beating of a University of California professor and his wife. Zambrano had told his friend Luis Reyna about the beating and then, afraid that Reyna would be a witness against him if the case went to court, killed him. Zambrano was charged with decapitating Reyna in addition to the attempted murder of the professor and his wife.

In another killing to silence a crime, Stanley Davis, twenty-seven, murdered two Los Angeles student sweethearts in 1985 to keep them from telling police he had stolen their car. He was found guilty in September 1990 of two counts of first-degree murder. In order to commit a robbery, Davis and three others had stolen the young man's car, kidnapping the man and his girlfriend. They drove to a secluded field where Davis shot them with an Uzi, then set the car on fire.

One of the accomplices, age twenty-four, was granted immunity in exchange for testimony that Davis told him to shoot the students in the back of the head at close range, because "he didn't want no witnesses to the car stealing." The other two male accomplices, both twenty-three years old, were convicted of murder, kidnapping, arson, and grand theft auto. When the verdict was read, the parents of the dead students cried with relief. "It's been a long four years," the mother of the girl said, weeping.

Murders in Violent Bursts of Temper

In an Oakland mall in January 1990, two groups of young people had a volatile confrontation because a person in one group bumped into a woman in the other. Then the groups separated, but not before Michael Wallis, twenty-nine, saw James Craft, nineteen, flash a weapon.

Wallis called a friend, who brought an automatic rifle to the mall in a guitar case. Wallis took the gun, found Craft, and fatally shot him. He later found Jimmy Jones, a member of Craft's group, and shot and critically wounded him.

Even in the sanctuary of a Baptist church, tempers can flare and leave others dead. One man, angry with other members at a deacons' meeting, opened fire and killed two people and wounded another. The murderer was thirty years old.

In Mastic, New York, a father argued with and shot his eighteen-year-old daughter. For a time, believing that the daughter was still alive, the police attempted to negotiate with the father. When a shot was heard, the police entered the home and found both the father and daughter dead. The father, James Hyames, fifty-nine, had a history of angry outbursts. Married several times, he once shot his pregnant wife, who survived though the baby was lost. He was sent to prison for that attack. In another marriage he held his wife and two children hostage for two days, holding off police by gunfire.

When Ricky Tejada returned home from his night job in a San Francisco hotel in June 1994, he found a bloody scene. His three-year-old son was dead; his wife, his mother-in-law, and six-year-old daughter were tied up, gagged, and stabbed. His wife told police her brother had come to the house to ask for money and when she refused to give him any he got violent. He was arrested the next day.

Many family arguments erupt over the holidays. Larry Bartlett, thirty-two, an IBM designer, shot his eleven-year-old daughter, Kelly, on Thanksgiving weekend. He told police she had shot herself accidentally, but four months later, Bartlett was arrested.

Many murders resulting from a man's temper are over trifling things. In Santa Ana, California, when Alfonso Rodriguez took a cowboy hat off a man's head as a prank, he was shot and killed. Also in June 1989, in the same city, Eugene Robinson, thirty-four, knocked over a man's beer bottle and was shot and killed.

San Quentin inmate Alfredo Hidalgo was strangled by his cell partner, Michael Ferrie, because he snored.

Loud music apparently causes so much stress in some men it drives them over the edge. Two Los Angeles brothers were arrested when one of them killed their upstairs neighbors because of their loud music. This was not the first time the brothers had argued with the neighbors, a man and a woman, over the noise. When the building manager went to investigate the sound of the gun shots, he too was shot, though not fatally. The brothers had rented their apartment for thirteen years. The unharmed one-month-old daughter of the slain couple was taken to the social services department.

In another loud-noise incident the complainant was killed. Jose Hertago, forty-four, had been awakened by two men in their car playing loud music in the street across from Los Angeles City College. Hertago argued with them and went back to bed. But when he left for work at 5:00 A.M., the two men jumped him and beat him to death.

Some murders occur when a would-be car thief demands a car and the owner resists. Twenty-three-year-old Vincent Rogers of Los Angeles was waiting for a red light to change at an intersection when he was approached by men for the purpose of taking his Cadillac; he was killed when he refused.

Getting into an argument at the scene of a traffic accident can be fatal, as it was for Juan Rendon, thirty-seven, in Oakland. When his car collided with another car, Rendon pulled into a car-wash parking lot. Witnesses reported hearing shooting. Rendon was killed, and the suspects fled.

Hospital emergency rooms have become dangerous places. Without security, staff and patients are vulnerable to attack from anybody coming off the street. Such was the case in February 1993, when Damascio Torres went to the University of Southern California Medical Center in Los Angeles, angry because he thought he had been used in an AIDS experiment. He brought two handguns, a knife, and a rifle, aiming to attack those he thought had infected him with AIDS. Though his victims—three doctors—lived, he was convicted May 9, 1994, of attempted murder. There was agreement that Torres was delusional, but the jury concluded that he methodically thought out his plan and might have been even more dangerous if the SWAT team that captured him had not been successful.

Murder in Commission of Robbery

Even when it is not known if any money was taken, murders occur where money is dispensed. At the Any Kind Check Cashing office in downtown Los Angeles, Loretta Abeyta, twenty-two, an employee, was fatally shot and her coworker critically wounded after four men demanded money. Children who were with the women were not hurt.

In another case where robbery was probably the motive, four men in ski masks, all carrying AK-47 assault rifles, burst into a car stereo shop in Paramount, California, and shot and killed two, and injured two others.

In Alameda County a landscaper is being held in the stabbing deaths of two elderly people, Earl Garcia, seventy, and his wife, Doris, sixty-three. The landscaper had worked for the couple, who lived in a secluded area, on two occasions. Robbery is believed to be the motive.

When Sean Darnell Slade was on parole after a conviction of manslaughter, he and several accomplices staged a robbery of an armored car at a Home Depot store in Los Angeles County. An armed guard was shot to death in July 1992, for which Slade was given a life sentence on May 5, 1994. His male accomplices have not been apprehended.

In another case of a robbery gone awry, twenty-year-old U.S. marine Erik Wick was arrested for the murder of two people and attempted murder of another in a Newport Beach rare coin shop on June 8, 1989. The three victims were shot in the back, as in execution-style killings. Wick was absent without leave from his marine base at the time of the shooting. The police linked several valuable rare coins and a 9-millimeter semiautomatic weapon that Wick possessed to the murders.

When a young woman, eighteen, left her country home in Sebastopol, California, to start her adult life in San Francisco, she was excited and filled with hope for her future. On her first night in the apartment she rented with her cousin, Gloria Schoofs, Iyan Hughes was killed by a young man who broke into the apartment to steal her stereo. The man was a tenant in the same apartment building.

When the apartment manager found Hughes, after being alerted by her screams, and after he scuffled with a fleeing man, she was bleeding from multiple stab wounds. A kitchen knife lay bent on the floor. Thirty-one-year-old Daryl Johnson, a twice-convicted burglar, gave himself up. He was about to be evicted from the apartment because he was two months in arrears on his rent. He was held on $1 million bail.

Whether for a stereo or for $5, many young men kill for what they want. No doubt Valestir Green, twenty-five, Sean Gage, eighteen, and Donald Reed, twenty-one, arrested in the slaying of a young attorney in Oakland, believed they would get more than $5 when they set out to rob him. Erik Hendrikson was attacked on October 30, 1989, as he left his office to return home to his wife and three-day-old baby. Hendrikson was kicked and beaten to death by what an Oakland homicide sergeant termed was "a vicious pack that prowled the streets" looking for people they could rob to get money for marijuana, gasoline, or liquor.

An irony is that Hendrikson, a *magna cum laude* graduate of Yale and a Harvard Law School graduate, believed strongly in the need to protect the rights of criminals. As Alameda County Superior Court Judge Roderic Duncan said, "They were the people he really went to bat for."

It is becoming commonly known that people who use automatic bank teller machines do so at their own risk. After removing their money from the machines, they are then robbed and killed. The men who commit these crimes are not satisfied with just taking the money. They seem to need to murder the victim in order to eliminate the one person who could identify them.

In San Francisco, in August 1990, a college student from Ireland, Paul O'Meara, was beaten to death with a baseball bat. His four assailants had watched him leave an automated teller machine. O'Meara's companion, waiting for him in a car, jumped out and shouted at the assailants, who then fled, dropping the bloody bat as they ran. The four men, described as being in their twenties and thirties, had taken no money from O'Meara because the automated teller machine had been closed. O'Meara's parents were to arrive from Ireland the next day to meet his fiancée.

On April 4, 1994, in a New Jersey Popeye's Famous Fried Chicken, two young men committed a robbery. In doing so, they rounded up three employees and forced them into a freezer and shot them dead. A wounded employee was able to call police after the robbers left. The men, Cuhuatemoc Peraita, seventeen, and Robert Melson, twenty-two, were arrested two hours later and charged with murder. In another fast-food robbery gone bad, two brothers in their twenties were arrested on May 23, 1994, after they had killed a seventy-one-year-old patron, wounded four others, and took twenty-five hostages in a Denny's.

When a husband and wife from Germany stopped in their rental car at a viewpoint near Palm Springs, California, on May 15, 1994, the woman was shot to death in the course of a robbery. The man, badly wounded, managed to drive his car to get help but was unable to tell others what had happened until an interpreter could be found. Nine days after the incident, two males from a nearby town were arrested for the crime.

Murder for No Known Motive

It is said there is a motive for everything, but in some cases of murder, the motives are obscure, or at least not yet revealed.

Neighbors in the affluent suburb of Whittier, California, said Thomas Morgan, forty-three, was depressed because he had been unemployed for several years. That's why he shot his parents and his brother. The police arrived in response to the brother's telephone call and airlifted the bleeding man to the hospital. A neighbor remarked that Morgan must have gone off the deep end.

At the Acorn Housing Project in Oakland, Shawn Garth, twenty-three, sprayed the project's guard station with bullets and killed Reese Davis. He was convicted in April 1989 of that murder and of attempted murder of two other guards. He provided no motive for his rampage.

In Hollywood, Florida, a gunman entered a bus and killed the driver and fired into the back of the bus, killing a passenger. He commandeered an automobile by shooting a driver sitting at a traffic light. This happened in front of a supermarket around noon on a hot July day in 1989. Police believed the gunman used an automatic weapon.

Even police officers go berserk. Two of them killed a club bouncer after getting drunk. In their thirties, Gabriel Bedoya and John Koch went to Chicago from Milwaukee on May 27, 1994, as they said, for a good time. While there, they sprayed a Catholic cardinal's home with gunfire, fired shots at a condominium and a hotel, and entered into an argument with the bouncer at a bar, shooting him dead.

In Germantown, Wisconsin, in June 1990, Peter Chapman, thirty-nine, reported to the police that his son had been abducted. Actually, the father had buried his eleven-month-old son alive, for no known reason. The autopsy revealed that the son had suffocated as he tried to scratch his way through the dirt. The circuit judge denied the father's request to attend his son's funeral.

Even extreme precaution against attack is sometimes not enough. In one of the toughest areas in Los Angeles, Jorge Dailey, Sr., sixty-eight, a retired restaurant worker who worked in the Calvary Baptist Church Bargain Thrift Shop, would not permit anyone to come into the store unless he knew them. He had been robbed several times and was extremely cautious. Yet someone did gain entrance and clubbed him to death. No robbery occurred, and no motive was determined.

CHAPTER 3

WHITE-COLLAR CRIME

White-collar crime is said to be, for the criminal, the most profitable of crimes, and also the safest. Some investigative experts believe white-collar criminals "get away with about $200 billion a year," according to a March 1986 *Scholastic Update*. That figure is considered to be more than the profit from all other types of crimes. Yet white-collar criminals make up only 5 percent of the prison population because so few are caught; if caught, few go to prison; if sent to prison, few serve lengthy sentences.

White-collar crime is defined as the taking of bribes, manipulation of stocks or bank information, false advertising, toxic waste dumping, tax fraud, concealment of product defects, the selling and buying of secrets, and wire and mail fraud.

Federal White-Collar Crime

In crimes committed against the federal government, 20,000 cases were investigated in the first six months of 1988. In 1985,

10,777 defendants were convicted of federal white-collar crime, 795 of those for tax fraud. Persons convicted of white-collar crimes received shorter average sentences than other federal offenders. White-collar criminals are most apt to be sentenced to probation or fined. Counterfeiters are most apt to receive longer sentences.

Monetary fines imposed on convicted felons in federal courts are often unpaid. According to an Associated Press report based on Justice Department statistics in October 1989, "More than 35,000 Americans convicted of federal crimes owe the United States $600 million." Efforts to collect fines for federal crimes have not convinced many felons to pay what they owe.

The following is quoted from the U.S. Department of Justice Bureau of Statistics' Special Report of September 1987:

Although white-collar offenses are less visible than crimes such as burglary and robbery, their overall economic impact may be considerably greater. Among the white-collar cases filed by U.S. Attorneys in the year ending September 30, 1985, more than 140 persons were charged with offenses estimated to involve over $1 million each, and 64 were charged with offenses valued at over $10 million each. That is a total of $780 million. In comparison, losses from all robberies reported to police in 1985 totaled about $313 million.

The appropriate definition of white-collar crime has long been a matter of dispute among criminologists and criminal justice practitioners. A particular point of contention is whether white-collar crime is defined by the nature of the offense or by the status, profession, or skills of the defendant. The 1981 *Dictionary of Criminal Justice Data Terminology* defines white-collar crime as nonviolent crime for financial gain committed by means of deception by persons . . . having professional status or specialized technical skills.

In general, defendants of all types [of crimes] were predominantly male, white, non-Hispanic, and younger than forty, and had not attended college. White-collar defendants, however, included higher proportions of women, nonwhites and persons over forty than did nonwhite-collar defendants. White-collar defendants were also less likely to be Hispanic, and they were more likely to have attended college.

With respect to specific white-collar offenders, higher proportions of those charged with tax fraud (93 percent), lending and credit fraud (81 percent), counterfeiting (76 percent), and regulatory offenses (90 percent) were white than were other types of white-collar and nonwhite-collar defendants. Women were a larger proportion of those charged with embezzlement (41 percent) and forgery (30 percent) than those charged with white-collar crimes overall (26 percent), though males had a higher percentage in each case.

Two-thirds of those arrested for tax fraud were over forty . . . those charged with tax fraud, lending and credit fraud, and embezzlement were substantially more likely to have attended college than were other types of defendants. In contrast, those charged with forgery were less likely to have attended college than all other defendants.

Federal investigators spend more of their time investigating white-collar crime than any other category of crime. Also, more prosecutors' time is spent on white-collar crimes than other crimes. Though there are higher conviction rates than for other crimes, sentences for white-collar crimes are fewer and shorter.

MISCELLANEOUS BUSINESS/CORPORATE WHITE-COLLAR CRIME

Corporate crimes are deemed by some to be less heinous because they seem less personal. They may be crimes against institutions like banks, or crimes against the government. Persons committing these crimes in corporations are seldom held accountable. When E. F. Hutton was fined more than $2 million and ordered to pay $4 million to the banks it had defrauded, no individual employee was cited for the crimes.

In Russell's book, *Corporate Crime and Violence,* he suggests several things that should be done to curtail corporate white-collar crime. He suggests prison sentences with a minimum of one year and a maximum of fifteen years and establishing guidelines for judges, whose sentencing is too lenient. Fines don't work since the potential monetary gain usually far exceeds the fines, and the penalties for most corporations are $5,000. Many corporations do not even pay their fines.

Also, Mokhiber says to treat white-collar criminals like criminals. Do not house them in "country-club" prisons. Quoting from his book: "The price-fixer should be housed next to the burglar, the company official whose drug company knowingly marketed unsafe drugs that killed people should be housed with other murderers. . . . A side benefit of ending this separation will be the improvement of prison conditions for all inmates. The white-collar criminals will insist on improvement."

Most corporations are the darlings of their states, which give them their charters. Corporations help support states in their payment of income, sales, and property taxes. For states to penalize their corporations is to threaten their potential tax base. States cannot be relied upon to regulate the corporations within their boundaries. Therefore, Mokhiber suggests that all corporations be obliged to have federal charters and federal regulations.

Racketeering

With the anti-racketeering law known as RICO—the Racketeering Influenced and Corrupt Organizations Act—prosecutors may arrest suspects and seize property more easily than before the enactment of the law. The success of this law is evident in the increased number of racketeering charges brought to court.

RICO enables prosecutors to focus on *patterns* of criminal acts, rather than on individual acts. If anyone has been involved in a criminal activity twice in a ten-year period, from murder and extortion to mail or wire fraud, RICO can target that person for racketeering charges. RICO has come under attack by corporations as being too all-inclusive, yet the U.S. Supreme Court has twice refused to limit RICO's power, leaving that up to the Congress.

There is currently strong support in Congress to limit the racketeering act, putting the burden on plaintiffs to prove that the person being brought to court is a major participant in the wrongdoing. An opponent of pending legislation, specifically Pam Gilbert, legislative director of Public Citizens' Watch, says, "This legislation is a bailout for white-collar criminals." Others agree that legislation concerned solely with the major participant could let others involved in white-collar crime escape indictment—namely accountants, lawyers, and investment bankers, participants who had no central role. Rep. John Conyers of Michigan said, "The major participant provision will let off the guys who cooked the books and the lawyers who helped put the schemes together."

Racketeering laws were used to convict two sports agents in Chicago in April 1989, Norby Walters, fifty-eight, and Lloyd Bloom, twenty-nine. They were accused of writing contracts with college athletes that violated NCAA rules, of using donations from organized crime, and of using threats of violence against at least one athlete—if he broke his contract Bloom would have someone break his leg. The mail fraud and racketeering charges stemmed from their defrauding two universities.

Stock Market Fraud

IVAN BOESKY

On May 24, 1990, Ivan Boesky's three-year prison term for insider trading ended after he had served nineteen months. Boesky had previously revealed that he had made a deal with the government allowing him to deduct from his taxes $50 million of the $100 million he had paid in settlement. He was also permitted to retain millions of dollars he had gained from insider trading. In May of 1990, he admitted arranging for briefcases of cash to be used as payoffs for tips on insider trading. He was a principal witness in the trial of Michael Milken.

At the heart of the Securities and Exchange Commission's case against Boesky and Milken is the charge that the two men were involved in insider trading, stock price manipulation, rigging of corporate takeovers, and tax fraud. According to a Security and Exchange Commission memorandum of May 1988, Boesky and Milken met in July 1986 to determine how they would conceal the origin of the $5.3 million payment from Boesky to Drexel Burnham Lambert, the stock exchange company headed by Michael Milken. This $5.3 million payment was made about two months before the fall of investment banker Dennis Levine, which triggered the whole insider trader scandal on Wall Street. Drexel said the payment from Boesky was for consulting services, but the SEC said it was a prearranged deal and that the payment was in exchange for insider trading information. Milken denied any connection to any such scheme.

MICHAEL MILKEN

The target of ninety-eight indictments of criminal racketeering and securities fraud, conspiracy, mail fraud, and aiding and abetting tax fraud, Michael Milken, forty-four, was considered the driving force behind Drexel Burnham Lambert's fabulous growth, selling high-yield and high-risk junk bonds to finance corporate takeovers.

Before any indictment of Michael Milken was under way, a woman was convicted in the insider trading scandal. Lisa Jones, twenty-six, who worked in the same trading room as Milken, was convicted of five counts of perjury and two counts of obstructing justice. She was not accused of securities fraud.

When questioned by the grand jury investigating Drexel Burnham Lambert about possible fraud, Lisa Jones said she knew nothing about parking stocks. "Parking stocks" is a scheme to conceal the real ownership of securities to avoid taxes. Although Jones claimed not to know of this scheme, prosecutors presented a tape of telephone conversations in which she discussed parking stocks.

One prosecutor, when criticized about his harsh treatment of Jones, said, "She is nobody other than a foolish young woman who made a dumb choice despite numerous opportunities to make the right choice."

William Hale, who testified against Jones, presented her "as a scared and confused minor employee who had been intimidated by government investigators and wasn't aware that she was involved in any illegal activity," according to the *Los Angeles Times*.

The case of a woman convicted in the stock market scandal is mentioned here to compare the severity of her prison sentence for perjury to that of the sentences of the men whose crimes caused the collapse of numerous companies. Her prison term may exceed that of Ivan Boesky, a major player in the insider trading scandal.

Michael Milken was indicted on March 29, 1989. On November 21, 1990, Judge Kimba Wood, after a lengthy presentencing hearing, sentenced Milken to ten years in prison, saying, "Your crimes show a pattern of skirting the law, stepping just over the wrong side of the law in an apparent effort to get some of the benefits from violating the law without running a substantial risk of being caught. . . . This kind of misuse of your leadership position and enlisting employees whom you supervised to assist you in violating the law are serious crimes warranting serious punishment and discomfort and opprobrium of being removed from society. . . ."

Judge Wood said in court that from the evidence in the pre-sentencing hearing she was convinced that Milken committed many crimes besides the six felony counts to which he had pleaded guilty. One of those crimes include Milken's order to his employees to destroy documents, in what amounted to an obstruction of justice.

Specifically, the government claims that as early as 1983 Milken led his company, Drexel, to trade on inside information and to manipulate the prices of stocks.

In 1985, Drexel arranged for Ivan Boesky to buy shares in Harris Graphics Company, in which Drexel already owned a 22 percent share. When Harris was taken over, profits on the deal personally netted Milken $6.5 million. In 1987, as a result of his stock-manipulation skills, Milken earned $550 million from Drexel. Earning huge sums of money is not a crime, but the government claims numerous deals to make it were illegal, which is a crime. Milken's personal profits from his manipulations netted him untold millions on top of his commissions from Drexel. His sentence is for ten years. (Compare this with a seven-year sentence given to a twenty-three-year-old man in Indianapolis in April 1991, for stealing a hamburger and french fries from a female customer at a McDonald's restaurant.)

If a faltering company wanted to expand, Milken would arrange for Drexel to sell bonds for that company. These bonds would pay high interest but were not backed with security, hence the term "junk bond." As long as the company flourished and could pay the high interest on its indebtedness, there was no problem. Milken made money making these bonds possible.

Also, if one company wanted to buy out another, the first company could sell bonds supplied by Drexel and arranged by Milken for any amount of money, often not represented by the value of the company. These bonds, which were sold to eager buyers including teachers, grocers, and retirees, would yield a high interest and were therefore attractive purchases. They generated millions for a company that wanted to buy controlling stock in another company. However, the high interest payments on their junk bonds drove many companies into bankruptcy.

The number of companies whose assets are measured in junk bonds cannot be known. But the worry is that too much of business capital is overinflated and in a time of recession may be disastrous. When people try to make good on the bonds they purchased, on which they depended, what then?

Many people love Michael Milken. He became known for contributing generously to charities. He even set up an education foundation to give grants to teachers and principals. However, now that Milken is a convicted felon, many educators are turning down grants from the Milken Family Foundation.

Many business people are grateful that he helped their companies grow and prosper. But just as many victims of hostile takeovers, companies whose employees were fired by new owners, are bitter. Fred Hartley, chairman of Unocal, the petroleum company based in Los Angeles, which successfully fought off a hostile takeover by T. Boone Pickens, said, "Junk bonds were destroying the financial system of the country. And Milken initiated the whole concept." Nineteen of the thirty-nine companies that defaulted on paying interest on their junk bonds were Drexel companies. Many companies flourished, but many floundered.

One Drexel employee said, "Greed was out of control. We wanted to do more and more deals and get more and more fees."

In November 1990, regulators working on S&L (Savings and Loan) losses filed claims against Drexel Burnham Lambert in an attempt to recover $6.8 billion the regulators claim was lost by about fifty S&Ls that failed because they bought junk bonds from Drexel. The S&L regulators say that Drexel and Milken made payoffs to S&L managers if they agreed to sell their junk bonds. Oversimplified, when junk bonds proved to be worth very little, the S&Ls failed. Drexel and Milken and the lack of regulation are being blamed for the failure of the S&Ls. The government claimed that the principal culprit in the S&L crisis was Drexel and the junk-bond market it created. Drexel's amazing financial success, the government said, was directly attributable to the unlimited amount of federally insured money it tapped, knowing the funds would be covered by the taxpayers if loans were defaulted.

With over 13,000 lawsuits filed against Drexel—$20 billion claims against the company—creditors may settle in a tentative agreement. The firm, with $2.8 billion in assets, could emerge as a going business. Under Chapter 11 bankruptcy proceedings, Drexel has been permitted to operate.

In April 1990, Milken pleaded guilty to six felony counts related to insider trading and agreed to pay $600 million in penalties to settle fraud and racketeering charges. While he was awaiting a hearing to determine what crimes he may have committed in addition to those he had admitted to, Milken resigned from Drexel and formed his own company, raising capital for many businesses.

Milken's assets are estimated to be over $1.2 billion. He and his brother, Lowell, are in partnership in at least eighty companies. It would be extremely difficult to determine his full worth since he has so many limited partnerships in many resorts, bars, and other businesses. It is possible that Drexel may turn over Milken's file to the Federal Deposit Insurance Corporation. In exchange, the FDIC may share with Drexel some of the $6 billion it is seeking in lawsuits against partnerships set up by Michael and Lowell Milken. Some of these partnerships, Drexel says, were compensation to a loyal employee, but some may have been secretly created, possibly at the firm's expense. Therefore, Drexel feels it has a claim against these partnerships.

THE INSURANCE INDUSTRY

The far-reaching effects of Michael Milken's influence were felt in April 1991, when Executive Life Insurance Company was taken over by the state insurance commission of California. Under the direction of Fred Carr, sixty, Executive Life, investing in junk bonds purchased from Michael Milken, was able to pay policy holders higher returns. In this way Executive Life grew into a $50 billion company, and Frank Carr became one of the largest buyers of junk bonds. In 1989, Carr received more than $2 million in income; in 1990, however, his income package was $612,500: Executive's stock had become virtually worthless because the company had invested heavily in junk bonds sold by Michael Milken. However, he had an agreement that if Executive Life or its parent company, First Executive, changed hands, he would receive $6 million. Executive Life has not employed Frank Carr since regulators took over, though he is still chairman of First Executive.

Executive Life was Michael Milken's most important customer. According to the *Los Angeles Times* article, "The Costly Comeuppance of Fred Carr," April 12, 1991, "The willingness of First Executive and certain large savings and loans to be steady buyers of junk bonds was credited as an important factor in keeping Milken's juggernaut going." But when the junk-bond market collapsed, and policy holders increasingly surrendered their Executive Life insurance policies—the equivalent of a run on a bank—it became apparent that the parent company of Executive Life, First Executive, might seek bankruptcy.

Regulators of the insurance company placed a moratorium on policy surrenders, though they continued to make pension, medical, and death payments. However, those payments were put in jeopardy when the Internal Revenue Service demanded $643 million in back taxes from Executive Life for the years 1981, 1982, and 1983 after the state had seized the company. The reaction from State Insurance Commissioner John Garamendi included the statement: "We have not had time to evaluate the merit of the IRS claim, but I cannot understand why they would wait so long to take action on liabilities alleged to have been incurred as long as a decade ago. Wealthy investors and traders earned hundreds of millions of dollars on Executive Life transactions, and not a peep was heard from the tax police. Now that we have conserved the company to salvage the life savings of smaller investors, the IRS has moved with lightning speed to cannibalize the vulnerable carcass of this company."

As of December 1990, Executive Life had income from premiums amounting to $94 million and liabilities of $3 billion. Upward of 60 percent of Executive's assets were in junk bonds purchased with the help of Michael Milken. When the junk-bond market failed in 1989, the company reported a $466 million loss in the last quarter of that year. There is some question as to the validity of state audits made by men who, after high ratings were issued, were then hired by First Executive. One man, William Sanders, was given a contract with a guaranteed salary of $300,000, plus bonuses of $100,000 in 1990, and $200,000 guaranteed in 1991. This is similar to the situation at American Continental Corporation when the accountant who had given the parent company of Lincoln Savings and Loan a clean bill of financial health was hired by American Continental at $900,000 a year.

At least $250,000 was spent in 1990 by First Executive for lobbying California state legislators to block a cap on junk bonds held by the company. The influence of Michael Milken's high-yield, high-risk junk bonds continues to rumble throughout the financial industry, destroying institutions and the financial security of untold numbers of investors. The effect of the junk-bond market collapse on retirees is frightening. Many who worked for companies that invested workers' pension funds in Executive Life Insurance have their retirement years threatened by lack of funds. Executive Life successfully marketed annuities by giving good returns based on high-yield junk bonds. Revlon, for instance, with 3,000 retirees, was said to be concerned about its ability to meet its obligations to former employees. The government guarantees pension plans in case a company goes broke, but if the company transfers pension funds to insurance annuity programs, the retirees lose government protection. Executive Life is being sued in a case that accuses directors, the accounting firm, and two rating agencies, Moody's Investors Services and Standard & Poor's, which gave the insurance company high ratings, and the two Milken brothers for defrauding tens of thousands who bought annuities and policies from the company.

The effects of these high-yield junk bonds are being felt among buyers of municipal bonds in Ventura and Riverside counties in California. Government agencies like the county boards of supervisors invested about $33 million in bonds with Executive Life, which is now expected to be able to pay only about twenty-five cents on each dollar invested. School districts, county maintenance programs, and other county entities lost money.

OTHER CASES OF STOCK-MARKET FRAUD

They start young on Wall Street. At twenty-three, David Bloom persuaded many clients to invest $10 million in his company and then invested their money as he saw fit. But he didn't buy stocks. His scheme was to send account statements to his clients that always contained good news. Then he spent the money to buy $5 million in paintings, a $830,000 Manhattan condominium, a house on Long Island, two expensive cars, and jewelry.

With a degree in art history from Duke University, he

wisely invested in good art, which then appreciated. When a client wanted to drop out of Bloom's investment company, Bloom simply went into the accounts of other customers and got their money.

When confronted with his crime, Bloom agreed to a settlement with the Securities and Exchange Commission to give up $8 million in assets. The money from the sale of these assets will be returned to his investors. The day after Bloom signed the agreement, he was charged with mail fraud.

When one of Wall Street's best-known figures, fifty-year-old Salim Lewis, pleaded guilty in August 1989 to three felony counts of stock fraud, it sent shock waves through the investment industry. Lewis was scheduled to go on trial the following month. The federal prosecutors' case stemmed from an allegation that Lewis had asked two employees of a brokerage firm, Jeffries and Company, to purchase over 400,000 shares of Fireman's Fund stock in order to drive up the price. Fireman's Fund had no knowledge that its stock was being used illegally.

Boyd Jeffries of Jeffries Company in Los Angeles had pleaded guilty to securities fraud in 1987. He turned state's evidence and implicated Lewis.

Another stockbroker implicated by Boyd Jeffries was Paul Bilzarian, thirty-eight, chairman of Singer Company, a large military contractor. Bilzarian was convicted in June 1989 of nine counts of securities fraud, together with making false statements to the government and conspiracy. Known as a corporate raider, buying up corporations, Bilzarian was also involved with the Jeffries Company and specifically concealed stock purchases that were part of his takeover operations. Singer Company was not involved in the fraud.

Following are the penalties for the various stock market violations:

- Robert Freeman, insider trader, two months prison, two years probation, $1 million fine

- Salim Lewis, securities fraud, three years probation
- Paul Bilzarian, securities fraud and tax evasion, four years prison, two years probation, $1.5 million fine; is appealing the case
- Martin Siegel, insider trader, two months prison
- Boyd Jeffries, securities violations, five years probation, $250,000 fine
- Ivan Boesky, securities fraud, three years prison, $100 million fine; allowed to deduct $50 million of this from his taxes
- Dennis Levine, insider trader, perjury and tax evasion, two years prison, $362,000 fine
- James Shrewing, securities fraud, six months prison; is appealing the case

In addition to the above, a California money manager central to the conviction of Michael Milken, David A. Solomon, forty-six, agreed in November 1990 to pay $7.9 million to settle charges against him for insider trading, income tax fraud, and other violations, which he committed with Michael Milken. Solomon provided information to the government against Milken that was above and beyond the information already provided by Ivan Boesky. Solomon Asset Management, Inc., was one of Milken's biggest buyers of junk bonds. The Securities and Exchange Commission's complaint alleges that Solomon defrauded his investment clients and personally gained from arrangements and information provided by Milken.

Commodities Futures Fraud

In one sweep, a federal grand jury indicted forty-six commodity traders in Chicago, August 2, 1989. In the commodities futures market at the Board of Trade or the Mercantile

Exchange, traders sell corn, beans, Japanese yen, German marks, stocks, and U.S. government bonds. They make contracts to deliver these financial instruments or commodities at a future date at a specified price. Known as "futures," these exchanges amount to billions of dollars a day. The volume of transactions are so great as to influence world trade markets.

Traders pay as much as $500,000 for membership on the commodities exchange. The FBI, in order to learn about corruption in these commodities markets, infiltrated the inner circles of the traders, spending large sums of money on expensive apartments and clothes for its spies, who tape-recorded incriminating evidence that led to the indictment of the forty-six men.

Some of the indictments included withholding certain commodities, in one case soybeans, from open trading in the pits. The soybeans were offered to "friendly" traders secretly, and these traders then paid a kickback to the brokers. Some traders made deals before the trading opened for competitive bidding. There were twenty-one indictments for fraud in the Japanese yen–trading pits alone.

One of the men indicted for fraud in dealing with the Japanese yen is Ray Pace, thirty-four, brought to trial September 1990. Though many of the traders become wealthy at a young age, Pace was merely making a living. He was paying $3,500 a month to rent a seat to trade in the Japanese yen pit. He is accused of defrauding customers, but maintains he was only doing what everyone else was doing.

He is also accused of racketeering. Under RICO, prosecutors can seize the property of an indicted person before a trial, to keep those indicted from selling off assets that may become part of the restitution if the accused is found guilty. Of the twenty-one men indicted in the Japanese yen pit, seven have pleaded guilty.

Other Corporation Fraud

THE NORTHROP CORPORATION

When Northrop Corporation pleaded guilty to thirty-four criminal fraud charges and agreed to pay $17 million in fines, the government agreed to drop 141 charges and also not to prosecute two Northrop executives. Joseph Yamen, sixty-two, vice president and general manager of Northrop's precision products division in Newton, Massachusetts, and Leopold Enger, sixty, also vice president, were put on administrative leave with pay when the charges were filed. Northrop was indicted in April 1989 for falsifying tests on components for nuclear-armed cruise missiles and pleaded guilty February 1990. Northrop was also cited for defrauding the government by improperly testing parts for Harrier jets used by the navy.

This was the criminal case against Northrop. A civil suit, brought by the two whistle-blowing employees who brought the fraud to the company's attention and then were fired for alerting federal authorities, was settled in June 1991, with the corporation's agreement to pay $8 million in fines. In addition to the $8 million, Northrop agreed to pay each of the whistle-blowers, Leocadia Brajas and Patricia Meyer, a total of $750,000 for wrongful termination. The total cost to Northrop for this fraud will be approximately $36 million.

Even though Northrop pleaded guilty in February 1990, and agreed to pay the $17 million in fines, the government continues to investigate the corporation's operations. In May 1990, federal agents raided three Southern California Northrop plants to determine if allegations were true that they were supplying inferior parts for navy jet fighter planes and if the navy was overcharged.

There is currently a partial suspension of offering contracts to Northrop from the Defense Department. In July 1990, the Justice Department recommended that the Pentagon place a ban on defense contracts with Northrop. The air force, how-ever, was urging that Northrop be allowed to continue doing business with the Pentagon. According to certain documents presented at a hearing by the House Energy and Commerce Committee, the Pentagon was attempting to protect Northrop from criminal liability.

Previously, in 1987, when Northrop was being investigated for systematically falsifying tests for the cruise missile and for the navy's Harrier jet, the armed services wanted to reduce some of the safety requirements. This served to undercut attempts that were made by the Justice Department. However, Howard Hyde, a senior engineer in Northrop's precision prod-ucts division, acknowledged that he participated in falsifying test results for the rate-sensor assemblies that stabilize the jet aircraft. He faces a maximum of fifteen years in prison. Hyde and four other men were accused of falsifying test results on the rate-sensor assemblies for which the government paid $1.6 million. Allegedly, phony paperwork was sent to the govern-ment indicating that the sensors had passed the tests, when in fact they had not.

The United States attorney urging the barring of Northrop from defense contracts is William Fahey, chief of the section on corruption and government fraud in Los Angeles. "If any case," he wrote in a department memo, "cries out for debar-ment, this is the case. If ever the American people deserve to be protected from the type of reckless and potentially life-threatening conduct, this is it."

The cases against Northrop influenced the Pentagon's deci-sion to buy the new F-22 fighter plane in April 1991 from Lock-heed. Northrop's F-23 was competing with Lockheed's F-22, but the contract was awarded to Lockheed for 648 planes that will counter enemy radar—at a cost of $60 billion. When it came down to the wire, it is possible that Northrop's falsifica-tion of records on nuclear weapon guidance systems and con-tract suspensions influenced the decision in favor of Lockheed, even though Lockheed has also received accusations that they built planes with defective parts.

CALPROTECH CORPORATION

Now defunct, the Calprotech Corporation must pay $1 million in fines for defrauding the government on military hardware parts. Specifically, they are accused of covering up defects and issuing false documents attesting to the performance of circuit boards used on helicopters and tanks. The former chairman of the Anaheim electronics company, David Ross, an ex-marine, was sentenced to three years in prison and fined $25,000.

As in other companies that falsified test reports, Calprotech allegedly told its employees to keep testing parts until it found parts that passed the test. Some circuit boards had been shipped out with test certificates from other boards.

TELEDYNE

On April 26, 1994, Teledyne was ordered by the Justice Department to pay $112.5 million to the government and to four whistle-blowers. Two men alerted the Justice Department in 1990 that the defense contractor was illegally testing eight to ten million relays, small switches necessary in military equipment. Another two men testified that padding of contracts gave Teledyne an illegal edge over competitors, because they could then negotiate downward when necessary.

HUGHES AIRCRAFT CORPORATION

In another whistle-blower case, the government and corporate papers seem to uphold the accusations of an employee that the Hughes Aircraft Corporation, a subsidiary of Northrop, shifted the cost of its radar systems for the navy's F-14 fighter and the air force's F-15 fighter to the air force's B-2 Stealth Bomber, which was being developed on a "cost-plus" basis. In this manner Hughes would appear to be making money no matter what the cost.

LOCKHEED CORPORATION

After a six-week trial, jurors delivered a verdict against Lockheed that ordered the corporation to pay $45.3 million in damages to three whistle-blowers, former employees who claimed that the gaint military cargo plane C-5B, which transports planes to Saudi Arabia, was built with defective parts. When the employees complained about the parts, they were fired.

A fraud and corruption case against Lockheed is under way in Atlanta, Georgia. A federal grand jury indicted Lockheed on June 22, 1994, for allegedly paying more than $1 million to a member of the Egyptian parliament, which helped Lockheed obtain a contract from Egypt for a $79 million sale of three C-130 planes.

Influence Peddling and Bribery

Concerned with fraud in the $150 billion-a-year Pentagon procurement process, government investigators began a three-year investigation that they referred to as Operation Ill Wind. Several major defense manufacturing corporations have been indicted for bribery, fraud, and conspiracy. Federal prosecutors continue to build their case against defense consultants and Pentagon procurement officers. In the course of their investigation, Navy Investigative Services and the FBI "searched the homes and offices of four dozen defense contractors, consultants and government officials," according to the *Los Angeles Times*.

One such procurement officer, who recently confessed to selling confidential information about a navy contract to a defense consultant, is Stuart E. Berlin, fifty-one, who pleaded guilty to fraud, conspiracy, and bribery. He claimed that over a period of ten years he had taken tens of thousands of dollars in bribes for information that he sold to defense contractors and defense consultants. He confessed that in one particular case, with authority to buy navy equipment, he funneled information to Fred H. Lackner, fifty-two, and a retired navy officer, William Parkin, sixty-five, who had set up his own consulting firm. These two men then sold the information to Teledyne and Hazeltine Corporation, in a conspired effort to help those corporations win valuable navy contracts.

After Teledyne was awarded a navy contract for $24 million, a Teledyne subsidiary reportedly paid Lackner and Parkin $160,000 for the information. The fee was to be split between Berlin, Lackner, and Parkin, but Lackner and Parkin apparently lied to Berlin about the amount of the fee, paying him only a small amount. These three men tried the same scheme with Hazeltine Corporation, and Lackner and Parkin once again paid Berlin less than his agreed-upon share of the "influence" money. Parkin appeared in court haggard after a failed suicide attempt.

For their part in the scheme, Teledyne agreed to pay the government $4.3 million for what the corporation called a "corrupt and illegal arrangement." Two Teledyne executives, George Kaub, fifty, vice president in charge of contracts, and Eugene Sullivan, fifty-eight, Teledyne's former vice president of finance, were given short sentences for their part in the conspiracy, wire fraud, and false statements. Kaub could have been sentenced to forty years in prison and fined $2 million, and Sullivan could have been sentenced to twenty years and fined $1 million. Kaub's light sentence was suspended, however, all except six months, and he was fined $300,000. Sullivan's sentence, except for three months, was suspended. Teledyne blamed its problems on Michael Savaides, Teledyne's former Washington marketing manager, who was sentenced to six months in jail for conspiracy to commit bribery.

In another case of bribery, Thomas Muldoon, fifty-nine,

was convicted of bribery and conspiracy for funneling bribes to a former Marine Corps civilian contracting executive, Jack Sherman, who pleaded guilty to the charges that he had taken bribes. The Whittaker Corporation subsidiary pleaded guilty to being a part of the bribery scheme and paid a fine of $3.5 million.

In its thirty-ninth conviction in Operation Ill Wind, federal prosecutors convicted William Sanda of conspiracy, wire fraud, and stealing and converting government property for himself. Sanda worked with William Parkin, providing UNISYS Corporation with confidential reports on particular Pentagon information. Parkin agreed to give Sanda information that would help UNISYS get the contract of up to $100 million if Sanda could pay him for the information. Though UNISYS never did get the contract, Sanda received a $33,000 consulting fee, which he shared with Parkin.

The longest sentence so far as a result of Operation Ill Wind was given to William Galvin, fifty-nine, who got thirty-two months in prison for arranging payments to Melvyn R. Paisley, who was then assistant secretary of the navy. Galvin also made monthly payments to a friend of Victor Cohen, who was then a deputy assistant air force secretary, knowing some of the money would go to Cohen. According to court papers, Galvin made the payments to influence the Pentagon to award a contract to Loral Electronics Corporation.

Garland Tomlin, Jr., fifty-nine, a program engineer at the Space and Naval Warfare Systems Command, retired in 1985 after he had taken $400,000 from Sperry Corporation and $75,000 from Honeywell for confidential bid information.

Jerry Manning, fifty-two, also a former navy engineer, admitted he gave a defense consultant information about bids for a $20 million navy electronics contract.

Many men and corporations were convicted for influence peddling, bribery, conspiracy, and wire fraud related to military purchasing. With a $150 billion military procurement budget, Pentagon bribery, and other crimes that lead to lucrative contracts, will persist. There is legislation pending in Congress that would bar the top 2,500 Defense Department officials from working with any of the country's biggest defense contractors for two years after they end their employment with the Pentagon. This is in a bill that would also attempt to eliminate the close ties military contractors have with the Pentagon by establishing an independent acquisition corps.

A few others indicted in Operation Ill Wind are: Joseph Colarusso, who pleaded guilty to conspiracy and wire fraud to gain a contract for Hazeltine when he was vice president; Charles F. Gardner, who pleaded guilty to bribing a Pentagon officer for UNISYS when he was vice president; James G. Neal, who pleaded guilty to bribing a navy official for UNISYS where he was employed as a consultant.

ZZZZ Best

Barry Minkow at sixteen was considered a business genius when he built a carpet cleaning company, which he had started in his parents' garage, into a business worth $200 million on Wall Street. At age twenty-three, he ended up accused of fifty-seven counts of fraud, having bilked investors out of $25 million.

After a three-month trial Minkow still claims he was a pawn of the Mafia, selling investors stock in a company that did not exist and claiming to restore fire- and water-damaged buildings. His accounting books held entries for money never received for work never done. He was sentenced in March 1989 to twenty-five years in prison and ordered to pay $26 million in restitution. The prison term stands as the longest ever given in Los Angeles for a white-collar crime. Prosecutors said his trial was the most significant white-collar crime in the West.

The sentencing judge described Barry Minkow as having

charisma and the gift of gab, dangerous, and without conscience. Minkow convinced lawyers, accountants, and Wall Street brokers of his ability to restore damaged buildings. He was reportedly earning $43 million a year from insurance companies at the same time he ran a legitimate carpet cleaning company with twenty-one offices in three states.

Minkow claimed he was a tool of the Mafia, though he later told the judge that wasn't true. When he needed more money he went to Drexel Burnham Lambert who underwrote $40 million in junk bonds with which ZZZZ Best could buy KeyServe, a company that got its carpet cleaning referrals from Sears Roebuck. With legitimacy established, Minkow would not have to fake any more restoration jobs. Stock in ZZZZ Best soared, and all was going well until some customers complained of overcharges on their credit cards. An accountant, Norman Rothberg, reported that he believed ZZZZ Best was fraudulently conducting business. When pressured by Minkow's employees, Rothberg accepted a $15,000 bribe to say he made up the story. But the damage was done and collapse imminent.

Mark Morze, Minkow's vice president who created fictitious papers to prove they were repairing buildings and took potential visitors on tours of buildings that were fixed up to look as though they were being repaired, probably came away with $3 million. He admits to $1 million on his 1987 tax return.

While the ZZZZ Best fraud all but slipped from public consciousness, Barry Minkow was serving his time in jail, where he became religious. Then, on May 3, 1994, the Securities Exchange Commission announced it had obtained a consent decree against Maurice Rind, the last remaining suspect in the case. Rind, accused of padding figures regarding the company's worth, which enabled it to gain a stock exchange listing, is obliged to pay the government taxes on the $720,000 he earned illegally, plus interest. However, as Rind's financial records show no assets, the government will probably not receive any money.

Other men involved in ZZZZ Best who were convicted are: Tom Padget, thirty-eight, sentenced to eight years; Mark Morze, thirty-eight, sentenced to eight years; Mark Roddy, thirty-seven, sentenced to five years; Daniel Krowpman, forty-three, sentenced to three years; Brian Morze, forty-two, sentenced to three years; Jack Polevoi, forty-one, sentenced to eighteen months; Jerry Pelovoi, forty-one, sentenced to eighteen months; Norman Rothberg, fifty-two, sentenced to one year; Charles Arrington III, twenty-eight, sentenced to six months in a halfway house; Edward Krivda, thirty-one, sixty days in a halfway house; Eugene Lasko, fifty-seven, sentenced to thirty-eight days in a halfway house.

Crime in Church and Synagogue

On April 21, 1994, $1.5 million was awarded to a couple in Dallas, who were defrauded by TV evangelist Robert Tilton. The couple, Mike and Vivian Elliot, claimed they had donated $3,500 for Tilton's crisis center, but that the money had been used instead for Tilton's personal luxuries. They accused Tilton of breach of contract.

Not paying $525,000 in income tax on money taken from church funds resulted in a conviction in federal court in North Carolina for PTL aides James and David Taggart in July 1989. They were convicted of conspiracy to defraud the government and impede the IRS and for filing wrong tax returns from 1984 to 1987. They spent $1.2 million on condominiums, jewelry, and designer clothes from money sent as donations to Jim and Tammy Bakker's PTL Ministry. A New York shoe store salesman said the brothers spent about $100,000 on shoes in four years. Other testimony revealed the brothers bought $320,000 in jewelry and crossed the Atlantic several times on the Concorde.

This is just one conviction in what became almost an epidemic of con artists making money by enticing people into religious investments. John Baldwin, president of the North American Securities Administrators Association, says religious swindles are rampant. Fraud has accounted for about $20–$30 million from people of *all* religious faiths.

Steven Streit, the treasurer of a Baptist church in Alabama, took $18 million from investors. Robert Rash of the Alabama Securities Commission says Streit never invested any of the money, though he printed bogus accounting sheets that he mailed to his investors, with a quotation from the Bible on the bottom of the page.

Ray Comstock, a preacher and former Sunday school teacher of a Baptist church in Los Angeles, was accused of fleecing members of his flock for $10 million. He guaranteed 36 percent interest to 600 investors on returns of Treasury bills. Comstock's prison term was four years for violating securities laws.

A second trial for Rabbi Abraham Low of La Brea Avenue in Los Angeles produced a conviction based on a conspiracy to launder drug money. The jury was not convinced that he had actually laundered the money, or that he was engaged in bank fraud, though the government claimed Low had met with undercover FBI operators five times.

The most notorious scam artist among religious TV evangelists is Jim Bakker, whom the prosecutor was to call the biggest con man. With tearful appeals for money, he built a religious theme park, a $129 million a year ministry, and a satellite TV station. He was sentenced to forty-five years on twenty-four counts of fraud against his followers, who numbered in the millions.

The prosecutor, Jerry Miller, pointed out how Bakker raised about $160 million with his promises of lifetime three-day-a-year lodging at Heritage USA for a donation of $1,000. Bakker's devotees, many of them elderly and on fixed incomes, subscribed to his scheme. Bakker diverted $3.7 million of this money into high salaries and luxuries, including a $600,000 home in Palm Desert, California; another home in Tennessee; a $600,000 condominium in Florida; three Mercedes-Benzes; $265,000 to PTL secretary Jessica Hahn to quiet her about their sex fling; a $5,000 Christmas tree; an air-conditioned doghouse; and a houseboat.

Bakker's second-in-command, Richard Dortch, fifty-seven, in a plea bargain pleaded guilty to fraud and conspiracy and was sentenced to eight years and fined $200,000.

On December 14, 1990, Bakker was ordered by a jury in Charlotte, North Carolina, to pay $129 million in a class action suit filed by 145,000 "lifetime partners" in Bakker's Heritage USA theme park. Those filing the lawsuit in 1987 claimed that Bakker had conspired with other administrators in the religious organization to set up secret bank accounts to give himself, his wife, and other ministry leaders large bonuses. The attorney for Bakker said it is unlikely that the people who lost their money will ever get any of it back because, as he said, Bakker owns nothing.

In February 1991, an appeals court set aside Jim Bakker's sentence of forty-five years, though the court did not set aside the conviction. The judge who reviewed the length of time Bakker was to stay in prison said Bakker had offended the sentencing judge's religious beliefs and for that reason was given such a long sentence. The sentencing judge, Robert Potter, was quoted as saying, "Those of us who do have a religion are sick of being saps for money-grubbing preachers." Bakker was subsequently sentenced to eight years and released to a halfway house on July 1, 1994, after serving four years. He has since been released on probation.

Miscellaneous White-Collar Crime

Promising returns of 12 percent or more on investments, Gary Naiman, fifty-six, was able to entice more than 2,300 investors in San Diego. To pay such high interest he made unsafe loans to developers and others. When the real estate market collapsed and the borrowers could not repay the loans, Naiman's Pioneer Mortgage Company could not pay investors their high-interest rate nor could it pay back the money, which amounted to $200 million.

On May 12, 1994, Gary Naiman was arrested on mail fraud and money laundering after a three-year investigation by the IRS and FBI. He is accused of transferring one couple's funds from a safe account (covered by federal deposit insurance) to one in which he had a partnership and fraudulently misleading his investors as to the status of their investments. Many retirees who put their life savings in Pioneer Mortgage Company have had to move in with relatives and live in humiliation. On October 10, 1994, Naiman pleaded guilty to money laundering and federal fraud. He may be fined $1 million and spend forty-five years in prison. He must also repay his victims.

General Electric Company was fined $10 million in the federal government's case against it for defaulting on a contract for providing mobile combat computer systems. The company also agreed to pay approximately $20 million in order to settle several suits.

The company overcharged the Army $15 million and did not report cost savings on the $240 million contract. Convicted were General Electric officials Gerald Leo, fifty-two, sentenced to ten months in prison and fined $15,000, and James Badolato, forty-two, sentenced to five months and fined $10,000.

In another case, John O'Brien, sixty, the chairman of the aerospace Grumman Corporation, resigned when he became the target of a federal investigation of corruption.

In yet another case of a company cheating the government by selling either untested or defective parts, VSI, a subsidiary of Fairchild Industries, was charged with fraud. For fifteen years, VSI omitted or falsified tests on jetliner and military planes, specifically on bolts, which keep aircraft in one piece. VSI agreed to pay $19 million in fines and costs. James Ryan, quality assurance manager, and Aram Marderian, supervisor of the company's metallurgy laboratory, each admitted to conspiracy and fraud. A *San Francisco Chronicle* article of May 12, 1990, stated, "According to the U.S. attorney's office, the company systematically generated fraudulent testing documents for products that had never been tested, and in some cases, for bolts the company knew were defective."

In San Francisco in June 1989, Bill Trout, a part-time employee, was arrested at the Bank of America for stealing $500,000 in checks made out to the IRS. He whited out checks made to the IRS and substituted the name of a fictitious business. He became the target of a federal investigation of corruption.

On counterfeiting charges, five men in New York were arrested in August 1989 when $17 million in counterfeit cash and $4 million in phony traveler's checks were seized by government authorities.

In Oklahoma City, September 1989, a former president of Southeastern Oklahoma University was sentenced to ten years in prison for defrauding the school of more than $3.4 million. Leon Hibbs, fifty-nine, diverted money from student scholarship funds and gave it to friends and relatives and bought personal items for himself. He "repaid" the money by putting his family on the payroll. He then took their salaries and recycled them back into the scholarship fund.

Among the computer whiz kids—almost all of whom are male—is twenty-five-year-old Kevin Mitnick, who pleaded guilty to computer fraud in March 1989, having gained access to secret computer information. He was sentenced to one year in prison. Said by prosecutors to be as dangerous with a keyboard as a bank robber is with a gun, he is seen as committing criminal mischief.

In May 1983, three men were indicted in masterminding a

scheme that bilked the Bank of America of $95 million. The defendants urged twenty institutions to put money in mortgage pools and issued guarantees against any borrowers defaulting. Almost all borrowers, however, did default. Because Bank of America was the trustee for the mortgage pool, it assumed the loss and filed a lawsuit in an attempt to gain back the $95 million.

The music recording business engages in white-collar crime when promoters bribe disc jockeys at radio stations to play their records and falsely send the ratings and popularity up. One such promoter to be convicted was Ralph Tashjin, forty-one, who pleaded guilty to one misdemeanor payola charge and two tax fraud and obstruction of justice charges.

Another music industry fraud case resulted in a fifty-one-count indictment against Joseph Isgro, forty-three, of Glendale, California. He was accused in December 1989 of racketeering, conspiracy to defraud Columbia Records and impede the IRS, making bribery payments to radio stations, and tax and mail fraud. Others indicted with Isgro were Raymond Anderson, forty-nine, former executive of Columbia Records, and Jeffrey Monka, thirty-one, charged with paying kickbacks and using mail fraud against Columbia Records.

In New York, high-salaried commuters were nabbed in February 1990 for using counterfeit train tickets. One, a corporate lawyer, was said to have lost his cool when the conductor became suspicious. This led to the arrest of twelve men, among them a vice president of an insurance company and several more in the six-figure income bracket. The special commuter tickets ordinarily cost about $120 a month, but counterfeits sold for half that.

The Wedtech scandal led to the conviction of Robert Wallach, fifty-five, for defrauding Wedtech stockholders. He was accused of accepting $425,000 from Wedtech Company, New York, to influence government purchasing agents in Washington and gain more defense contracts. The U.S. Court of Appeals threw out the conviction, claiming that one of the witnesses, Anthony Guariglia, former president of Wedtech, had lied under oath. While Wallach's attorney believes the case is over, the government has said they will retry the case. Guariglia was sentenced to twenty-seven months for perjury. Wedtech partners John Mariotta, Fred Neuberger, and Mario Mareno were all sent to prison.

Another white-collar criminal who started young was Lamont Coleman, student body president at San Francisco State University. He misappropriated $7,000 of student funds and was convicted of that theft in February 1990. His sentence was three years probation, six months county jail time, and restitution of $1,500.

Others student leaders who have come to the attention of law enforcement are: Chris Martinez, twenty-one, former student president at College of San Mateo, California, who used a student government requisition form in an attempt to buy a $42,000 Mercedes-Benz; Michael Bang, former student body president of Grossmont College, San Diego, who pleaded guilty to embezzlement of $36,000 of student funds, which college officials say he spent on hotels, limousines, drinks, and meals.

The Savings and Loan Crimes

INTRODUCTION

The best case for making the point that men are not cost-effective is found in the group of almost entirely male criminals who are now costing U.S. taxpayers an anticipated half *trillion* dollars. This amounts to more than the total cost for all of the following: the Vietnam War, the Marshall Plan, bailouts for New York City, and Lockheed. These men are involved in the worst financial scandal in the history of the United States. Men fraudulently and premeditatively, or at the very least greedily, siphoned off savings and loan depositors' money to their own advantage, knowing that the government, or more precisely the American taxpayers, would make good on their crimes and/or indiscretions, or lax management.

This is in no way a definitive analysis of the S&L crisis. It is simply a brief summary of a complex financial fiasco brought about by deregulation of the S&Ls, which gave the companies unlimited use of depositors' funds. Before deregulation, S&Ls were limited to investing only in thirty-year fixed-rate home mortgages.

In California the chasm between sensible investing of depositors' funds and irresponsibility was widened with the enactment of the Nolan Act and the Bane legislation. The Nolan Act, signed by Gov. Jerry Brown, gave California-chartered S&Ls permission to make investments in any kind of business venture. The Bane legislation, signed by Gov. George Deukmejian in 1983, permitted S&Ls to invest more freely in out-of-state investments and weakened restrictions on insider trading and on making loans to people on the board of directors of S&Ls. Tom Bane, a Democratic state assemblyman, received $513,000 in campaign contributions from S&Ls. Pat Nolan, a Republican assemblyman, received $154,000 (according to an article in the *San Francisco Chronicle* of October 19, 1990, by Robert Gunnison). After the Nolan Act and Bane legislation, contributions from S&Ls climbed from $480,979 in 1981–1982, to $1.2 million in 1985–1986.

There are several questions that should be answered: How much of this fiasco was criminal? Who would be punished? Where did the money go?

Naturally, people want an accounting. If directors of S&Ls made fortunes that bankrupted their companies, why can't these fortunes be seized and credited to the government, which is now picking up the whole tab for investigation, selling seized S&Ls, and prosecuting criminality where it finds it? The answer is that the government, through the newly created Office of Thrift Supervision, is seizing property, but only after lengthy court trials.

The loudest cry from the public is for the people who caused this great problem to be punished. Punishment is being meted out, but fraud cases take a long time to prosecute, and, contrary to popular belief, fraud, i.e., actual criminal intent, figured in only $5 billion of the $500 billion estimated cost, according to Carl Close, a research associate with the Washington, D.C.–based Competitive Enterprise Institute, writing in the *San Francisco Chronicle* on August 16, 1990.

Currently there are 21,147 criminal referrals for possible S&L fraud. These cases take years to prosecute and they are expensive. The Financial Institutions Reform Recovery and Enforcement Act of 1989 initially provided $50 billion to cover S&L losses, but a year later, regulators asked for $100 billion, and much more is needed. As more and more commercial banks fail, they are not paying funds into the Federal Deposit Insurance Corporation, funds that the Resolution Trust Corporation uses to cover deposits in failed S&Ls.

It was during the Reagan years, in an effort to "get government off the back of businesses," that the S&L industry was deregulated. When S&Ls no longer had to restrict their investments to home loans, there were few to oversee what was happening to individual deposits. In this way deregulation opened the doors for corruption. U.S. banking regulator and chairman of the Federal Deposit Insurance Corporation William Seidman said on "Face the Nation" that deregulation in conjunction with deposits that were federally insured gave S&Ls "a credit card on the U.S. with no limits." He said, "We did everything we could to make this a disaster. First, we allowed these institutions to operate without true capital standards. Second, we gave them the right to invest in anything they wanted to. And, third, we provided no supervision over what they were doing."

In 1991 there were 4,000 legal cases against S&L officers but not enough investigators to search out and prosecute. As of October 1990, nearly 500 S&Ls were under control of the fed-

eral government, which had seized $240 billion in assets.
Fraud was found in more than half of those failed institutions.
Seventy-five percent of the money spent by FDIC in 1988 ($29
billion) was to depositors in failed or troubled S&Ls in Texas.

One of the many people who took advantage of the 1982
deregulation was Kenneth Kidwell, who took over his father's
Eureka Federal S&L and immediately made $400 million in
loans to Nevada casinos—loans that were never repaid. Before
deregulation, Kidwell could not have made these loans with
depositors' money. Because the deposits were insured, the federal government must now make good to the depositors. And
the federal government is all of us, paying and paying. Kenneth Kidwell is not held accountable. Right now the looted
funds, as claimed by the authors of *Inside Job: The Looting of
America's Savings and Loans*, are waiting to be reinvested in the
purchase of the failed S&Ls that the federal government has
closed and must sell, some at great loss.

Phony land deals, inflated appraisals, and borrowers who
didn't exist were the ingredients of the S&L fraud. Congressional members have been implicated, accepting campaign
contributions and "going easy" on any investigation of a particular S&L.

Even though many S&Ls have been seized by government
regulators, many of their administrators are still receiving
extremely high salaries. These salaries are based on contracts
made between the company and employee when the employee
was hired, contracts nearly impossible to break. It is difficult to
dismiss a top-level employee who has a contract. A case in
point is in two government-controlled failed S&Ls in Orange
County that still have six former officers on the payroll. Since
the government seized these companies, it is the government
that is paying for this nonwork. A person sent by the government to manage the Franklin Savings Association received
$220,000 for six months' work.

Donald Cook, chief executive officer of the Resolution Trust

Corporation, which was set up to resolve the S&L crisis, defended the high salaries. Cook told the chairman of the House S&L bailout task force that of 351 government-seized S&Ls, executives were retained at 211 of these because their contracts could not be broken legally. The RTC's regional director in Kansas City was quoted in the *San Francisco Chronicle* on June 16, 1990, as saying, "Some of these sweetheart management deals they cut for themselves . . . are almost ironclad legally." One House committee member said no one above the level of a secretary or a teller should be retained in a failed S&L.

The S&L crisis happened on the Republican watch, but it involved many Democratic legislators who received large contributions from owners of S&Ls who wanted regulators kept at bay. Mary McGrory, in her article, "Seidman, S&L Man in the Middle," writes of "the lying, cheating, stealing industry. . . . The thrift industry hurtled merrily toward ruin." William Seidman was quoted saying, "It was like building a nuclear plant without safety devices. If you don't have them it's going to melt down and take you with it."

Possibly the S&L industry will be re-regulated. On April 11, 1991, the Federal Deposit Insurance Corporation chairman, L. William Seidman, recommended to the House Banking, Finance and Urban Affairs Committee that banks (so far not S&Ls) be prohibited from making loans on raw land and that developers be required to bear 25 percent of the costs of real estate projects in order for the banks to lend money on their projects. These were requirements before the 1974 deregulation. Reinstating these controls would provide more realistic assessments of real estate lending by banks.

CENTRAL FIGURES IN THE S&L SCANDAL: NEIL BUSH

They say that the Democrats picked on Neil Bush, thirty-five, the then president's son, for political reasons. Nevertheless he was on the board of directors of the Silverado S&L in

Denver when loans were approved to Bill Walters and Ken Good, friends of his wife who were also investors in Bush's oil exploration company. Neil Bush did not disclose either his relationship to these men or the fact that he would profit from the loans.

The Silverado S&L has since collapsed, with Walters defaulting on a $100 million debt and Good defaulting on $8 million. Neil Bush and other Silverado directors were sued by the Federal Deposit Insurance Corporation for $200 million, but in May 1991 there was a settlement for $50 million. Most of the settlement money will be paid by insurance firms. The agreement asks for the officials of Silverado to turn over their $23 million "war chest," which had been set up in 1986 with Silverado money as their personal legal defense fund. The failure of the Silverado S&L is expected to cost taxpayers $1 billion.

Ken Good had hired Neil Bush to be on the board of directors of his company at an annual salary of $100,000 a year, an unusually high salary for an S&L director, the usual being $22,500 to $25,000. Neil Bush is the owner of an oil exploration company known as JNB International. While Good was borrowing from Silverado S&L, Neil Bush's oil company received more than $1 million from Good, and Bush's salary from JNB was raised from $50,000 to $120,000.

Silverado S&L was taking a loss on the $8 million loan to Good at the same time Good was planning to purchase a controlling interest in Bush's JNB International with $3 million. Bush did not disclose this to the S&L. The effect of the infusion of this money into his company was to reduce Bush's liability at another bank from $750,000 to $100,000.

Where did Silverado S&Ls money go? Federal investigators say it went to six- and seven-figure salaries and huge bonuses. In one year, 1985, senior managers in Silverado S&L were paid $2.7 million in bonuses. Money was also lent on undesirable land such as a 1,200-acre parcel overlooking a toxic waste dump on which Silverado paid $25 million and which is estimated today to be worth $6 million.

Though Good defaulted on his loans and claims he has a negative net worth, it was reported in September 1990 that the Congressional House Banking Committee learned that he owns a $450,000 home in Florida; an $800,000 note from his former company, Gulfstream Housing Corp., which was secured by his home in Vail, Colorado; and $3.3 million in unsecured notes from numerous trusts.

Others named in the government complaint are a Silverado chairman, Michael Wise; a former director and majority stockholder, Russell Murray; a former chief lending officer, James Metz; and a former outside counsel, Ronald Jacks. Murray, Metz, and Wise agreed to a ban on their ever again engaging in banking business, but Neil Bush claims he did nothing wrong and will not agree to remove himself from future banking business.

Though Neil Bush loomed as an important figure in the S&L scandal, he is actually only a bit player compared to the many who were indicted for greater crimes. Actually, Bush's actions don't constitute an act that the Office of Thrift Supervision considers a violation. But it was his socioeconomic class and gender that caused this problem for this country. And guilty of a crime or not, he is seen as fair game for those who are angry, not only at the debacle but at the slowness with which the prosecution proceeds. Even so, he is accused, along with other officers in the civil suit against Silverado S&L, of "gross negligence" that contributed to the Silverado collapse.

In December 1990, an administrative law judge who works for the Office of Thrift Supervision ruled that while Neil Bush was on the board of directors of Silverado S&L he failed to disclose his business association with Good and Walters when Silverado S&L made large loans to these men. The judge ruled that Neil Bush had violated conflict of interest rules and should be barred from engaging in any future activities with financial companies. Neil Bush's attorneys appealed the ruling. U.S. Rep. Robert Gonzales, chairman of the House Banking Committee, said that the judge's rulings appeared to be correct. "Frankly," he was quoted as saying, "my own opinion is that he was a little minnow swimming with a bunch of barracudas."

In April 1991, the director of the Office of Thrift Supervision, T. Timothy Ryan, upheld the judge's ruling that Neil Bush had behaved wrongly by "engaging in unsafe and unsound practices and breaches of his fiduciary duties involving multiple conflicts of interest." In June 1992, Neil Bush decided not to appeal the government's order, which imposed light restrictions on him if he should become a director of a bank or S&L.

CENTRAL FIGURES IN THE S&L SCANDAL: CHARLES KEATING, JR.

Another failed thrift is Lincoln S&L, based in Irvine, California, which Charles Keating took control of in 1984. Federal regulators disclosed that on March 2, 1991, they sold the Lincoln S&L deposits and its twenty-eight branches to Great Western for $12.1 million, although the total cleanup of Lincoln S&L cost taxpayers approximately $34 million.

When Lincoln S&L was being examined by the Federal Home Loan Bank Board, examiners claimed there was interference from senators who were protecting the S&L. These senators were Democrats Alan Cranston of California, Dennis DeConcini of Arizona, John Glenn of Ohio, and Don Riegle of Michigan, and Republican John McCain of Arizona. Together they had received a total of about $1 million in campaign contributions from Charles Keating.

On February 28, 1991, all but Cranston were cleared by the Senate Ethics Committee. Though the committee reported that two of the men "gave the appearance of being improper" and two had "exercised poor judgment," the committee found that Cranston, who had received over $800,000 in donations from Keating, had participated in an "impermissible pattern of conduct" by intervening on Keating's behalf with federal bank regulators investigating Lincoln S&L.

In 1987 M. Danny Wall ignored an order to close Lincoln S&L and instead transferred the examination to Washington. As William Seidman, then FDIC chairman, said Lincoln S&L should have been closed in 1986 because it practiced the worst money-lending policies, buying raw land and junk bonds.

The case against Keating is the largest yet filed by the Resolution Trust Corporation, established by President Bush to clean up the S&L financial catastrophe. The suit against Keating sought triple damages and named Keating's wife, children, and his brother as defendants. He was accused of "illegal, fraudulent and imprudent schemes" that destroyed the S&L. The lawsuit further charged that depositors' money at Lincoln was used to pay "the racketeering defendants and other insiders excessive compensation, and to fund the personal, political and charitable convictions of Keating."

One of the schemes for siphoning funds from the S&L for personal gains, the lawsuit contended, was Keating's use of S&L depositors' money in his own American Continental Corporation, one of the country's largest builders. Keating transferred $200 million to American Continental to build an Arizona project, the Phoenician Resort. American Continental floated bonds and sold them to Lincoln S&L. The lawsuit referred to interference, presumably by legislators on Keating's behalf, that delayed examination of the financial solvency of Lincoln S&L and gave the "racketeering defendants additional time to exacerbate their frauds."

Keating was also accused of transferring depositors' money out of the country into personal accounts in Switzerland, the Bahamas, and Panama. Investors in his American Continental Corporation initiated a class action suit in an attempt to reclaim more than $100 million in foreign accounts. The suit alleged that Keating's son established accounts in Zurich, Switzerland, and Dusseldorf, Germany, into which he paid $20 million for "unknown reasons." Also, according to this class action suit, Keating allegedly sent $25.5 million in Lincoln S&L money to a company in the Netherlands for unexplained reasons, and sent $17.5 million of Lincoln money to a company called Trendvest Ltd., in the Bahamas. Keating has a home in the Bahamas. He is also said to have a Panamanian company, Southbrook Holdings, with $10 million in Lincoln funds, and, the suit continues, Keating has accounts in at least six foreign banks in Europe.

When American Continental Corporation began selling debentures to cover its losses, they were sold in twenty-nine Lincoln S&L branches, and 22,000 people, mostly retirees, purchased them. By buying debentures in an S&L that advertised federally insured deposits, the purchasers assumed that they were buying safe, insured investments. Keating and others in this fraud are charged with requiring employees to steer depositors away from the insured investments and into the junk bonds. When Lincoln was seized by the federal government in April 1989, Keating immediately declared his American Continental Corporation bankrupt to protect it from creditors, especially the 22,000 people who had purchased over $200 million of nonrated high-risk securities.

In May 1991, the law firm of Sidley and Austin agreed to pay $4 million as a settlement in a class action lawsuit that contended that certain law and accounting firms managed to manipulate statements and figures to show the S&L in a better light than it deserved. The law firm also agreed to an additional $30 million in the event of future settlements. The suit for bondholders and shareholders of Lincoln S&L is also directed at the accounting firms of Touche Ross & Company and Arthur Young and Company.

The Office of Thrift Supervision filed an additional claim against Keating and five business associates, including his family, to recover $40 million of S&L assets. Part of that money is owed Lincoln depositors for Keating's purchase of the Hotel

Pontchartrain in Detroit, which he must have known was a losing business venture but gave limited partners tax write-offs.

This suit is in addition to another suit brought by the Office of Thrift Supervision for $1.1 billion in civil racketeering that accuses Keating of "illegal, fraudulent and imprudent" schemes that allegedly destroyed Lincoln S&L and cost taxpayers more than $1.1 billion. The $1.1 billion case may stretch out for years, while the $40 million suit is apt to be prosecuted more quickly.

Keating says deregulation was the cause of his problems. In 1982 the federal government deregulated S&Ls, but in California, the Nolan Act gave S&Ls authority to invest in limitless ways. In an interview with a reporter from the *San Francisco Chronicle*, Keating said, "It gave the buyer of a charter of a Savings and Loan in California the greatest financial charter, in my opinion, that ever existed. You got government-insured funds, about which I made no secret, to invest as I saw fit."

The junk bonds that Keating sold to unsuspecting Lincoln S&L depositors were purchased from Drexel Burnham Lambert, which was an undisclosed partner in Keating's Lincoln S&L. Drexel is the company that, with Michael Milken in its high-risk bond department, nearly collapsed under the weight of its unsecured debentures.

On June 5, 1991, thirteen of the counts against Keating were dismissed by a superior court judge, but the rest of the case remained intact. Keating's lawyers maintained that he could not be held responsible for his employees selling junk bonds. The prosecution maintained that Keating knew what was going on and that there was willful misconduct. As of this writing, Keating is serving ten years in prison for securities fraud and twelve years and seven months for federal racketeering.

In July 1991 federal regulators opened hearings in efforts to recover $130.5 million from Keating and six others, exploring four transactions: $94 million loss from a tax-sharing arrangement between American Continental and Lincoln; $24.2 million loss on the Hotel Pontchartrain in Detroit; $12.3 million loss from financing arranged for an American Continental stock option plan; and $4.4 million loss from the Hidden Valley Ranch real estate deals south of Phoenix. The six others are former American Continental executives: Judy Wischer, Robert Kielty, and Andre Niebling; Keating's son, Charles H. Keating III; and Keating's sons-in-law Robert J. Hubbard, Jr., and Robert M. Wurzelbacher, Jr.

In a kind of last roundup of the previously owned Keating Lincoln S&L, federal prosecutors filed a criminal complaint against Ray Fidel, a former Lincoln president, charging him with securities fraud related to marketing junk bonds at Lincoln S&L.

INDICTMENTS AND CONVICTIONS

As of March 1989, "of the 11,000 S&L cases the Federal Home Loan Bank Board has referred to the Justice Department in the last two years for criminal prosecution, less than 200 have resulted in convictions." That was the statement made by Charles Schumer, Democrat, New York, chairman of the House subcommittee examining the S&L scandal. After the General Accounting Office's report to the House Judiciary Committee appeared in March 1989, an Associated Press report said, "white-collar crimes, not poor economic conditions or deregulation, are the root cause of the savings and loan crisis."

Of the twenty-six failed S&Ls examined by the GAO, as of March 1989, charges had been filed against 182 people for criminal conspiracy, theft, fraud, and embezzlement. Twenty-three were convicted of these crimes and sentenced to prison, but most were suspended with probation, according to Fredrick Wolf, assistant comptroller general for the GAO.

William Oldenburg purchased an S&L company based in Utah and Hawaii, which had over $600 million in deposits. He was indicted in January 1989 for gross mismanagement of funds, conspiracy, and mail and wire fraud to buy overinflated bonds with State Savings funds. He was accused of defrauding the S&L of $26 million. In 1977, Oldenburg had bought 363 acres of land in Richmond, California, paying $874,000. In 1984, State Savings, under Oldenburg's ownership, bought the property from him for $26.5 million. When regulators seized State Savings they sold the property for $5 million, the market price.

James Rossetti was president of State Savings in Utah while it was owned by Oldenburg. Rossetti, who was indicted with Oldenburg, pleaded guilty to nine counts of conspiracy, misapplication of bank funds, and two counts of wire fraud. He agreed to testify at Oldenburg's trial and faces up to forty years in prison. On May 28, 1991, the case against Oldenburg was dismissed after two hung juries could not agree on his guilt or innocence.

Nicholas Muccino, a former director of the failed State Savings, was indicted along with Oldenburg and Rossetti. As part of a plea bargain with federal prosecutors, Muccino withdrew his guilty plea to a felony charge of making a false statement to a federal bank examiner and changed it to a plea of guilty to aiding in a misdemeanor.

It was reported in the *Los Angeles Times* in April 1991 that Don R. Dixon used his Texas S&L for his "personal piggy bank." In 1982 he bought a small S&L for $5.8 million and built it up to a $1.7 billion empire before it was seized by federal regulators in November 1987. They concluded that over 96 percent of their $1.4 billion in assets were in default.

Don Dixon and his wife flew to Paris by private jet, paid for with depositors' money. The S&L had five airplanes and one helicopter to move the business associates of Don Dixon around the country. He also used S&L money to pay for $1,000-a-night prostitutes for his business associates. Taxpayers will lose an estimated $1.3 billion on this company.

Dixon was held without bail until his sentencing, which

occurred in April 1991, when he was convicted by a federal court jury in Texas of twenty-three counts of fraud and misuse of the funds of the Vernon S&L. Though Dixon faced a sentence of 120 years in prison and a $5.75 million fine, he was sentenced to five years and ordered to pay $611,000 in restitution. This light sentence shocked federal officials.

Seven other Vernon S&L officers have been convicted of criminal charges. For those who say these criminals are getting off too easy, at least one is not. Vernon's chairman, Woody Lemons, was sentenced by a U.S. district judge to thirty years for receiving more than $200,000 in loan kickbacks, the longest sentence so far for any executive convicted in S&L fraud cases. The comparison of the light sentence for Dixon with the heavy sentence for Lemons prompted federal officials to complain that Dixon was far more responsible for the collapse of the S&L than Lemons and was getting off too easily. During the sentencing, U.S. District Judge Joe Fish told the courtroom that he did not believe Dixon should be punished for the $1.3 billion failure. Edwin Gray, one of the first regulators to crack down on the Vernon S&L, asked the question, "If not Don Dixon, then who? And why not Don Dixon?"

When a woman is convicted of fraud in a S&L failure, that news makes headlines: WOMAN SENTENCED TO TWENTY YEARS IN PRISON FOR S&L COLLAPSE. Janet Faye McKinzie, forty-one, of Newport Beach, California, was convicted of racketeering, wire and bank fraud, and interstate transportation of stolen securities for North American S&L. Together with North American chairman Duayne Christenson (who died when his car crashed into a bridge railing shortly after North American S&L was declared insolvent), Janet McKinzie was accused of bilking dpositors of $11 million for personal use and $5.6 million for false billings of construction for North American that never occurred.

Other than Janet McKinzie, virtually every person convicted of S&L crimes is male. As one study, headlined in the July 1990 *San Francisco Chronicle*, as: WHITE MALES LINKED TO S&LS said, 88 percent of S&L officers of failed thrifts are white males, and of those, 99 percent own their own homes and 92 percent have more than three credit cards. White males in the United States number only 39.8 percent, but 88 percent of the heads of failed S&Ls are white males, a higher percentage than their proportion in the population. These statistics are from the National Institute for Research into Crime Origins.

The study made a correlation between white males raised in two-parent families and those who are indicted or convicted in S&L fraud. The researchers believe that in a two-parent home, the white male needs to overcome a sense of inferiority. In addition, it could be said that the son is competing with the father, or that the parents have enjoyed each other's company to the exclusion of their son. In any event it appears that the single-parent home is not contributing to bank fraud to the extent that the two-parent family is, nor are the homes of minorities. The researchers said, "Maybe if we can find the pathology in the white male culture, we can intervene with preventative programs before the entire federal treasury collapses."

Edwin T. Birney III, thirty-seven, of Dallas, was indicted on seventeen counts of bank fraud for his role in the failure of Sunbelt S&L. He was accustomed to giving extravagant parties, even with elephants, and offering $100,000 loans on the spot. He also financed the purchase of thirty-four Rolls-Royces for the Bhagwan Shree Rajneesh.

In December 1990, Edwin T. McBirney III agreed to plead guilty to fraud and help federal investigators search out others who had been involved in the S&L scandal. Even though federal regulators limited his penalty to $7.5 million for restitution and $8.5 million to help settle the civil suits in exchange for his guilty plea, he still may be sentenced to fifteen years in prison for bank fraud.

As of November 1994, 78 percent of 580 thrift fraud convicts received prison sentences, according to the University of California, Irvine, report titled "Fraud in the Savings and Loan Industry: White Collar Crime and Government Response," a study sponsored by the U.S. Department of Justice's National Institute of Justice. Of those sent to prison, 4 percent were sentenced to ten years or more, with a median sentence of less than two years. The average sentence was 36.4 months, less than for a burglar or a car thief. In 1988, failed S&Ls accounted for more than $8 billion in losses, but fines totaled only $348 million, and only a fraction of that was collected.

A few other indictments or guilty pleas include:

Robert Franks, former president and director of North Park S&L, Richardson, Texas, in a scheme to defraud his S&L by obtaining a loan of $138,000, using another person's name, to pay interest on a $2.95 million loan that he personally guaranteed.

John H. Roberts, Jr., former president and owner of Summit S&L, who pleaded guilty to bank fraud in which he diverted up to $4.5 million of depositors' money for his personal use (including buying himself an airplane).

The former vice president and loan officer of Sunbelt S&L pleaded guilty to conspiring to defraud the Federal Home Loan Bank Board and the IRS. He did not report money received in a Sunbelt S&L real estate deal to the IRS.

Former chairman of the board Kenneth Hood was also the president and only stockholder of Century Investments and the vice president of Western Savings and Loan; as the *San Francisco Chronicle* reported, "He pleaded guilty to conspiring to defraud the Internal Revenue Service by creating artifical losses to offset income."

The *San Francisco Chronicle* article "Probe Shows Fraud Key in S&L Failures" does not mention by name the the former chairman of California's Brookside Savings, who "pleaded guilty to four counts of falsifying bank records and misapplying funds."

Robert Ferrante, forty-one, the previous owner of Consolidated Savings Bank of Irvine, California, which collapsed in 1986, was indicted along with eight others on February 15, 1991. Ferrante's indictment included the charge of making loans to development companies in which he had a personal interest, and loans to friends and family. The other eight are: Ottavio Angotti, fifty-four, president of Consolidated; Lee Bartholomew, fifty-nine, lawyer for Consolidated; Raymond Arthun, forty-two, former treasurer; Eric Bronk, forty-four, lawyer; Peter Sardagna, forty-seven; William Crowder, forty-two; Sigmund Kohnen, forty-three; and James Allee, thirty-six.

On February 27, 1991, Michael Parker, forty-three, and Jefferson Worthy, thirty-three, were indicted for having defrauded the Columbia S&L, which is now insolvent. Parker, a former vice president of Columbia, is charged with forty-six counts, and Worthy of forty-three counts in a leveraged leasing scheme. Parker allegedly paid Worthy $1.5 million in kickbacks from the leases that Worthy recommended to Columbia, though the leases often were fraudulent. Parker established his own company, Parker North American Corp. of Costa Mesa, California, which allegedly received $31 million in cash from Columbia. Prosecutors requested that Parker be held without bail because he might leave the country. They also asked for permission to seize Parker's assets, which they believe were purchased with money illegally obtained.

In September 1990, Oliver Trigg, Jr., forty, was indicted on charges of conspiracy, bank fraud, money laundering, and tax fraud. He was convicted and sentenced in April 1991 for taking money from Family Savings and Loan in Whittier, California, one of the largest black-owned S&Ls in the country, to buy the S&L for himself. He was sentenced to seven years and five months in prison.

THE REWARDS FOR COMMITTING S&L CRIMES

As if it isn't bad enough that taxpayers will be paying possibly $500 to $600 billion to pay for the fraud and mismanagement that became the S&L crisis, add to that the news that some of those who caused it are living in the lap of luxury.

One such case is that of Bill Walters, who, with the help of Neil Bush, obtained loans on which he defaulted to the tune of nearly $100 million, causing the failure of the Silverado S&L in Denver. Though he told a congressional committee that he was broke, a trust, which controls a $1.9 million home and a $250,000 ocean-front mobile home at Laguna Beach, had been set up in his wife's name. In addition, he owns a $1 million condominium at an exclusive club in Indian Wells, California.

While a new home was being renovated in Newport Beach, Williams and his wife spent several months at the Four Seasons Hotel there, which charges $250 and up a night. A lawsuit filed in Santa Ana, California, claims that Bill Walters's wife, Jacqueline Walters, and lawyers administering the family trust "knowingly and willfully conspired and agreed among themselves to devise a common scheme and design to hinder, delay and defraud [Bill Walters's] creditors . . ." Jacqueline Walters received millions of dollars of assets from her husband, all put in her name. Before she married Walters she was his secretary; the court claims she has no assets of her own. Therefore, what is now hers is actually his, which is owed to his creditors.

Since Walters claims he is $196 million in debt, one might ask where his money went. He borrowed $96 million and defaulted on that loan. People are no longer thrown in debtors' prison for nonpayment of debts, but public sentiment is that there should be some punishment for a man whose nonpayment of his debt contributed to an S&L collapse that will cost the taxpayers $1 billion.

For Charles Keating, who symbolizes the extent to which the S&L scandal was carried, money was no object. His five daughters and their husbands were all on the payroll. His son who had held only one job before, as a busboy, was given a salary of $1 million. One son-in-law earned $1.3 million, another $520,000. Keating paid himself a salary of $3.4 million a year.

The federal government estimates that, from 1985 to 1988, $44 million went to Keating's family. He paid enormous salaries to his office staff, thanks to federally insured deposits. He had private planes, three mansions, and used gold leaf in the hotel he built in Arizona, the Phoenician Resort. There, he installed Italian marble costing $14 million and hung $25 million in original art. It was built at such an expense that each room cost $500,000. The Phoenician Resort is now owned by the government. Trying to make it a go, the government is only getting about $50 a night for each room.

David Paul, who headed the Centrust S&L in Miami, Florida, had a yacht built costing $7 million, a $13 million Rubens painting, and gold fixtures in his bathroom, according to NBC News in August 1990. Bailing out Centrust will cost taxpayers $2 billion. This amount would have been much less if the S&L could have been closed two years earlier, but Paul, like Charles Keating, had friends in high places. U.S. Sen. Bob Graham reportedly told the banking regulators to "lay off" the Centrust S&L in Miami.

In October 1990, the regulators made judicial moves to take about $31 million from David Paul, blaming his "insatiable vanity and greed" for the failure of Centrust S&L.

WHERE DID THE MONEY GO?

Stories of fraud grab the headlines, especially as people are desperate to find someone to blame. The cost is actually going to be around $157 billion, but interest over the next forty years brings the bill to around $500 billion.

Developer Conley Wolfswinkel of Mesa, Arizona, borrowed $52.5 million from Western S&L to build a sixteen-story office building. The loan was not paid back to the S&L. The S&L folded because there were no more funds and depositors were asking for their money. The government regulators took over the building and sold it—for only $20.3 million, a $32 million loss to taxpayers. No doubt the building was overappraised and never should have commanded a $52.5 million loan to begin with. How much of any excess money went as kickbacks to various people will probably never be known.

When developers wanted to build Stonebridge Ranch near Dallas, First Texas S&L lent $325 million for the project. First Texas was closed by regulators when they had no more money to pay interest to their depositors. After a lengthy search for investors, Stonebridge Ranch was then sold to the Japanese for the highest price they could get, $61 million. Here was another loss the taxpayers would have to pay the depositors of First Texas S&L—$264 million.

Sherman Maisel, former Federal Reserve Board governor, is quoted in an Associated Press article written by Robert Dvorchak and Scott McCartney, September 11, 1990: "It was like staking poker players to piles of chips while allowing them to keep any winnings, even as the government agreed to pay all the losses." Other losses resulted from excessively high interest rates designed to attract more depositors. Their money was then loaned to real estate developers for overappraised developments.

High salaries to S&L executives, for numerous branch offices with costly decorations, for jets and yachts, and luxurious company parties also contributed to the problem. Mortgages that were fixed at a low rate years before 1983 were not returning money at the rate at which interest was later paid to new depositors. S&Ls that were trying to attract money by paying high interest rates were often those least able to afford to pay the high rates. Also contributing to the collapse was the amount of interest paid by FDIC to help failing S&Ls survive, rather than paying off depositors earlier and closing the S&Ls.

In all of this are accountants and lawyers and advertising executives who glorified a prospectus for investors, and who either camouflaged or mystified profit and loss statements in order to attract investors into government secured deposits. If the government is going to secure, with money, taxpayers' deposits in an S&L, then the government has the moral and ethical responsibility to oversee what happens to that money. One could make a case for the government being fraudulently negligent. To say that only 5 percent of the loss is from fraud depends on what one calls fraud. It is difficult to discern what is not fraud in this picture.

To answer the question about where the money went, James Barth, former chief economist for the Office of Thrift Supervision, says it went "down a deep hole." The money didn't just disappear, he says, it went into real estate deals and junk bonds, among other things.

The Resolution Trust Corporation was set up in 1989 to sell failed S&Ls and their assets. These assets are almost entirely business loans that were not repaid and include such ventures as race horses or methanol plants. About $18 billion in assets held by the government is in real estate, and $2.5 billion is in junk bonds. About $50 billion is attributed to fraud. In 1991 there were 3,000 criminal fraud cases against the operators of S&Ls.

Because failing S&Ls were slow to be closed, losses amounted to about $40 million a day. Also, because higher interest rates were paid to attract money into failing S&Ls (especially in Texas), this rate was paid directly to depositors. This contributed an additional cost of about $342 million to the total the government will have to pay back to depositors.

Losses in real estate account for a figure impossible to calculate. If an S&L made a mortgage on a house at an inflated price and the real estate market fell, the S&L is stuck with both an unsalable house and the unpaid mortgage. When the Texas real estate market failed, it took the overextended S&Ls with it.

As of 1990, the government had 30,000 foreclosed proper-ties from the over 400 S&Ls it closed. It is expected that another 500 will be seized and until that happens, it is impossi-ble to know where all the money went. Kenneth Howe, in the *San Francisco Chronicle* of June 14, 1990, wrote, "Until the R.T.C. finally sells off the assets from those failed thrifts—and finds out how much money it can get for them—the full cost of the bailout won't be known."

The Resolution Trust Corporation in Colorado Springs, Col-orado, is commissioned to sell off assets in Colorado from failed S&Ls that the government has seized. In Colorado Springs alone, the U.S. taxpayers own nineteen apartment houses, thirteen shopping centers or malls, fifty-two ware-houses, and one huge ranch of 25,000 acres—for which West-ern S&L lent Frank Aries $200 million without requiring his signature. When the S&L went under, the ranch cost the U.S. taxpayers $235 million but the Resolution Trust Company says they'll be lucky to get $40 million. Frank Aries lost nothing, because his corporation went bankrupt. Asked by Steve Kroft on "60 Minutes" about his transaction with Western S&L, Aries said he never signs anything, adding "That's the way we do business in America." It is costing the taxpayers $100 million a year to care for the property.

WHO'S GETTING THE FAILED S&LS?

Western Savings and Loan of Colorado Springs was sold recently to the Taiwanese. Appraised at approximately $40 mil-lion, the S&L sold for $8 million.

"Easy pickin's" is what the failed S&L sales by the govern-ment are called, and James Fail is the epitome of the person picking up the pieces at windfall prices. Putting up only $1,000 of his own money, he was loaned $70 million to buy Bluebon-net S&L of Arizona. Bluebonnet is a conglomerate of fifteen failed S&Ls that the government combined into one company. With the sale, there is a $1.85 billion federal subsidy that guarantees against losses on assets.

A federal subsidy in the case of the purchase of a failed S&L is called a "yield maintenance agreement." This guarantees that all bad, money-losing assets of the failed S&L will be kept profitable at a declining rate for ten years.

When Silverado S&L of Denver collapsed, leaving the taxpayers with a $2 billion bill, it merged with Colorado's Columbia S&L. In 1990, because of the merger and being able to take advantage of the federal subsidies for Silverado losses, Columbia made a $48 million profit.

A few months after government regulators sold New York luxury condos that they had claimed as government property because of a failed S&L, the real estate developer who purchased the condos put them on the market at a 400 percent markup.

Lincoln S&L, owned by Charles Keating, has now been sold to Great Western, which paid $12.1 million, acquiring more than $2 billion in Lincoln assets. Taxpayers will pay $2.6 billion for cleaning up Lincoln, which makes it the costliest in the financial scandal, exceeding University Federal Savings in Houston, which cost $2.58 billion. What this does for Great Western is increase their banking branches to 241 in California and increase their deposits to nearly $30 billion.

American Savings of California, worth $16.3 billion, was purchased by the Robert N. Bass group of Texas for only a $410 million down payment, and last year it reported a 30 percent return on that down payment. First Gibraltar of Texas, worth $9.7 billion, was purchased for about $315 million and posted a 33 percent return in 1989. Additional tax write-offs combined with federal subsidies were worth about $91 million. Not bad for a $315 million investment.

But is this a crime? Yes—the subsidies have to be considered a crime against the taxpayers. Not all failed S&Ls made a profit. Some fail again. But with government help that seems almost impossible.

There has been some urging by congressional committees to buy back the failed S&Ls sold in what are now known to be bad deals because they were sold too cheaply and because of the federal subsidies. In the long run that may save money, but there's no money for buy-backs. As Rich Thomas said in the July 30, 1990, *Newsweek*, "The shrewd vultures who swooped down in 1988 are feasting."

Ever hoping to understand and do something about the S&L crisis, Congress passed legislation in October 1990 that authorizes the Department of Justice to appoint an "S&L fraud czar." With an eight-member commission, it would establish and coordinate all ongoing activities for S&L inquiry.

In July 1991, the Center for the Study of Responsive Law, Washington, D.C., charged that the men who had purchased the failed S&Ls had made large contributions to the key members of the House and Senate banking committees. In the last weeks of 1988 the 192 failed S&Ls that were sold cost the taxpayers $73 billion, according to the study. The General Accounting Office had previously concluded the cost would be from $39 to $69 billion. Savings and loans are sold by RTC at 50 percent or less of the appraised value of the property, according to a July 1994 Associated Press review of land transactions across the country. The RTC has claimed it sold properties at low prices because real estate values have fallen and the selling price was the best they could get. That has not proved true for those who bought the failed S&Ls and then turned around and sold them for a soaring profit. For instance, when Keating's 17.5 acres were sold by the RTC for $875,000, the buyer, Bob Frank, resold it for $1.225 million on the same day.

This most expensive of crimes, white-collar crime, involves intelligent planning, a predetermined plot to deceive, and a lax system of regulation, whether it be in the management of school funds or the largest banks in the country, or even in the management of the country itself. Where there is something to be criminally gained in the white-collar area, there are those who will scheme to get it. And almost all are educated, upper-middle-class white men who were raised in two-parent families.

CHAPTER 4

ENVIRONMENTAL DESTROYERS

Toxic Waste

The laws that were set up in the 1970s to protect the environment were weakened in the 1980s as administrations became pro-development rather than pro-environment. In the mid-1980s people became aware of the deteriorating condition of the ozone layer caused by fluorocarbons, the killing effect of acid rain, water pollution, global warming, and toxic waste dumping violations.

In spite of opposition, in 1980 Congress established the Superfund, under the administration of the Environmental Protection Agency, which was designated to clean up the country's worst toxic areas. The toxic waste cleanups were originally projected at a cost of $5 billion over five years. Ten years later the costs are projected at $1 trillion—a figure that two studies agree on, one from Salomon Brothers brokers and one from Hirschhorn and Associates, a Washington environmental consulting firm. It is now expected that it will take *fifty years* to clean up the areas. From the National Priorities List of the 1,236 most hazardous areas established since 1983, only 220 sites had been cleaned up as of June 1994. Approximately $200 billion will probably be used to pay corporate attorneys' fees for thousands of lawsuits, not for any actual cleanup. According to chemical industry and environmental group sources, $12 billion has already been used for what are known as "transaction costs"—legal fees.

What has been generating the huge number of lawsuits is the phrasing in the law that holds one company responsible for the cost of cleanup if it can be proved that that particular company used the site for dumping, even though many other companies may have used it as well. Other violators may not have been cited because they are no longer in business or because they have avoided being identified with the toxic dump. The corporations that are identified resort to litigation to prove they are only one of maybe thousands of firms that have used the site and therefore should not be wholly responsible. The Superfund Act includes what is known as "retroactivity," that is, being responsible for dumping toxic wastes that were not illegal at the time of the dumping; the Superfund act also includes "joint and several liability," which means each company is liable even if only a small portion of the toxic waste was dumped by one individual company.

In October 1986, the Superfund was reauthorized for another five years, but no change in the law was made. Banks and insurance companies now find themselves liable for cleanup costs on properties in which they have a financial interest. The insurance industry may expect $400 billion in liability claims because of corporate dumping. This, some experts say, could be a death blow to the insurance industry. Banks that acquire buildings, often through foreclosures, also face costly cleanup fees on properties that previous business owners have polluted.

The toxic waste cleanup program is doing well in the area of deterrence: corporations are dumping less pollutants. In 1989, according to an EPA report, 22,650 businesses released 5.7 billion pounds of toxic waste into the environment, 1.3 billion pounds less than in 1987. David Morrell, a toxic waste expert and historian of the Superfund, was quoted in the *San Francisco Chronicle* as saying that corporations are more willing to pay lawyers' fees than pay for the cleanup, hoping that if they stall long enough in the courts, they may not ever have to pay. Compared to costs for cleanup, lawyers' fees are cheap.

Aware of the people's concern, George Bush, when elected to office, declared himself the "Environmental President" and appointed William Reilly as head of the Environmental Protection Agency. Reilly had previously been head of the World Wildlife Fund/Conservation Foundation, which received corporate donations from Dow Chemical, Monsanto, Du Pont, Exxon, Union Carbide, General Electric, Ciba-Geigy, and Shell Oil.

The environmental "watchdog" organizations, known as the Group of Ten, include the National Wildlife Foundation, Sierra Club, Environmental Defense Fund, Natural Resources Defense Council, National Audubon Society, Wilderness Society, Environmental Policy Institute, Defenders of Wildlife, National Parks and Conservation Association, and the Izaak Walton League of America. These are the groups, along with local citizens' action groups, that try to keep corporate polluters in check.

How are they doing? Surveillance is a constant struggle, and money for cleanup is hard to come by. Though dumping of toxic waste is a crime, it is often difficult to catch the criminal, especially if it is a small company hiring a man with a pickup truck to get rid of a few barrels of waste, which he may do along a country lane or down a remote sewer drain.

Illegal dumping kills people. It's not like being robbed, when you know instantly you've been victimized. It takes time to destroy life with this kind of crime, but this crime is as deadly as any other kind of murder. As the larger corporations are caught dumping, corporate executives are being indicted.

In Jacksonville, Arkansas, the Vertex Corporation was accused of letting barrels of dioxin leak from their plant into the ground. For years dioxin seeped into the Arkansas River and then into the Mississippi River. It takes fourteen seconds for a fish exposed to dioxin to die. Dioxin cans were also placed in landfills, and when it rains the chemical seeps into property where children play. It pollutes the well water.

The EPA says there is no health problem, that people are simply getting hysterical. Now they are planning to incinerate dioxin and people are scared. What happened to the Vertex Corporation? It was sold to another company and is now in the hands of federal receivership. This is only one of many similar situations that a resident of Jacksonville says is a "massive failure of government to protect its people."

Corporations in California release more toxins into the environment than any other state, about six billion pounds a year. Nationwide, in 1987, twenty-two billion pounds of toxic chemicals were released into the air, ground, or sewers, and all of these releases are still legal. (There is now a computer database for use by citizens who want to know what harmful chemicals are being released in their communities. It is available through the National Library of Medicine; for information, call 800-535-0202.)

NON-NUCLEAR U.S. MILITARY TOXIC DUMPING

While numerous corporations are criminally liable for illegal dumping of toxic waste, the government of the United States is the biggest toxic polluter in this country, producing more waste than all five chemical companies put together. The National Toxic Campaign Fund, an environmental group based in Boston, in March 1991 identified more than 14,000 likely pollution sites nationwide that will cost approximately

$200 billion to clean up. This includes 1,579 army, navy, and air force bases in the States, Puerto Rico, and U.S. territories. In these installations there is contaminated groundwater and toxic sludge in unlined areas. This information was gathered from the Pentagon's own records—the National Toxic Campaign Fund is the first group to put it all together.

Where nerve gas was developed in Denver, the army arsenal left a sludge of toxic by-products. In Indiana, where shells were tested, not only were over a million shells left still unexploded, but some contained radiative uranium.

In Jacksonville, Florida, the naval air station released twenty hazardous chemicals into the ground, taking them off base and haphazardly dumping them. These chemicals dissolve grease off airplanes. On the landfills where these chemicals were dumped, people built homes.

For forty years the army arsenal in Milan, Tennessee, dumped dynetrolylent, which causes cancer in animals. This seeped into a lake and into drinking water so that wells had to be closed. When the EPA declared it the most hazardous dump, the army tried to get the EPA to downgrade the category.

In Tucson, Arizona, 600,000 people who use the underground water now fear that it is poisoned from Hughes Aircraft Company, which pumped waste into the desert. People are dying of leukemia and brain tumors. On one street there are twenty-three cancer cases. Toxic waste killed cattle on Indian reservations. The air force gave Hughes a contract worth $30 million to clean up the toxic dumps. So Hughes is being paid to clean up its own toxic mess and will probably make a profit doing so.

In Baltimore, Maryland, three civilian managers of the army's Aberdeen, Maryland, proving ground were sentenced to three years' probation for knowingly storing dimethyl polysulfide, ethyl acetate, and hydrazine in containers that leaked for years. They were warned often by inspectors and told to correct the problem. Prosecutors claimed that in some cases these hazardous chemicals were poured into drainage pools that ran into the sewers. The three men convicted, the highest ranking civilians at the base, were William Dee, fifty, Carl Gepp, fifty-two, and Robert Lentz, fifty-one. This was the first time that officials were convicted for ignoring federal environmental laws.

Unless corporations or the military are caught red-handed they seldom admit responsibility. And even when corporations are caught, mandatory sentences are not imposed. In April 1990, the U.S. Sentencing Commission proposed strong guidelines for imposing stiff mandatory fines for companies convicted of illegally dumping toxic waste. But the then attorney general, Richard Thornburgh, under pressure from corporation lobbyists, withdrew his support for mandatory punishment for corporations.

Littering

How to stop it? Who's doing it? What does it cost?

Texas has found at least a partial solution. Texas pride! Throwing litter into a trash can is "The Texas thing to do!" The Texas Department of Highways and Public Transportation began an advertising blitz to reduce the expense of picking up highway litter. Using sports stars and TV personalities, the commercials were aimed at young men, who, research says, are the likely litterers. One of the ads shows a young man they call "Bubba," in a pickup truck. The Texas anti-litter campaign costs $3 million a year and includes roadside landscaping.

In California, litter expert Daniel Syrek, who heads the Institute for Applied Research in Sacramento, says Texas is on the right track. Previous ads trying to persuade people to stop littering featured cute little animals saying, "Please don't litter." Syrek urges, "Never use the word 'please.' People who litter don't understand the word."

This proved to be true to a *Philadelphia Inquirer* columnist Clark DeLeon. When he saw four teenagers in a car with New Jersey license plates throw two beverage containers out their car window, DeLeon got out of his car and handed the trash back to the boys, asking them to please take the beverage containers back to New Jersey. An article in the *San Francisco Chronicle* describes the incident: "The litterbugs were quick to respond. DeLeon required six stitches for a cut below his right eye where his glasses dug into his cheekbone when they hit him."

In California eighty-five tons of litter end up on the state's streets. On state highways, paid workers and volunteers pick up 176,000 cubic yards of litter each year. While the Texas anti-litter ad campaign costs about twenty to fifty cents per resident per year, California's anti-litter campaigns cost less than a penny a resident. But picking up the litter is estimated to cost California taxpayers $125 million a year, or about $4.50 per resident.

According to Syrek's studies, more than half of litter is deliberate and is committed by males under thirty. Littering is a group thing and it is *macho*. One radio ad campaign to reduce littering featured girls who said that boys who trash California turn girls off. Unfortunately, this, the one ad directed to the actual litterers, had a budget of only $20,000 and no money for purchasing time on the radio.

So in California alone, where young males are said to be the principal litterers, these men are costing the state $125 million per year. How much are they costing the country?

Graffiti

Writing on walls with spray paint or wide felt pens causes millions of dollars in damage to municipal buses, schools, office buildings, and tenement apartments. It lowers the value of the property and usually indicates that a gang has moved in to claim territory.

In one case in California, the name *Chaka* appeared 10,000 times, spray-painted on buildings from Orange County in Southern California to San Francisco. Eighteen-year-old Daniel Ramos, who is referred to as a "tagger," was arrested and pleaded guilty to defacing more than $500,000 in property. The Southern Pacific Railroad yard had approximately $30,000 worth of graffiti—Chaka's—on its cars. It was surmised that because the cars travel throughout the country, they were desirable targets for Ramos's tag.

A sting operation in San Jose, California, netted law enforcement nine adults and thirty-seven juveniles as taggers. Those caught had answered an ad for a nonexistent job that required artistic writing skills. Candidates then took the supposed employers to the graffiti they had painted on public walls to prove how artistic they were. To their surprise, they were charged with vandalism. The next day, of the forty-six charged on June 7, 1994, twenty-nine were arrested. Their graffiti cost the city $80,000. On July 4, 1994, five males, ages eighteen to twenty-two, drove 340 miles from Southern California to San Francisco with red paint, which they used to deface buildings with gang symbols. When they were caught, literally "red-handed," they were booked on felony mischief charges.

Nuclear Plants

NUCLEAR WEAPONS PLANTS

Eighteen miles from Denver, Colorado, is the Rocky Flats Nuclear Weapons Plant, which makes plutonium triggers. It is owned by the U.S. Department of Energy, but run by Rockwell International. The plant is the target of allegations that it discharged toxic chemicals into two creeks that run into drinking water supplies. The FBI, after three infrared surveillance flyovers, discovered that the plant's plutonium processing incinerators were being operated illegally after having been shut down for safety violations.

In June 1989, the Colorado Department of Health issued twenty-five violations against the plant, among them citations for not monitoring groundwater and incorrect storage of nuclear waste. In addition, the Justice Department charged that the Energy Department and Rockwell International had consistently interfered with governmental authorities who tried to enforce water and air pollution laws.

Only ten days after the EPA refused permission for the Rocky Flats Nuclear Weapons Plant to use a particular pond for dumping nuclear waste, there was evidence that the pond was again being used for that purpose.

Rockwell International received an $8.6 million bonus from the Energy Department in May 1987 for "excellent management," even though the Energy Department said some of the plant's waste management was illegal and that radioactive contamination was a problem.

As recently as November 1990, the Energy Department was accused of building an $86 million plutonium processing center in South Carolina without public hearings or a review of the environmental effect. Though the Energy Department has agreed to be open and honest about their activities, only by chance was it discovered that the plant was about to go into operation without public scrutiny. The center, which produces plutonium for use in nuclear weapons, had been under construction for the past seven years. Money for this center was included in annual congressional appropriations, but hardly anyone knew about it until environmentalists began to study the appropriation bills. A lawyer for the Natural Resources Defense Council, Dan Reicher, said he will sue the government unless there are public hearings and a formal environmental impact report is begun.

It has been projected that it will take approximately thirty years to clean up the waste from nuclear weapons plants, but the Congressional Office of Technology Assessment concluded in a report, released February 10, 1991, that it may take much longer than that. The contamination from four decades of arms productions may have rendered the lands near the plants as wasteland, never habitable again.

The most pressing problems are liquid nuclear wastes at Hanford, Washington, and Savannah River, South Carolina. At Savannah River thirty million gallons of radioactive effluents are released into the seepage basin each year, according to Marvin Resnikoff of the New York Radioactive Waste Campaign. Other focus points are 11,000 pounds of uranium buried at the Portsmouth Gaseous Diffusion Plant near Piketon, Ohio, since 1954; the plutonium-contaminated ground at Rocky Flats near Denver; and the uranium at Fernald, Ohio. In his book, *The Generation Time Bomb*, Resnikoff cites 36,000 pounds of uranium released into rivers and 23,000 pounds released into the air since 1954 at the Oak Ridge Tennessee National Laboratories.

Costs for cleanup around nuclear arms plants range from $80 billion to $110 billion, according to the General Accounting Office. Anne Erlich and John Birks, the editors of *Hidden Dangers: Environmental Consequences of Preparing for War*, claim the costs will be higher and that the problem is out of control. The Environmental Protection Agency cannot bring a suit against the Department of Energy for violations. The U.S. Department of Justice, according to the authors of *The Bomb Factories: Out of Compliance and Out of Control*, appears to have been protecting the polluters.

The report from the Congressional Office of Technology Assessment urged that Congress set up a national commission to oversee cleanup rather than have it managed by the Energy Department. One of many concerns is that the Energy Department is lacking in knowledge about the health threats associated with nuclear waste.

NUCLEAR ENERGY PLANTS

When Charles McDowell reported on nuclear energy plants on the Public Broadcasting System's "Washington Week in Review," he said that these plants have been growing more and more unsafe over the past four decades. The situation is so critical that some plutonium and tritium plants have had to be shut down completely. "The FBI actually had to raid nuclear energy plants to find out how bad they are. It is serious. It is grave. Toxic waste is carelessly stored."

Since the Soviet nuclear accident in Chernobyl in April 1986, antinuclear movements have grown stronger. But as yet they are no match for the lobbyists of the corporations that run these plants.

Clean Air

In March 1989, the Sante Fe Springs Oil Refinery and three executives were fined $177,750 for knowingly polluting the air. Actually, the executives paid only $11,750 each for the crime and for failure to correct the violations. The company paid the rest.

In November 1990, Congress passed a Clean Air Act, which addresses the four major sources of air pollution: tailpipe emissions; smokestack emissions, which transmit acid rain; cancer-causing airborne toxins; and flurocarbons and other chemicals that harm the earth's protective ozone layer. The cost for this bill is about $25 billion a year. Specifically, the law imposes strict requirements on almost all industries to reduce their harmful airborne emissions and strengthens environmental laws that have been allowed to erode since 1977, the last time Congress passed a significant environmental protection law. The penalties for violators can be as high as $25,000 per day, and there will be criminal prosecutions for corporate executives where they knowingly pollute and endanger health.

Miscellaneous Corporate Pollution

When Lockheed employees complained to the Occupational Safety and Health Administration that they were suffering from illnesses they attributed to exposure to hazardous chemicals at the plant, the corporation was cited by U.S. safety officials for over 400 violations of health and safety standards. Safety officials said that Lockheed should be fined $1.5 million. The citation stated that Lockheed "willfully mislabeled or failed to label many in-plant containers of chemicals."

When a strike force of policemen, district attorney's investigators, public health officers, and sanitation inspectors invaded the Diceon Electronics plant in Chatsworth, California, the two top executives, Ronald Mathews and Peter Jonas, did not know that nine months later they would have felony complaints filed against them for illegal disposition of hazardous waste into the sewer system.

In California in 1984, violations of hazardous waste control became a felony, permitting prosecutors to send offenders to prison, the only effective way to deter these criminals. If the punishment is only a fine, often the company pays it. Fines previously were considered just the cost of doing business. But now that prison time is an element, corporations are looking more carefully at their policies. Jail has a chilling effect on business.

When Tom Billecci realized that benzene, toluene, and chromium were released into the San Francisco Bay by his employer, Unocal Corporation, an oil refinery in Rodeo, California, he took his information to governmental agencies. None paid any attention. He was especially concerned about a three-day spill he had witnessed in 1979 where phenol was released into the bay. He and his father fished in those waters, and he was concerned about the destruction of marine life.

He finally told his story to the Sierra Club, whose legal

defense department filed a suit against Unocal in February 1990. Unocal agreed to a $5.5 million settlement for thousands of violations. Billecci was the prime witness, testifying that when companies monitor their own pollution, they can control what is being tested. If a sample is dirty, they throw it out. After Billecci's deposition, the suit was settled out of court. Unocal admitted to no crime. Billecci says, "All I was trying to do is help the company improve the environment and not use the bay as a private dumping ground. If they were really concerned about the environment they'd be glad I brought it to their attention." Billecci does not work for Unocal anymore. Unocal has spent $67 million improving their waste-water treatment facilities.

In April 1989, the multimillion-dollar cleanup of the Chico, California, groundwater supply came to a halt because the funds ran out. The carcinogens suspected of polluting the groundwater are PCE and TCE, solvents used in dry cleaning and engine degreasing. Victor Industries, an alleged culprit, refused to go along with the state order to come up with a plan to clean up the chemical pollution caused by their plant. With the state Superfund out of money, the cleanup program waits.

Hazardous work conditions are revealed in *Behind the Silver Curtain*, by Denis Hayes. He points out that though many workers have come a long way from digging coal in dirty mines to the dust-free "clean rooms" of computer factories, garbed in sterile costumes, these cleanliness precautions are to protect the product, not the worker.

The so-called "bunny suits" that workers are required to wear do not protect them from the deadly chemicals that are used to make disks and chips. Often these chemicals are odorless, tasteless, and colorless and may not affect the worker for years. And though the companies have spent billions to improve the technology, almost nothing has been spent to study the effects of the chemicals on the workers in their environment.

Chemical Waste Spills

In one year alone, Union Carbide had thirty toxic leaks into the environment. One, a gas mixture of methylene chloride and aldicarb oxime for Temik Pesticide, caused 135 people to be treated for related health problems. The next day Union Carbide's plant in West Virginia spilled 1,000 gallons of fluid used in hydraulic brake fluid.

On that same day a truck spilled 500 gallons of liquid hydrazine, ethylenediamine, ammonium hydroxide, and sulfate compounds on the freeway near Alexandria, Virginia, forcing 600 families to be evacuated.

Later that year, in Camden, New Jersey, a forklift punctured a storage tank of toxic, flammable liquid, causing the hospitalization of ten people. And in Arizona a cargo of thirty chemicals on a freight train derailed, exploded, and burned.

Oil Spills

EXXON OIL CORPORATION: *VALDEZ*

Except for the purposeful dumping of oil into the Persian Gulf during the Gulf War, the Exxon *Valdez* oil spill is the deadliest oil spill in history and one of the three largest man-made disasters in history. The other two man-made disasters are Union Carbide's explosion in Bhopal, India, and the nuclear plant meltdown at Chernobyl. All three have been likened to the nuclear bomb explosion at Hiroshima.

On March 24, 1989, at 11:00 P.M., Captain Joseph Hazelwood, forty-two, turned his ship, the *Valdez*, over to what may have been an unqualified third mate, who ran it onto a reef in Prince William Sound, causing a rip in the hull and spilling eleven million gallons of crude oil into the bay.

Hazelwood, who became known as the number one environmental enemy, had been under treatment for alcoholism. Though he had lost his license for driving a car because of alcohol, he was still allowed to command a ship. He had been drinking before the accident, but no one testified that he was out of control. However, a prosecution alcohol expert testified at Hazelwood's trial in March 1990 that he had tested at one and one-half the alcohol limit and was in an alcohol-impaired state. Alcohol impairment is not based on what one observes, the expert said, but on scientific evidence.

Hazelwood was fired by Exxon and later indicted on felony counts that held him responsible for the massive devastation. He was exonerated in court and relieved of his captain's license for one year.

Though Exxon has spent $2 billion on oil cleanup, more than 1,000 miles of shoreline are still covered with oil. In findings summarizing fifty-eight field studies, as of April 1991 the wildlife death toll was estimated at 3,500 sea otters, 350,000 birds, 22 killer whales, and 200 harbor seals. It is estimated that wildlife will need seventy years to recover. With storms and tides, the sea continues to regurgitate new oil.

Exxon was indicted on five criminal charges carrying fines of more than $700 million. Exxon said it would fight the charges. The corporation reported a profit of $3.51 billion in 1989, after deducting $1.7 billion for the oil cleanup and for possible civil judgments.

Exxon has since filed claims against the federal government saying the coast guard was responsible for the oil spill. The court papers from Exxon say the coast guard failed to provide adequate navigation services to the *Valdez* when it hit the reef.

In March 1991, the federal government and the State of Alaska reached a tentative settlement agreement with Exxon in a plea bargain, with Exxon pleading guilty to misdemeanor charges. This was to be based on the approval of the U.S. District Court. Under the agreement, felony charges against Exxon would be dropped, and Exxon would pay $1.1 billion. However, in April 1991, U.S. District Judge H. Russell Holland threw out the $100 million criminal fine saying, "The fines which were proposed to me were simply not adequate."

As of mid-1991, it was believed that the settlement would collapse. Exxon could be liable for criminal penalties for as much as $700 million. If there was no ceiling on the criminal fine, it was doubtful Exxon would agree to the $1 billion settlement. On May 2, 1991, the Alaska House of Representatives rejected Exxon's deal, voting that Exxon should pay $1.2 billion in civil and criminal fines within a year, instead of spreading it out over ten years. On May 4, 1991, the settlement deal between Exxon and the federal government and the State of Alaska fell apart.

Five years after the spill, the trial against Exxon—with 14,000 plaintiffs, including commercial fishermen and others seeking $3 billion in damages plus punitive damages—began in the U.S. District Court in Anchorage, Alaska. Exxon projects itself as a good environmental citizen having paid $2 billion for cleanup and promising another $1.3 billion for natural resource help over ten years.

The jury, however, on June 13, 1994, ruled in favor of the fishermen, saying Exxon's Captain Hazelwood was to blame and was responsible for the recklessness. The 14,000 fishermen can now decide how to allocate the $15 billion.

All of the above occurred because one man carelessly allowed his ship to spill eleven million gallons of oil into Prince William Sound.

OTHER OIL SPILLS

In 1987 there were 257 oil spills around the world; in 1988 there were 342 spills; in 1989 there were 368 spills; and by February 1990 there were already 110. It was in February 1990 that 400,000 gallons of Alaskan crude oil spilled from a tanker owned by British Petroleum Oil Shipping Company, USA, which assumed responsibility for the spill.

In one weekend in June 1989, there were three oil spills in the United States. One in Rhode Island released 420,000 gallons into Narragansett Bay. One in Delaware released 800,000 gallons into the Delaware River. And one in Texas released more than 200,000 gallons into the Bayport Ship Channel. Each oil spill was the result of a mistake in navigation. The expense to the coast guard and the states involved, and to the marine life and wildlife, is incalculable.

CHAPTER 5

HATE CRIMES

Hate crimes are more lethal than other crimes in that they result in hospitalization four times more often.

Hate crimes are perpetrated against one another by all races, nationalities, and religions: whites versus blacks, blacks versus Hispanics, Chinese versus Japanese, Christians versus Jews, etc. Regardless of the victims, media reports indicate that most hate crimes are committed by young white men. It would be difficult to know by looking at someone if they are prejudiced, except perhaps for those known as "skinheads," who declare their prejudice by the way they dress and the way they shave their heads.

Skinheads

Generally these young men, in their late teens or early twenties, conform to the group consensus, wearing bomber jackets, T-shirts, Levi's with suspenders, and steel-toed boots. The boots are useful for kicking the ribs of blacks, Jews, gays,

Asians, and Hispanics after they have thrown them to the ground. Swastikas are the tattoo of choice for the skinhead.

From a group of about 300 in 1986, skinheads have multiplied to what the Center for Democratic Renewal estimates to be about 3,500, spread over about 200 U.S. cities. They are a part of a total pool of about 15,000 to 20,000 hate participants who make up groups such as the Ku Klux Klan, the paramilitary The Order, Nazi organizations like the National Socialist Vanguard, and the anti-Semitic Christian Identity Organization. All believe whites are superior to what skinheads term the "mud" races. Most of the hate groups meet at Hayden Lake, Idaho, for the annual conference of the Aryan Nations Church, a neo-Nazi organization.

The young men in hate groups are often recruited from families that have abandoned them or families so strict that the boys abandoned them. When parents require blind obedience from their children, such as "You do that because I said so," the child may later seek out an organization that also requires blind obedience. These children become good subjects for leaders who want to use their pent-up hostility for their own purposes. Hitler used the blind obedience of his generation of Germans, who had been raised in the mode of "Children should be seen and not heard," and "Spare the rod and spoil the child." People who had suffered frequent beatings from their parents were able to turn their repressed anger on the Jews. In such a way, skinheads are looking for a leader they can be submissive to, who will tell them who to vent their anger on.

Skinheads first organized in England in the 1970s in reaction to the influx of black immigrants. When immigrants appear to be getting jobs and jobs are scarce, it offers an excuse for violence for some restless, poorly educated, poorly trained young men. Turning their enormous adolescent energy to hate, they can wreak havoc in communities—and even on TV shows. When the skinheads were on the Oprah Winfrey show they called her a "monkey." She said she had never felt such evil and hatred in her life. When they were on the Geraldo show, they broke his nose.

A flyer with slogans of "Young Nazis" and "Skinheads" covered with swastikas was circulated in Hollister, California, explaining the skinhead viewpoint. It is reprinted here with spelling and grammar errors included.

> The attitude of a skinhead is generally ready to fight and on guard at all times . . . Skins do not usually go around and start trouble. Its only when people start to make the jump on skins. When that happens, the skins end up winning! Skinheads are mad and tired of the system screwing them over . . . Skinheads are the All American white youth. They love mom and love their flag. The dress of the skin is rough, smart and clean . . . All in all, the skinhead uniform is working class, ready to fight because our heads are shaved for battle . . . Skinheads are against nonwhite immigration because, these people take our jobs and land and give nothing in return. Skinheads are Anti-Semitic, because we know the Jews have extorted us for there personnel means. Skinheads are anti-abortion, we all know that abortion is another form of genocide, the nonwhite races and the Jews sit and laugh at our self-annihilation.

Peter Lake, a journalist who infiltrated a white supremacist group, reported his experiences in the University of California, Davis, *Cal Aggie* of February 8, 1989. He said that these groups, "most notably the Identity Church Movement," hold that "Eve mated twice: once with the devil and again with Adam. The offspring from the Serpent became the Jews; when the Jews mated with the beasts, they produced the . . . blacks and Orientals. The story of Cain and Abel shows how the Adamic race was murdered by Jews and sets examples to white Christians to arm themselves and defend themselves against the Jews."

Lake said that white supremacists believe that Jews and blacks do not have souls. "As soon as you deny someone their humanity, say that someone doesn't have a soul . . . then you can do anything you want to them." Lake observed that "often the younger skinheads are controlled by the more well-established white supremacists."

Aside from hating other races, what harm have these white supremacists and skinheads done? To recount just a few incidents, in July 1988, Ken Allen, twenty, and three other skinheads told a black woman in San Jose, California, she would have to pay a "nigger toll" to pass by them. They also told her they were going to "string you up on that tree." Allen was convicted of false imprisonment—restricting the woman's freedom on a public street—and sentenced to two years in prison.

When a transient, Isiah Walter, forty-one, was sleeping in a park in Tampa, Florida, two brothers, Scott McKee, eighteen, and Dean McKee, sixteen, stabbed him to death. The father of the two boys said his sons became skinheads after a summer in Southern California. Dean McKee received a life sentence in prison, but his brother received only five years because he gave evidence about their actions.

Mike Martin, eighteen, leader of the Reich Skins, terrorized a Hispanic family after he kicked in their apartment door in Granada Hills, California. He had been followed by about a dozen chanting skinheads. When neighbors appeared to help the family, Martin made his escape, protecting himself with his .38 semiautomatic weapon. He stayed in jail six months for this intimidation.

"Go back to Hong Kong," was shouted by three Nazi skinheads to a Chinese man, Hock-Seng Chin, in Portland, Oregon. Chin was attacked, and when he collapsed he was kicked by the steel-toed boots. Two of the skinheads received prison sentences.

When Philip Rowe, a member of the Reich Skinheads, and several friends were hitchhiking and got picked up by a Hispanic woman in Van Nuys, California, they slit her throat and left her for dead. She lived. Rowe was charged with attempted murder.

Skinheads and other hate groups appeal not only to racists but to an economic class. They come from working-class homes, in an economic climate where their opportunities are diminishing. Skinheads blame the minorities for the lack of job opportunities for whites. Their leaders appeal to working-class youth by exploiting their contempt for the rich.

Tom Metzger, fifty-four, a leader of the decade-old, neo-Nazi White Aryan Resistance organization, is one man who is using the skinheads to further his own political ideology. A former member of the John Birch Society, a member of the anti-Semitic Christian Identity group, and a former Ku Klux Klan Grand Dragon, Metzger is currently recruiting members to the Aryan Youth Movement with his White Power Network, which includes a newspaper, weekly cable TV show, and call-in phone lines, all espousing white supremacy.

National media attention was paid to Portland, Oregon, in November 1988 when an Ethiopian named Mulegta Seraw, twenty-seven, who was planning to attend Portland State University, was beaten to death by three neo-Nazi racists, members of East Side White Pride. Friends who tried to help Seraw were injured by the skinheads.

For the attack on Seraw, Kyle Brewster, nineteen, was sentenced to twelve to twenty years; Kenneth Mieske, twenty-three, who admitted beating Seraw with a baseball bat, was sentenced to life in prison. The third man is still awaiting his trial. Literature from Tom Metzger's White Aryan Resistance Movement was found in the possession of the assailants. The three skinheads were out on the town at 1:00 A.M. afer meeting with two of Metzger's lieutenants.

After the murder trial, a civil suit was filed by the Southern Poverty Law Center, holding Tom Metzger and his son John, twenty-five, president of the Aryan Youth Movement, responsible for influencing the men convicted of Seraw's death. One of the witnesses for the prosecution testified that he had gone to Portland at the request of Metzger a couple of years earlier to organize young men into skinhead groups. He said his job was to teach them how to provoke racial violence. He said he had specifically instructed the men who were later convicted of Seraw's death.

When the jury voted that Metzger, his son, and the skinhead murderers must pay the family of the murdered man a combined total of $12.5 million, Metzger's remark was that now he would be a martyr for white America. "We are telling the white underclass that is growing out there that this kind of thing is coming to their door next." Metzger is appealing the case with the help of the Patriots Defense Foundation, American Association for the Advancement of White People, and the White Separatist Movement. In May 1991, he went on welfare because, he said, his assets were seized to pay the judgment against him. He received $960 for his first check and commented, "It seems strange not to go to work, but now I can do full-time work on my politics."

After hundreds of leaflets from the White Aryan Resistance were distributed to doorsteps and car windows in Castro Valley, California, more racial attacks occurred. This area is considered ripe for recruitment by white supremacist groups dedicated to inciting whites to rise up against their minority neighbors. Many minorities give up and move away, as did the Chinese grocer and Korean liquor store owner who, after they had been beaten and ridiculed by youth groups who hung around their stores, feared for their families' safety.

In October 1988, the Anti-Defamation League issued a report bringing attention to the rising number of skinheads and their crimes. The report reads: "The rise in the number of skinheads has been paralleled by an increase in the number of violent crimes they have committed, including homicides and numerous shootings, beatings and stabbings directed against members of minority groups." The report calls for careful monitoring of the group's activities, which range from vandalism to murder.

Anti-Semitic Attacks

Although skinheads are anti-Semitic and cause problems for Jews, not all attacks on synagogues are perpetrated by skinheads. In one day in San Francisco in June 1989, there were three attacks against the Jewish religion with no known reference to skinheads. An incendiary bomb was detonated at Beth Sholom Synagogue; at Adath Israel Synagogue, windows were broken; and at the Holocaust Memorial, excrement was smeared on the walls. No one was apprehended for any of these crimes.

In New York, three teenagers were arrested for attacking three Jewish students. Charged with first-degree assault and violations of civil rights were Anthony Sorrentino, eighteen, Joseph Guben, sixteen, and James Dynes, seventeen. Two of the attacked students were hospitalized.

The Anti-Defamation League reported an increase from 1987 to 1991 in anti-Semitic attacks such as arson, bombings, cemetery desecrations, and swastika paintings on homes and synagogues. In February 1991, at university campuses in California, such as UC Berkeley, UC Santa Cruz, UC Santa Barbara, and Stanford, either actual attacks or threats on Jews were reported in increased numbers compared to attacks in 1990.

Anti-Black Attacks

Blacks have been the victims of hate crimes in this country for over two centuries. Crimes against them range from cross burnings in front of their homes to lynchings and other murders. More than 50 percent of all hate crimes in this country are directed at blacks. Hate crimes against blacks, or African Americans, would be an entire book.

To name just one incident, in Louisiana, Kentucky, the FBI arrested a man in May 1990 who told his friends he was going to kill as many blacks as he could at the Kentucky Derby, then he would kill himself. He had previously been convicted of burning a cross on a black family's lawn. In his home, police found a mechanism that could convert an AK-47 rifle to make it fully automatic.

Anti-Asian Attacks

As more Asians enter this country and pursue education and jobs, they also become the focus of anger by white people who believe Asians are taking something away from those whose families have been here for generations.

After Patrick Purdy opened fire on children in a Stockton, California, elementary school, it was said that he did it because he hated Asians. He complained to a Stockton bartender two weeks before the shooting that the Vietnamese were getting jobs and welfare assistance, and he blamed immigrants for his own failure. He told the bartender he had an AK-47 rifle and, as he left the bar on that particular night, said, "You're going to read about me in the papers." Previously he had complained that "those damn Hindus and boat people own everything."

The investigation of Purdy's background revealed that he had no known connections with any hate groups but had acted on his own. His killing of five children and wounding of thirty-one prompted a report from the state attorney general's office. The tone was set with the statement: "Violence and hostility against Asian/Pacific Americans is a growing trend in this state." The long report concluded that though Purdy had many problems, it was his racist anger that culminated in the death of those he saw as his enemy.

Six Japanese students sat on the lawn of Teikyo Loretto Heights University in Denver, Colorado, one of the U.S. campuses that is operated by the Japanese. They were singing and strumming guitars when they were approached by four white men swinging baseball bats and cursing them in English, which the Japanese could not understand. The Japanese suffered severe injuries, open head wounds and bruised ribs. Two of the four young American men who attacked the Japanese were brothers. In the homes of these brothers the police found bats and sticks, a copy of the book *A Clockwork Orange*, a novel about gangs of boys who rough up other boys, a book with information about the Ku Klux Klan, and a Ku Klux Klan membership card.

Anti-Gay Attacks

"We would never make a decision to go beat up fags, but if we're walking down the street and some guy passed that looked 'queer,' we'd let him have it." This is a quote from an average teenager in Gary Comstock's *Violence Against Lesbians and Gay Men*. "Gay bashing" is the act of seeking out and intimidating or physically abusing homosexual men and women. This includes assault, harassment, vandalism, and abuse by police. Gay bashing sometimes ends in murder. The crime of Donald Miller, forty-nine, should more likely be included in the chapter on murder in this book, but his is a classic example of a hate crime.

Donald Miller received the death penalty in May 1990 for the bludgeon-slaying of four homosexual men he met in bars in Southern California in 1980 and 1981. Justice David Eagleson wrote that the evidence clearly indicated "the defendant kept a pipe in his car for use as a weapon and that on four separate occasions he met men in gay bars, invited them to his car for marijuana or sex, drove them to nearby side streets and without warning struck them on the head with a pipe and killed them." In addition to the four murders, Miller was identified by three other men as the man who had lured them to his car and attempted to murder them.

San Francisco leads the nation in the number of attacks on gay men and lesbian women, according to the Community United Against Violence. In 1990 there was a 199 percent increase over the number of attacks in 1989. Approximately 85 percent of attacks against homosexuals do not get reported to police because of what is perceived as police discrimination against homosexuals. Many gays may not have revealed their homosexuality or may not want to make it public by reporting abuse against them. Also, as Comstock explains in his book, the "gay basher" has little to fear from the police because the police are among the most frequent attackers of homosexuals.

The National Gay and Lesbian Task Force Policy Institute reported an overall increase of 42 percent in hate crimes against homosexuals in 1990 in cities that included Los Angeles, San Francisco, Chicago, Boston, and Minneapolis-St. Paul.

Anti-Arab Attacks

With the invasion of Kuwait by Iraq, hate crimes against Arabs increased from one incident in January 1990 to fifty-eight incidents in January 1991. Most cases involved vandalism or graffiti. In some predominantly Muslim communities, stores owned by Arab-Americans were targeted and windows broken. Threatening phone calls were made to mosques, and anti-Iraqi hate literature was distributed to Arab-Americans.

General Information

In an era when affirmative action has been downgraded, and as this nation becomes a nation of minorities and faces economic hard times, racial hatred and its associated violent crimes are expected to grow, according to the chairman of the state attorney general's Commission on Racial, Ethnic, Religion and Minority Violence, Monsignor William Barry. While violent crimes, such as Purdy's shooting the Vietnamese and

Laotian children, get considerable media attention, other more subtle hate crimes exist that quietly destroy people's lives. For instance, in a nearly all-white school in the Walnut Creek area of California, a Chinese student argued with a female student. The girl's boyfriend rammed the Chinese student's car. Then the home of the Chinese was sprayed with derogatory racial remarks. The same words about the Chinese student were sprayed on the walls of the high school and, as his mother said, "all over town." When the Chinese student's mother complained to the police she was told that it was just a case of "two boys fighting." Is this another case of boys-will-be-boys? The Chinese boy dropped out of school.

In cases of vandalism or battery, the penalties can be converted from misdemeanors to felonies if racial hatred is the motive. Few victims know about the severe civil and criminal penalties that can be imposed.

In the San Francisco Bay Area, concern about the rising number of hate crimes has prompted communities to call meetings in attempts to curtail cross burnings, swastika-painting, and racist graffiti. "Die Jews" and "Niggers go home" have been spray-painted on walls in King School in Hayward. The high school in Hayward was sprayed with Ku Klux Klan sprawlings as well. In Castro Valley, a black woman was awakened one night to see a flaming cross burning on her lawn.

Pending legislation in California would double a prison sentence for a misdemeanor hate crime from six months to one year; for a felony hate crime, add one to four years and increase penalties from $10,000 to $25,000. Punitive damages would no longer have a limit.

While the number of hate crimes is small compared to the number of crimes of other natures, it is the direction of hate crimes that is of concern. A December 9, 1990, *Los Angeles Times* article by Judy Pasternak entitled, "How Hate Comes to a Boil" and subtitled, "Animosity toward those who are 'different' turns from thought to deed" pointed out that in counties where hate crimes are specifically categorized, as in Los Angeles County, there is a rise in the numbers of these crimes. The Center for Democratic Renewal, which monitors hate crimes across the United States, notes an alarming increase in crimes directed at people who are "different"—a different color, different religion, or different sexual preference.

A poll taken in August 1993 in the Los Angeles area revealed that among hate crime victims 21 percent were Asian, 12 percent white, 14 percent black, and 16 percent Hispanic. A more recent accounting by the Los Angeles County Commission on Human Relations reported that as of May 1994 gay men have become the primary targets of hate crimes. Also, included in the more recent survey was the fact that Jews account for 15 percent of the victims of hate crimes. More than 43 percent of all hate crimes entail some kind of violence, especially now, when anti-immigrant sentiments surface from politicians.

Even a seventy-year-old man, an Armenian who came to the United States to live with his son, is not immune to hate crimes. Jumped by a man lying in wait behind bushes, Sarkis Shavaladian was allegedly beaten by a forty-five-year-old homeless man who shouted that the Armenians were taking jobs away from people born in this country. Edmond Antone pleaded not guilty April 7, 1994, in Los Angeles municipal court, but will be prosecuted for a hate crime since that appears to be the only motive for injuring his victim.

The executive director of the Human Relations Commission in Los Angeles says, "The tension level is up. We still haven't learned to live together."

CHAPTER 6

DRUNK DRIVING

Every twenty-four minutes a drunk driver kills someone. Ninety percent of drunk drivers are male. Nationwide, there were 18,000 alcohol-related deaths in 1993. Only one in 1,300 drunk drivers is caught, and more than half of those had previous drunk driving arrests, according to a CNN report on April 30, 1994.

Drunk driving is the second leading cause of death for young people, the first being violent crime. Since 1980 there has been a 30 percent decline in drunk driving fatalities, largely because of public awareness made possible by Mothers Against Drunk Driving (MADD), which has 400 chapters and three million supporters.

Over the past twenty years, as cited in the California Department of Motor Vehicles Handbook, 50 percent of auto deaths were caused by alcohol. In California alone there were 302,298 drug and drunk driving convictions reported to the Department of Motor Vehicles. In 1992 drunk drivers caused 22 percent of all fatal car crashes, compared with 30 percent in 1982. Behavior is changing as the public becomes more aware of the tragedy of drunk driving.

Persons Arrested for DWI, 1991

Characteristics	Percent now inmates
Male	87%
Female	13%
White	90%
Black	9%
Other	1%
Under 18	1%
18–24	25%
25–44	61%
45–54	9%
55–64	3%
65 & over	1%

U.S. Department of Justice Bureau of Statistics

Before they were arrested for DWI (driving while intoxicated), drunk drivers had consumed approximately six ounces of pure alcohol, or the equivalent of twelve bottles of beer or eight mixed drinks, in four hours. Typical of many drunk drivers, they have no idea what the legal alcohol level is. They drive faster than legal limits and take more risks.

Repeat offenders are allowed to drive for months while awaiting trial. Suspended licenses don't seem to have much effect. In Orange County, offenders who have had their licenses suspended in the courtroom are rearrested in the courthouse parking lot as they proceed to drive away. Officials in Orange County say this method is the only one used to catch drivers who drive with suspended licenses.

The California Department of Motor Vehicles estimates that 400,000 California drivers with suspended licenses continue to drive. Those driving with suspended licenses are often repeat offenders in drunk driving cases. Except for one woman, all of the people caught by the Orange County method (arrests in the parking lot) have been men.

There are those who argue that tough laws against drunk drivers are not what will make a difference, that most repeat offenders are alcoholics who need treatment, not jail. It is estimated by a public defender in San Francisco that half of the people arrested for drunk driving are alcoholics, and of those arrested twice, 80 percent are alcoholics.

In Manteca, California, a man with seven previous drunk driving convictions and one vehicular manslaughter conviction was arrested for felony drunk driving and felony hit and run. He is accused of running over a man as he walked on an interstate frontage road. The driver was speeding at about 75 miles per hour with a blood alcohol level between .15 and .19.

In California a person is legally drunk when the blood alcohol level is .08 or higher. That amounts to about five drinks in two hours, depending on a person's weight. As a member of Mothers Against Drunk Driving remarked, "We're not talking about a falling-down-drunk standard. Alcohol impairs you in ways that are not always visible, like a person's mental function. You don't have to be drunk to be involved in a drunk driving crash." People in California who have been convicted of drunk driving more than four times in the previous seven years can be tried in court for a felony and may serve up to three years in state prison.

A man who lived in Sacramento, California, and was on probation for prior convictions in 1987 and 1988 was sentenced to fourteen years in prison for the drunk driving deaths of three people and the injury of four others. He had a blood alcohol level of twice the legal limit and was speeding at 85 miles per hour.

If drunk drivers would stay on the road, it would be bad enough, but some lose control and end up on the sidewalk. This was the case in Pasadena where two mothers and their young daughters were waiting to cross a street when a drunk driver ran his car into all of them. The prosecuting attorney lined up ten glasses on the jury banister. Without saying a word, he filled the glasses with beer, held up four fingers then snapped his fingers four times to indicate that the accused had snuffed out four lives after drinking ten glasses of beer.

In another case of sidewalk drunk driving, a woman and six children were walking to Miramonte Elementary School in Florence, California, when a drunk driver drove up over the curb and ran over them, killing one seven-year-old.

Judgment is impaired when driving drunk. Mistakes like driving onto sidewalks, or driving on the wrong side of the road, or of driving the wrong way on freeway off-ramps occur. Such was the case in Lancaster, California, when a man drove his car west on the eastbound lane of Highway 18 on April 7, 1990. The driver was accused of second-degree murder after the head-on collision killed one man.

At times the citizenry becomes so enraged at drunk driving accidents that they take things into their own hands. In downtown Los Angeles, a drunk driver came off the Santa Monica Freeway at record speed and, as a witness said, "plowed right into two men and then continued on and hit two other cars. When the crowd tried to get him to stop, he just got out and started running." Jorge Urrutia was chased down and captured by the people who had seen it happen. Because one of the people he had hit was killed, he was arrested on suspicion of murder and for drunk driving.

Yet the police are vigilant. In one weekend in the San Fernando area of Los Angeles, there were 230 drunk driving arrests in nine hours. Arrests for drunk driving have been increasing in California because of the law that took effect January 1, 1990, lowering the blood alcohol level indicating driving under the influence to .08 from .10.

Nonetheless, it is difficult for a prosecutor to get a conviction from a jury for drunk driving. Unlike jury trials for other crimes, such as robbery, assault, or murder, many people who have been called to jury duty for a drunk driving charge have themselves driven after they have had a couple of drinks. They are reluctant to send another person to jail for "having a few drinks."

Vehicular manslaughter carries a penalty that usually entails several years in prison, but for Fernando Niebla, who had seven traffic tickets within a year after getting his license at eighteen, his sentence amounted to only 133 days. This was true even though one of his accidents involved the death of his friend, a passenger in the car when it hit a power pole. His sixteen-year-old friend was thrown through the windshield, which split his skull. Another friend in the car came out of the crash with his collarbone broken. Niebla said he and his buddies were going to buy hamburgers when they were hit by another car. According to police, however, there was no other car and Niebla's blood alcohol level was .12. However, the judge took Niebla's word for the circumstances of the accident, dismissed the vehicular manslaughter charge, and sentenced him to probation and 133 days for drunk driving.

In another incident, on May 15, 1994, a drunk driver's five-year-old son was killed in an accident, after the mother of the boy begged the drunk father not to take the boy for a ride. Now Pedro Guzman, thirty-five, spends his time in prison lamenting his son's death.

At least for those who are not incorrigible, public awareness is probably making a difference. The words *designated driver*, for nondrinking drivers, are finding a place in the general vocabulary for people out to do some drinking yet wanting to ensure a safe ride home.

There has been some effort made to hold others responsible for the alcohol consumption of drinkers who then cause accidents. However, the U.S. Supreme Court upheld a California law that shields bartenders and tavern owners from responsibility for accidents caused by customers who had been drinking in their business establishments. It is not that the Supreme Court endorsed the law, but rather that it said the law did not raise a constitutional issue and therefore the Court would not review the case. This was a major disappointment for Mothers Against Drunk Driving. As Vicky Cloud of that organization said, "Responsibility has to go beyond just the drunk driver for his actions; it has to extend to the server and the seller as well."

The basis for the law was the drunk driving death of a twenty-year-old boy as he was riding his bicycle along the Pacific Coast Highway in Newport Beach. He was struck and killed by a man who had just left a bar on the beach and was so drunk, as witnesses recalled, that he fell off the bar stool. His blood alcohol level after his arrest was three times the legal limit. He served sixteen months in prison for drunk driving.

Those who rejoiced that the law shielding taverns was upheld remarked that the California legislature decided correctly that adult customers should be responsible for their own actions. Efforts to pass laws holding others responsible for serving liquor to people who then cause accidents have met with severe lobbying by liquor and restaurant industries against such legislation.

Even with public awareness, new legislation, and the massive efforts of MADD, figures for drunk driving are not heartening. The change in the percentage of those driving under the influence shows that although older drivers are not arrested as often for drunk driving, there is an increase in the number of arrests for younger people. As alcohol is the drug of choice of young people, drunk driving will probably remain a serious problem and will cause many deaths.

Drunk Piloting

A related crime is developing in the airline industry—pilots who have consumed excess amounts of alcohol before flying passenger airplanes. Whether there is a carryover factor of automobile drunk driving to airplane flying is not clear, but the Department of Transportation is concerned and has been tracking pilots in regard to drunk driving convictions. In a study reported in *Jet*, November 1986, the department revealed that approximately 16,000 licensed pilots had been convicted of drunk driving since 1960. "And nearly half that number failed to admit their convictions on federally required medical reviews." As of this writing, drunk driving convictions are not cause for revoking pilots' licenses.

Newsweek, August 13, 1990, reported that each year between 5 and 10 percent of pilots killed in plane crashes have alcohol in their blood. In March 1990, the Federal Aviation Administration accused three Northwest Airlines pilots of flying under the influence of alcohol and suspended their licenses. This is the first known case of pilots of commercial airlines being accused in this kind of situation. The three men were arrested when the plane landed, after a tip from a passenger on the plane.

Federal regulations prohibit alcohol consumption by pilots eight hours before they fly. Northwest has an even stricter rule of twelve hours. All three pilots in the above incident submitted voluntarily to blood alcohol tests and failed. Their licenses were revoked.

In October 1990, the three pilots were convicted of flying a passenger plane while under the influence and were sentenced to federal prison. The captain was sentenced to sixteen months, the copilot and flight engineer each were sentenced to twelve months. Defense attorneys argued that their flying skills were not impaired even though the men had split seven pitchers of beer and fifteen mixed drinks at a bar the night before their flight, which left at 6:30 in the morning.

As of January 1991, the Federal Aviation Administration program matched the names of 680,000 licensed pilots with the possibility of alcohol-related offenses in their automobile driving records. Of pilots killed in plane crashes each year, 5 to 10 percent had alcohol in their blood.

Whether it is drivers on the highways who are under the influence, or pilots in the skies, drunk driving in either case is often deadly or seriously injurious. And almost all such drivers are men.

CHAPTER 7

ARSON

According to the Department of Justice, 87 percent of all arson fires are started by men.

When a three-story apartment building goes up in flames in the middle of the night and tenants, barefoot and wrapped in blankets, scramble for their lives, the first question firemen ask is, "Did everyone get out?" Then, as the building burns, and one of the firemen discovers some half-burned rags in a mail chute near the street, the second question they ask is, "Who could have done such a thing?" The search is on for an arsonist.

Where to look? The best place, according to specialists in arson crime, is to peruse the gathering crowd. Notice the faces of spectators who come to watch the blaze. "Arson is the only crime where the suspect sticks around," said John Orr, the captain of the Glendale Fire Department. That was his statement in July 1990, after sixty-seven homes were destroyed by an arsonist in Glendale, California; the temperature soared to 105 degrees with the combined effect of fire whipped by raging winds.

The arsonist was the arson specialist, Fire Capt. John Orr, who was arrested in 1992 for setting the Glendale fire and several others, including one in Fresno, where he was attending a conference for arson investigation. He is serving a thirty-year prison sentence.

On November 21, 1994, John Orr was charged with murder, accused of setting the fire in a South Pasadena hardware store in 1984 that killed four people, including a two-year-old boy. The publication of his book, *Points of Origin*, in which he fictionalizes an arsonist's attack, led to the investigation for which he may now face a death sentence. In the book he describes the arsonist as feeling fright and enjoying the excitement. It is not likely that an arsonist will be immediately detected by looking at the spectators, but all of those watching the fire should be questioned. Even if they are not suspects, they might have important information leading to an arrest. Long after the cinders have cooled off, arson fire spots are often staked out, because arsonists are known to return to the scene of their crime.

Many fires are set by "vanity pyromaniacs," men who want attention, or maybe want to become firefighters. Or possibly it was started by "true pyromaniacs," those who are thrilled by fire and sometimes sexually aroused by the destruction. This pattern harkens back to the way violence sexually arouses some murderers as they destroy their victims. Sex, for some men, means violence, and violence in turn means sexual arousal.

One stakeout paid off in the case of the arrest of Douglas Gerrie, thirty-six, of Carmichael, California, who was questioned in conjunction with a two-year investigation of several forest fires around Truckee. Gerrie was arrested at the scene of a fire near the Truckee-Donner housing subdivision.

The U.S. Fire Administration states that 50 percent of fires in the United States are set deliberately. Of the remaining fires, from 25 to 33 percent are later identified as arson fraud. Arsonists set fires for many reasons other than the thrill of seeing the blaze and the violent destruction. Many set fires for revenge, for insurance money, in anger in a love triangle, to cover up a crime, and sometimes for no other reason than for being mad at the world.

In times of economic hardship, fire for hire becomes an occupation. When business slackens and no buyers for that particular business are in sight, the owners can contract with an arsonist, whose wages are inexpensive. Some insurance companies do not want to take the time or money required to bring an owner to court. In many cases it is cheaper to pay the insurance claim.

But how does the desire to set fires start? When a research psychologist, Wayne S. Wooden, looked into this question in regard to children setting fires (*Psychology Today*, January 1985), he learned that there are four distinct types of juvenile fire setters. Some are young children up to ten years of age, playing with matches, who accidentally cause a fire; some are slightly older, with problems, and seem to be asking for help. Children in a third group not only have problems but could also be classified as delinquents: setting fires is an "adolescent acting out against authority." The fourth group includes the severely mentally disturbed of any age. Though this study did not classify the subjects by gender, all references to firestarters involve masculine pronouns. When females are involved in any arson, their gender was invariably pointed out.

Some fires are accidentally started by young boys, as in the case of a thirteen-year-old arrested in April 1989 for the $900,000 fire in a vacant San Francisco building, which the police and fire inspectors believe was being used as a boys' clubhouse. Another case in San Francisco involved four boys, one a twelve-year-old who was cited for starting a fire in an elementary school that caused $100,000 in damage. Two twelve-year-olds and one nine-year-old were scolded and released. Apparently, the four boys had been playing with matches when the fire got away from them.

Many young firestarters questioned in the Wooden research said they would like to be firefighters when they grew up, and that their favorite toy was a fire truck. Questioning adult firemen, a statement was made to them to which they could agree or disagree. The statement was, as compared to nonfiremen, "firemen are apt to have a history of firestarting." The researcher was startled to learn that 9 percent of firemen agreed with the statement. He noted also that though 9 percent is not very significant, it seemed to indicate that firemen who have a history of firestarting expect that other firemen also had a history of firestarting.

What do child arsonists burn? They burn their schools, after they have had some experience in burning other things. For instance, a fourteen-year-old boy who set his junior high school on fire had set his bathroom on fire when he was four and had set his kitchen on fire when he was twelve. Arson in schools is the most expensive crime against schools. While vandalism against schools amounts to about $600 million a year, 40 percent of that is due to arson caused by children who might have been angry at someone at the school, or just not doing well in their classes.

But anger over family problems also can result in children striking out with fire. One six-year-old boy, when he was told he was going to have to be "the man in the family" after his father was taken to prison, set a fire in the kitchen and then set his father's couch on fire. In the Wooden article, the boy was quoted as saying he set fires when he got mad at himself or when he felt stupid.

Among children firestarters, the mentally disturbed are probably the exception. Young firestarters are generally what would be called normal white middle-class youths. Wooden conjectures that middle-class youths do not generally have the accepted outlets for anger that other youths in congested urban or ghetto areas have. White middle-class children, he says, are socialized to repress anger and control their hostility, whereas urban, lower-class youths shout their anger at each other and at their parents; there is a certain amount of tolerance for physical punching and hitting.

What, then, is the anger outlet for the middle-class youth? "Passive aggression," says Wooden. This is the outlet for the boy who must control disturbing feelings if he is angry or feels unable to compete. Lighting fires is passively aggressive. Lighting destructive fires can give a powerless person a sense of power that he may not feel when he is with his parents or peers. Arson is an assertion of control, power, and superiority.

This idea is somewhat analogous to the findings of the study on the S&L scandal. Researchers pointed out that most of those crimes were committed by white males in two-parent families who may have had difficulty competing openly with fathers or other family members and who later compensated by accumulating wealth that gave them power and superiority.

When drawing a profile of an arsonist, "Look for a passive, unmarried man between the ages of eighteen and thirty, who lacks a capacity to confront people," says Dr. Allan Hedberg, a Fresno psychologist, referring specifically to an arsonist who sets wildfires in timberland. Hedberg, who has worked with convicted arsonists and who helps the Forestry Department in searching for arsonists, is quoted in the *San Francisco Chronicle* of July 26, 1988: "Big forest fires with massive fire trucks and pandemonium are a way of making a masculine statement for an unstable young man who in the past has been wronged."

The article continues with information that some wilderness fires are started by young male campers who have been drinking and start a fire on a dare. Other forest fires have been started by firefighters, who earn money fighting the fire. But, as Jerry Partain, the California state director of forestry says, the majority of wilderness firestarters "should be regarded as serial terrorists." There are about 200 wilderness arsonists in the state of California who use all sorts of firestarting devices such as matches, cigarette lighters, Molotov cocktails, and other incendiaries.

Compared with urban firestarters, who have to approach a building and may have to worry about smoke alarms or easier detection, wilderness arsonists have only to drop an incendiary device on the side of a country road and drive away. In California, an annual average of 1,250 fires are caused by arsonists, and only about 15 percent of the arsonists have been arrested and convicted.

A few of the crimes of arsonists include a June 1990 fire in San Bernardino County in which an elderly couple was burned to death in their home. During this fire, 285 homes were destroyed in the brush fire that was set during a 75 mile per hour wind.

Near Ojai, in Ventura County, an arsonist set a fire that destroyed twelve homes and about 120,000 acres of watershed land.

A repeat arsonist known as the "Stairway Arsonist" terrorized residents of San Jose during the summer months of 1989, torching older homes by lighting newspapers around the staircases. These fires were all started at night and usually resulted in tenants being rescued by firemen with ladders extended to upper-story windows. After fire gutted the San Carlos Hotel, the arsonist, who had been seen hanging around the hotel as it burned, was arrested and convicted. Guillermo Mendez, twenty-three, confessed to setting ten fires in thirty-six hours and was sentenced to eleven years in prison. He had no explanation for his crime except to say that he was "mad at the world."

Also in San Jose, the "Willow Glen Arsonist" had been striking dental offices. The California Dental Association periodical, *Update*, advised dentists to update their insurance. They were also advised to have sprinkling systems in their

buildings and a fire alarm system connected to a security system. These precautions couldn't keep the fire from starting, but
they could help to save the property. Some dentists, concerned
about their expensive equipment, began sleeping in their
offices.

In San Francisco, June 1990, a serial arsonist set twenty-two
fires near Russian and Nob hills, torching wooden buildings
with multiple apartments. Gasoline-soaked rags were shoved
through a mail slot in one of the apartment buildings and
ignited. Fifty people rushed out into the streets at 2:00 A.M. to
see their homes and their belongings go up in smoke.

Witnesses described a white male, twenty-five to thirty
years of age, hanging around the fire, but no one was apprehended. In the *San Francisco Chronicle*, Fire Inspector Ron Moehan said they had no motive to go on. "It could be the thrill of
it, or maybe anger at society, or even the feeling of power for
causing all this equipment and men to respond." Sixty firefighters and eighteen pieces of equipment were used in fighting the fire. While a lot of fires are set for revenge, this one did
not seem to be set for revenge. "This one looks like a guy walking around." But Moehan added, "We're out there. We're trying to get this man."

In another San Francisco arson case, police are looking for a
white male in his twenties, with a stocky build and long hair.
He is a suspect in an arson fire that caused $700,000 damage to
two buildings. Two witnesses described this man as leaving
the building after the fire started on June 30, 1989.

A Molotov cocktail thrown into the basement of a set of
three-story apartments in San Francisco caused a blaze that
brought ninety-four firefighters and sixteen pieces of equipment to the scene in the middle of the night in February 1990.

Throughout the city of Pomona, California, residents were
frightened during a twelve-day arson spree in February 1988.
Jaim Asoau, twenty-nine, known by firefighters as the "Fire-

bug," admitted responsibility for the twenty-seven fires in the city.

In Sunol, California, Michael Ryan, thirty, was arrested in October 1988 as a suspect in a fire that caused $1 million in damages. Ryan was allegedly seen filling a can with gasoline at a Chevron station before fire broke out there. The fire from the gas station spread to two historic buildings nearby.

In California's drought-stricken hills and towns, fires break out from lightning and causes other than arson, but two of California's worst fires, in Glendale and Santa Barbara, both in 1990, were deliberately set. In the Glendale fire, witnesses said they saw two men toss something into the brush. Later, in the area where this had been reported, investigators found a butane lighter wedged open with a pen. In the Santa Barbara fire, 524 buildings were destroyed and one person was burned to death.

A guard who was on duty at Universal Studios when the fire started on November 7, 1990, was arrested. Fire damage was $25 million and major movie sets were destroyed. Michael Huston, forty, was arrested after questioning as a suspect. He admitted to setting the fire with a cigarette lighter. Bail was set at $1 million. He was an employee of Burns Security Services and had been employed for one month. He claimed to have a split personality and said, according to the fire investigator, that it was the other person inside himself who started the fire.

Collecting on fire insurance may have been the motive for Jose Alonso, thirty-one, for setting his restaurant on fire in San Francisco in July 1989. Alonso was arrested in a private hospital where he went to receive help for second- and third-degree burns. He was allegedly seen leaving Sefi's Restaurant at 4:00 A.M., right after an explosion was heard in the building. Sefi's is below an apartment building that was engulfed in flames, leaving thirty tenants homeless. Many were removed from the building by firefighters with ladders. An anonymous witness telephoned the police to give information about Alonso.

In what may be anger at pro-choice women working in the Planned Parenthood clinic in Concord, California, David Martin, thirty-one, was arrested for setting fire to the clinic and robbing a Vietnam veterans' center of office equipment in the building next door in September 1990. After Martin confessed to the crimes, his bail was raised from $5,400 to $500,000 because of what Det. Frank Harper called "instability."

In a Seventh-Day Adventist Church in Burlingame, California, Pastor Paul Bray, Jr., thirty-two, was arrested for pouring gallons of gasoline on the structure and starting an early morning fire in June 1990. According to his confession, Bray was looking forward to getting insurance money. He was going to use the money to pay for remodeling the rest of the church. But the fire, which caused an estimated $1 million in damages, got away from him and caused much more destruction than he had anticipated. Arson dogs were used to sniff out the gasoline source.

Bray had been a suspect from the start of the investigation. When he could not verify where he had been the night of the fire, he confessed and led inspectors to the spots in the church where he had started the fire. He had been a pastor there for three years.

In what was considered to be arson for revenge against a landlord, a Napa man was arrested and sentenced to three years in state prison in connection with the fire in his girlfriend's apartment, where he had been living. The woman had asked Donald Maus, twenty-five, to leave because he had not paid her rent. She went to work that morning in May 1990, and Maus remained in the apartment to pack. Witnesses said that at six that evening they heard an explosion in the apartment and saw Maus drive away. Investigators found a gasoline can inside the apartment. Maus had the smell of gasoline on his shoes when he was arrested.

In New York, after being ejected from an illegal Bronx

social club after an argument with an ex-girlfriend employed as a hat-check girl, Julio Gonzales, thirty-six, set fire to the building. This revenge fire, on March 25, 1990, was one of the worst in New York in the past seventy-nine years. It killed eighty-seven people, most under the age of twenty-five.

In this building, called the Happy Land, there was only one door and people were trapped. In November of the year before, fire inspectors had issued an order for the building to be vacated because of its fire danger, but, as one patron of the bar said, "They close them down one week, they're open again the next."

Gonzales had been drinking that night and wanted to be with his ex-girlfriend. She had told him to go away. When he didn't, the bouncer threw him out, and Gonzales got angry. Gonzales set fire to the building with one dollar's worth of gasoline. He was remorseful after the fire. One year later, in March 1991, a $5 million lawsuit was filed against the Happy Land Social Club owner, the city of New York, the building owner, and the lease-holder by thirty-four private lawyers representing the victims.

In a sort of "boys will be boys" type of arson, what is known as "Devil's Night" fires flare across Detroit on Halloween. Devil's Night is an orgy of arson. In 1989 30,000 people patrolled the streets to prevent the disaster that occurs each Halloween, when youths roam the city and set trash cans, cars, and buildings on fire. After Halloween in 1989, 334 youths were arrested, mostly for curfew violation, but four for arson.

People in Detroit's run-down, poor neighborhoods were especially worried about fires that might be set in abandoned buildings. One woman who lost everything in her apartment, which was next to an old building, said that there were so many fires in the city that the fire truck couldn't get to her until everything she owned burned up. One old man had stayed up most of the night watching to see if anyone entered the abandoned building next to his house. At about dawn he retired, believing he was safe. Not long after he went to sleep neighbors roused him to tell him his house had caught fire from the burning building next door.

Devil's Night 1994 ended with three people killed and 300 juveniles arrested after their rampage of fire starting.

In Houston, Texas, a veteran policeman who had been named officer of the year in 1989 for rescuing people from fires, was arrested for setting fire to a parsonage of the Mt. Zion Baptist Church, the city's oldest black Baptist church. Sgt. Oliver Brown, sixty-two, was seen crawling out a window at the pastor's home just before the fire broke out.

From the hills of Malibu Canyon down to the Pacific Ocean, a huge blaze that began on November 2, 1993, lasted four days, killed three people, destroyed 350 homes, and caused $375 million in damages. Six months later two male firefighters, ages twenty-four and twenty-nine, were called to testify before a grand jury. They claimed they were just driving by when they saw the fire and tried to put it out, insisting that the fire had started from a downed electrical wire. But investigators saw no evidence of a downed wire and became suspicious. When all other possible causes of the fire were ruled out, the arson specialists concluded that the fire was caused by an open blaze, with the suspects allegedly planning to start the fire, to put it out, and to be hailed as heroes. But the fire got away from them. One witness, having seen the two men at the time of the fire, bolstered the suspects' testimony. On July 29, 1994, the prosecutors said they did not have enough evidence to file criminal charges against the two suspects. However, the investigation will remain open because murder is involved, and there is no statute of limitations for murder.

In another suspected arson case, fifty-five firefighters fought a fire in Concord, California, when a grocery store blaze engulfed three other businesses and caused structural damage and content loss estimated at $1.5 million. The son of the grocery store owner, Rupert Malik, thirty-five, was arrested after inflammable liquid was found in the store and he gave conflicting stories to investigators.

All in all, except for the S&L financial losses, arson crimes represent the largest crime-related financial losses in U.S. history, amounting to over $1.5 *billion* in 1991, according to the National Fire Protection Association, Quincy, Massachusetts, in its journal of September 1992, as reported in the U.S. Statistical Abstracts.

CHAPTER 8

CRIME IN GOVERNMENT

The saying goes that power corrupts, and absolute power corrupts absolutely. Once in a governmental position with power and authority, many elected or appointed governmental employees find it irresistible to enrich themselves with all the opportunities available to them. Most people do not become criminals after becoming public servants, but many do. These include judges, legislators, janitors, police and fire chiefs, mayors, and employees in governmental departments.

In 1991 there were 1,452 indictments of public officials violating federal criminal statutes. These included 803 in the federal government, 115 in state governments, and 242 in local governments.

Employees in governmental departments who handle huge sums of money are quite prone to corruption. The Pentagon has $150 billion a year to be spent for military equipment, and, as we have seen, there is ample opportunity for a Pentagon official to get a kickback from a defense contractor in exchange for awarding a huge contract. Though Operation Ill Wind was instrumental in bringing about approximately forty convictions in Pentagon fraud cases, the opportunities for fraud are built into the current procurement procedures, and investigators have a permanent job overseeing contract award practices.

Department of Housing and Urban Development

In HUD, another large department of the federal government, huge sums of money are awarded for housing in various geographical areas. In 1990 HUD was the focal point of an investigation. Compared to the S&L scandal, the scandal at HUD was rather small—involving a mere $2 billion. But then, the opportunities at HUD are not as limitless as they had been at any S&L.

The congressional investigation into political favoritism and fraud at HUD revealed that multimillion-dollar urban development grants were awarded to the geographical areas of lawmakers who had been particularly helpful to the Reagan administration. One of the key witnesses for the investigation was thirty-eight-year-old DuBois Gilliam, a Republican, who was sentenced to an eighteen-month prison term for conspiracy and receiving illegal gifts from contractors hoping to win approval on their bids. Formerly a top aide to Samuel Pierce, who was the director of HUD during the Reagan years, Gilliam told the committee that "politics was a big part of the way HUD operated, and Pierce was involved in all of that. So was the White House. There was influence from 1600 Pennsylvania Avenue."

Congressional investigators concluded that Samuel Pierce had misled the Congress about abuses in his HUD department. These abuses included favoritism to political friends with money received from his department. The investigators further concluded that Pierce hid the extent of abuses when he was head of that department for eight years. The report said, "At best, Secretary Pierce was less than honest and misled the subcommittee about his involvement in abuses and favoritism in

HUD funding decisions. At worst, Secretary Pierce knowingly lied and committed perjury during his testimony." Pierce indicated he had never told anyone to fund anything, but a series of witnesses contradicted that statement.

On loan defaults on coinsured mortgages, HUD faces a $650 million loss because of practices that are questionable. As in the Pentagon situation, where former Pentagon officials formed their own defense consulting businesses using knowledge gained while working for the Pentagon, so also did former employees of HUD, who left their government jobs and formed their own joint development ventures. One such company was called Winn and Associates, named after Philip Winn, who later became ambassador to Switzerland. With two other former employees of HUD, Philip Abrams and J. Michael Queenan, Winn and Associates built a 160-apartment complex, Sierra Pointe, in Las Vegas. The mortgage company for the project, Benton Mortgage, was accused after a federal audit of not using prudent underwriting practices and of not following HUD rules. The federal audit stated that the three former HUD officials reaped millions in "unjustified profits" and increased the costs because of questionable practices of a mortgage company.

Other HUD investigations reveal housing programs that include golf courses and marinas that will probably cost the taxpayers $177 million in loan defaults. A considerable portion of this monetary loss was the result of housing grants based on favoritism.

Elected Officials

Whether it is the position of governor, judge, mayor, legislator, or police or fire chief, all offices lend themselves to corruption.

In one year, three U.S. district judges were either impeached, indicted, or removed from the bench. In May 1989, the House of Representatives unanimously impeached U.S. District Judge

Walter Nixon of Mississippi for lying to a grand jury about what he knew concerning drug charges against the son of a millionaire who was a friend of his and for his efforts to get involved in the case to help his friend. He is in jail serving a five-year sentence, although he must be tried and convicted by two-thirds of the Senate before he can be denied his lifetime judicial appointment. In November 1989, the Senate voted overwhelmingly to remove Nixon as a judge of the U.S. District Court.

In a case involving a former governor, sixty-seven-year-old Arch Moore of West Virginia pleaded guilty to extorting $573,000 from a coal company, not reporting it on his income tax, and for other fraudulent activities.

No indictment of a city mayor received more publicity than did that of Mayor Marion Barry, fifty-four, of Washington, D.C. Indicted for drug usage, he was sentenced to six months in prison and fined $5,000 for his misdemeanor conviction for cocaine possession. When released he filled out papers to again run for mayor of Washington, D.C., and in November 1994 was reelected.

Daniel Rostenkowski, powerful longtime chairman of the U.S. Congress Ways and Means Committee, was indicted in May 1994 by the Justice Department on seventeen counts, including embezzlement, mail and wire fraud, conspiracy, and jury tampering going back over a twenty-five-year period. He claims that he is innocent and that he will be exonerated by a jury. The trial, which is pending, could take years.

Legislators have the opportunity to extort money from lobbyists in exchange for influencing the laws that will help the lobbyists' companies. In California, a nine-year sting operation by the FBI, the IRS, and the U.S. Attorney's office resulted in the indictment of State Senator Joseph Montoya, forty-nine, and his former top assistant, Amiel Jaramillo. For the sting, dummy corporations were set up, and men posing as rich southerners handed out money to Montoya to get him to pass legislation favorable to their corporations. Caught on videotape, Montoya was convicted of racketeering, extortion, and money laundering. He was also accused in a state lawsuit of using campaign funds for personal purposes and for not reporting over $60,000 in gifts or income. Prosecutors said he would sell his vote anytime he could make money by doing so. He was sentenced to six and a half years and must serve five and a half before he can be considered for parole.

Another legislator indicted and convicted for racketeering, extortion, and conspiracy is sixty-two-year-old California State Senator Paul Carpenter. Reportedly he would not discuss issues with people who came to his office unless their names appeared on his contribution list. He was sentenced in December 1990 to twelve years in prison. He fled to Costa Rica, fought extradition, but was returned to California to serve his twelve-year prison term. Carpenter agreed to accept $20,000 from a bogus company in exchange for legislation that would benefit that company.

In addition to Montoya, Carpenter, and Jaramillo, who were all caught up in the sting, two others pleaded guilty to corruption. They are former Yolo County Sheriff Rod Graham and his undersheriff, Wendell Luttrell. Final verdicts on June 16, 1994, resulted in the conviction of Senator Frank Hill for extortion, conspiracy, and money laundering. Convicted also was lobbyist Terry Frost, guilty of conspiracy to commit extortion.

One colorful police chief, Lonny Greywolf Hurlbut of San Juan Bautista, a town of about 1,900 that lies ninety miles south of San Francisco, was convicted of tampering with evidence. He and other officers added drugs to a drug arrest in order to increase the offense from a misdemeanor to a felony. Hurlbut was sentenced to a year in jail and a fine of $1,000. The cowboy police chief, who has suspended himself from duty for being drunk in public, has been reelected three different times in the last five years.

Other Government Officials

Police officers as well get caught up in criminal activity. In a story on "60 Minutes," in one housing project in Oakland, built and supervised by HUD, men were hired to prevent or curtail crime in the project and then stole money from tenants and planted drugs on them. They beat up people if they ran. There was no training for these housing police, and new recruits learned by example. They were required to meet a monthly arrest quota even if it required illegal arrests. The only way they could keep their jobs was to make arrests. Drug dealers were arrested, but since they seldom had drugs on them, drugs were planted on them. Deputies were fired if they refused to lie in court. When too many people began to come into area hospitals from beatings, the complaints went to the chief of police. Undercover police were sent in to learn just what was going on. As a result, one-third of the housing police were indicted and face prison terms of ten to sixty-two years.

Even fire chiefs, who would not seem to have such opportunities for fraud, can find ways to misappropriate public funds. Such was the situation in Ross, California, where forty-one-year-old Chief Richard Mollenkopf pleaded guilty to falsifying records so that he could channel probably as much as $200,000 into his own account. He also pleaded guilty to having the components of a bomb that police believe could have been used to blow up his brother-in-law's truck or house.

College executives have opportunities for embezzlement as well, as in the case of the former chancellor of the University of California at Santa Barbara, Robert Huttenback, convicted of embezzling $250,000 to make repairs to his home. Fined $60,000, he is appealing his conviction.

A former purchasing agent for the medical school at the University of California, San Francisco, John T. Glennon, thirty-five, was arraigned on charges that he embezzled $350,000 by setting up a dummy corporation and billing the school for equipment never delivered. The money that he embezzled came from the U.S. Department of Health and Human Services.

Also related to medical research, James Erickson, director of the U.S. Agency for International Development's malaria vaccine program, was indicted for embezzling $140,000 and diverting it to his own bank account.

And in the Food and Drug Administration, a chemist and an executive of a Denver drug manufacturing company were charged with bribery. Thirty-eight-year-old David J. Brancato, a chemist in the FDA, was charged with accepting $4,300 in bribes from two generic-drug manufacturers, Par Pharmaceutical, New York, and Quad Pharmaceuticals, Indiana. In Denver, a vice president of Pharmaceutical Basics, Raj Matkarai, was charged with offering $2,000 to Brancato's boss, Charles Chang, who was the chief of the generic drug division. The federal prosecutors promise a wide-ranging investigation into the approval process of generic drugs.

CHAPTER 9

RAPE

At least one rape a minute occurs in this country, with friends, neighbors, and relatives accounting for about one-third of the rapists. Generally 22 percent of rapists are strangers to the victim. For every rape reported, it is estimated there are ten rapes not reported. Along with murder, rape is the fastest growing crime in the United States. One in four women in Los Angeles County will be raped in her lifetime.

Of all rape victims, 51 percent are under eighteen years of age, and 16 percent of rapes are of girls under twelve, and of those under twelve, 20 percent have been raped by their fathers, according to a U.S. Department of Justice report released June 22, 1994. Almost all—96 percent—of girls under twelve who were raped were raped by family members and acquaintances. In 1992 another study, conducted by the Crime Victims' Research Center at the University of South Carolina, estimated that one in eight women in this country have been raped. The National Victim Center estimates that there are 683,000 women raped each year, compared to the 207,610 reported by the Justice Department for 1991. Rape is the most underreported crime, and fewer than 10 percent of rape cases go to trial, as reported by Peter Jennings, on the ABC report "Men, Sex and Rape," broadcast May 5, 1992.

Most states have laws that cite "criminal sexual assault," which includes penetration of a person's body by a foreign object and forced oral sex. Under these laws, a few women have been prosecuted for rape, according to Jane Larson, Northwestern University professor of law. But most were prosecuted for having participated in "criminal sexual assault" against men with men in a gang rape.

The U.S. Department of Justice Bureau of Statistics reports that 41 percent of rapes take place inside the woman's home, 13 percent on the street, 13 percent at friends', relatives', or neighbors' houses. The remainder take place in a variety of places, like parking lots, garages, laundromats, and elevators. Though based on only a small sample of 40,000 rape victims, the Justice Department statistics reported 36 percent of rapists in 1991 used a gun, and 35 percent used another weapon such as a knife or blunt implement.

Rape statistics indicate that the United States has a rape rate four times higher than Germany, thirteen times higher than England, and twenty times higher than Japan. A July 23, 1990, *Newsweek* article stated, "Sadly, sexual violence, too, may now be an emblem of the American way."

The following generalities about rape were culled from government statistics, psychological research reports, criminal records, and victims' reports: three-fourths of rapes are planned; victims are not chosen because they are attractive and are asking for it, but because they are accessible and vulnerable; rapists want victims who will submit and not fight back; a rapist may test his victim by walking close to her and/or talking to her. If she seems compliant he is more likely to move in on the attack; 50 percent of rapes occur in or around the victim's home and at any hour of the day or night; 50 percent of attempted rapes are completed; most victims are of the same racial, ethnic, or socioeconomic class as the rapist; one-third of rape victims know their attacker; black women are at greater risk of being raped than any other group of women. Prostitutes are ready and accessible victims of rape, considered throwaway people, and not expected to be believed by law enforcement.

Yet rapists are not all alike. Most react to their victims with no feeling whatsoever, having depersonalized them. Others have great remorse and suicidal feelings after their attack. Many have been abused as children and pass this abuse on to their victims. In an Oregon study of rapists in 1982, it was learned that 80 percent had been child-abuse victims.

Newsweek's article "The Mind of the Rapist" attempted to answer the pervasive question of why men rape. In the article, rape is described as being "the preempting of another person's body for the gratification of their own needs." Why men rape may be understood by studying men who have been convicted of rape. Whether it is a man who stops to help a stalled female motorist and then rapes her before proceeding home to his wife and children or a man who prowls the neighborhood looking in windows for potential rape victims, inside most of these men is a deep anger, a rage against something in their lives of which they may not be aware.

A consistent element in most rape is the lack of concern for the victim. As a consequence, the most difficult task in rape counseling treatment centers is to get rapists to develop a sense of empathy. This is almost impossible for men who are devoid of emotions other than anger or frustration. Most rapists can recount at least one horrible childhood experience. If, because of child abuse, many men commit violent acts in anger, or for the need of power, the question must be asked why this is not true also for the female child-abuse victim. (This question will be addressed in the concluding chapter of this book in a discussion on the different way boys and girls are parented.)

Some rape counselors see rape as a sexual act, and some see it as an act of aggression. The consensus is that it is both. As Nicholas Groth, who has worked with over 3,000 sex offenders, says, "We look at rape as the sexual expression of aggression, rather than as the aggressive expression of sexuality." Most rapists, he says, were not sexually deprived when they raped.

Groth indicates that rapists fall into one of three categories. They rape because of their anger, because of the need for power, or for sadistic reasons. Pleasure in humiliation gives power to men who feel generally incompetent. Sadistic rapists use torture instruments to increase the erotic pleasure. While many may say that these men are unbalanced, it is estimated that only 10 percent of rapists have a psychotic illness.

A counselor at the San Francisco Center for Women Against Rape, Dana Cayce, was quoted in an article by Stephanie Salter in the *San Francisco Chronicle*: "Rape still has more to do with society's attitude toward women and sex than it does with the act of the rapist." Being raped often implies to some that the woman must have been "loose." That is because a woman who willingly has multiple sexual partners is generally looked down upon, whereas a man with the same pattern is generally looked upon as simply fulfilling his natural drive. Therefore, the victim, if she chooses to report a rape, makes herself open to the suspicion that she was loose and wanted to be raped. There is even the myth that most women fantasize about being raped—a myth no doubt circulated by wishful-thinking men.

A victim reporting a rape must make public the most personal activity involving her body, which becomes known as "the crime scene." Often she is asked how she was dressed—in other words, was she "asking for it." One eighty-year-old woman with a wooden leg was awakened in the middle of the night by a young man who, after raping her, urinated on her, and then made off with her artificial limb. She was not "asking for it."

In spite of efforts to the contrary, there is still a "blame the victim" attitude when a rape is reported, which leaves a victim unwilling to report the crime committed against her. When sperm samples must be collected for evidence, it may be as traumatic for a victim to be treated by a male emergency room doctor as the assault itself. In some enlightened communities, rape crisis centers ensure that a victim is first treated by a woman and that a support group is available to help her through the healing process.

The statistics on rape are discouraging. Most rapists had abusive childhoods, 60 percent will be rearrested within three years, and a rapist is almost never cured. No treatment is known to be completely successful. Extended counseling while in prison and high motivation for change are a rapist's best chances of not raping again.

The head of the Oakland, California, police sex crimes unit, Captain James Hahn, quoted in the *Los Angeles Times*, April 11, 1991, said, referring to rapes on women who had been using drugs, "Those rapes are very difficult cases to prosecute. Often there's no question rape occurred, but it's very difficult to show to a jury. When does consent stop and force start? The reality is that sometimes you have to have some good injuries."

As the incidence of rape increases, women are learning to be wary, not to walk in unlit streets, to be unfriendly to strangers, and in a laundromat have bleach and detergent at hand to throw in an attacker's face. When women were little girls they were taught to be nice and to be helpful, not to hurt, not to be forward. These are characteristics dangerous for anyone to have when confronted with an attacker. A woman cannot be too careful. And as one-third of the victims know their attackers, even a friend or a partner on a date could become one.

Date Rape

Date rape, or acquaintance rape, accounts for half of the rapes committed, according to Carol Middleton, who heads the Self-

Defense Karate Association in Washington, D.C. The possibility of date rape requires that the woman learn how to forcefully refuse someone she had considered a friend, Middleton says. Frequently the man's attitude is, "This is my girlfriend, so why not?"

A problem inherent in date rape is that men often do not define forced sex as rape. In a 1979 California survey, 43 percent of the men of high school or college age said it was all right to force sex on a woman by the fifth date. In another report, from a University of California at Los Angeles psychologist, Neil Malamuth, men were asked if they would force sex on a woman if they knew they could get away with it. About 50 percent said they would. Asked if they would rape a woman if they knew they could get away with it, about 15 percent said they would. Yet, forcing sex "against their will" is the definition of rape. The word *rape* may be objectionable to a man who would force sex on a woman, but if he did force sex on his partner, he would be legally guilty of rape. The criterion for whether or not a woman has been raped is whether or not the woman is a willing partner.

How much of a protest is required to prove that sex was forced? If she's forced to have sex at knifepoint, should she scream? That could be fatal. If a woman on a date makes it understood at the outset that sex is not part of the date, that should suffice.

On college campuses date rape is increasing at an alarming rate. Parents have a genuine concern about sending their daughters off to college because of the prevalence of this crime. The male college student is increasingly a person to be wary of. A 1988 study showed that of the women raped on campuses, 80 percent of the crimes were committed by college students. A study by Dr. Koss, at the University of Arizona, showed that 11 percent of college women had been raped, and of those, 80 percent knew their attacker. Only a few men, even those who admitted they had forced sex on their date, believed they had committed a criminal act.

In a rape scene there is a difference in the perception of alcohol as a factor. If a woman has been drinking, she is seen as being responsible for what happened to her, but if her attacker has been drinking, he is seen as not being responsible for what he did.

In some cases the judiciary does not want to punish young rapists because going to prison may ruin their lives. Such was the case for David Caballero, a student at Lake Superior State University in Michigan who left his date in her dormitory raped, bruised, and bleeding. Though he claimed she consented to having sex with him, at his trial the judge said he did not believe Caballero. Yet the judge set aside what would have been a verdict of first-degree criminal sexual conduct and sentenced him to a fine and probation, saying if the defendant fulfilled the terms of the sentence his record would be expunged. The judge said he did that so as not to ruin Caballero's chances of becoming a policeman.

When women become disillusioned with the justice system, they sometimes take things into their own hands, as they did at Brown University. In September 1990, women students who had been raped by men on campus and who had not seen any action by the administration when the rapes were reported began to write the names of rapists on their restroom walls. Though the janitors erased the names every day, the names reappeared and new names were added. Women were warning women. The administration took notice, held meetings with women students, and agreed to follow up on reported rapes. The administration then encouraged men whose names were on the list on the walls to file formal complaints, but how could they, if the women who wrote the names were unknown?

How to prevent date rape, if all else fails? UCLA psychologist Neil Malamuth says to yell, "This is rape and I'm calling the cops!"

Gang Rape

Often date rape ends up being gang rape, known as a "gang bang" on campuses and in fraternity houses. One-third of gang rapes on campuses are perpetrated by athletes; fraternities are blamed for the other two-thirds. Many men involved in a gang rape would probably not rape on a one-on-one basis. It is the security of the group that gives a member of the gang rape a sense of protection and spurs him on. This is all part of the "boys will be boys" syndrome that starts early in a boy's life. This kind of peer activity often begins with knocking over a few garbage cans, later knocking over rural mailboxes, and eventually, sometimes, to gang rape. In the gang bang there is a camaraderie, a sort of rite of passage. The boys cheer one another on, each in time trying to outdo the other in various antics or in using foreign objects that they shove into their victim, the violence increasing as the rape progresses. Gang rape is more an act of boys joining together to prove their sexual power to one another. It has strong homosexual overtones, because in sharing the woman the men may be expressing their desire for each other.

Unlike other rapes, gang rape is seldom planned and is more apt to start on the spur of the moment. Such was the case when three men in their early twenties and another in his early thirties went to rob a drug dealer in Sacramento. Not finding him at home, they decided to rape his nineteen-year-old girlfriend, which they did repeatedly. The men were sentenced to life in prison for the assault and for kidnapping, since they took the girlfriend to Los Angeles. They will be eligible for parole in eight years.

The idea of raping the drug dealer's girlfriend comes from the age-old idea that women are the property of men. When the men could not rob the drug dealer, they did the next best thing as far as they were concerned, which was to rob him of his property—his girlfriend. This is the underlying motivation for gang rapes by soldiers occupying enemy territory during wars. Spoiling the women is spoiling the property of the enemy. Throughout history women have been raped in front of their fathers or their husbands, the ultimate spoiling of another man's property.

Gang rapes are committed usually by young men who are susceptible to pressure from their peers. To not participate in the rape would leave the men open to scorn. Then, if caught, the group bonds together in their stories of how the rape occurred, often further victimizing the victim with threatening phone calls or other intimidation. In her 1988 book *I Never Called It Rape*, Robin Warshaw explains that gang rapists are bonded to each other in the rape where "they prove their sexual ability to other group members."

An increasing number of gang rapes by closely knit groups of men in fraternities and athletic teams is of concern to the Association of American Colleges' Project. In their report in 1985 they reported gang rape to be kind of a team sport. One woman on campus at Florida State became intoxicated and then was raped by three men. She was then dumped on a fraternity porch with another fraternity's initials written on her thighs, her skirt up, and her pants down.

However, many gang rapes occur off the campus, as in the Glen Ridge, New Jersey, case where five white middle-class high school teenagers raped a seventeen-year-old retarded girl they had known since she was six years old. Two of the boys were cocaptains of the football team and one, a captain of the basketball team. While she was being raped by the five boys, eight other boys were watching. More so than in other rapes, gang rapists deny the use of force even after raping a woman for more than four hours.

Mentally impaired women are especially vulnerable to

gang rape. In Dedham, Massachusetts, four men claimed that a retarded woman seduced them. They were acquitted of rape but found guilty of battery and indecent assault. The four men were nineteen to twenty-two years old.

In Oakland, California, in April 1989, four men accosted a twenty-seven-year-old woman, threw her in the trunk of their car, drove to a deserted area, raped and sodomized her, then drove her to an apartment where they tied her to a bed and raped and beat her. She was rescued because a reserve police officer heard her screams and noted the license plate as she was driven away in the trunk of the car. Her assailants were thirty, twenty, seventeen, and fifteen years old. When arrested none had a previous police record.

A Philadelphia study of 646 rapes showed that almost half were committed by gangs of young men. Older men do not generally travel in gangs or participate in gang rapes. In 62 percent of the multiple-offender rapes (gang rapes), the rapists were under twenty-one years of age. Many people tend to absolve gang rapists because of what is believed to be young men's uncontrollable hormones. But power, not sex, is the driving force of the rapist. In prison, gang rapes establish the ruling hierarchy within the prison walls. Outside of prison, rape establishes the hierarchy between men and women.

Many gang rapes are committed within the range of a large audience. Since the rapes proceed over a period of several hours—four hours on average—and involve noise, cheering, and turbulence, it attracts a crowd of onlookers. Though gang rape is male or female, it is not a heterosexual act, in that men are enjoying one another's sexual prowess. Gang rape proves to the gang of rapists and the onlookers that the rapists are not homosexual, something many males need to prove. For them, gang rape verifies manhood.

Gang rape is a bonding of young men in the humiliation and domination of women. As in other situations throughout history where women themselves reinforce male domination of women, so also, in hearing about gang rape, many women, although they do not approve of the rape, do not condemn it to the point of outrage. If the public can put some of the blame on the victim, then those who hear about the rape are also absolved of a silent complicity in the act. In some cases there is almost a knee-jerk reaction. Questions are asked like, "What was she wearing?" "Why was she in that bar at that time of the night?" In the Glen Ridge case, several girls spray-painted congratulatory words after the names of the rapists on the sidewalks outside the high school. "We love you," they added. They, too, had been dominated.

When rape was on the rise in Israel during Golda Meier's term as prime minister, the governing body proposed a curfew that would require all women to be off the street by dark. Golda Meier asked, "Why enforce a curfew on women? They're not the ones committing the crime." Blaming the victim releases the public from any responsibility for a society that raises boys to grow up and degrade women in any way but especially by fouling their bodies.

The "wilding" incident in New York's Central Park on April 19, 1989, which began with about thirty teenage boys rampaging through the park, attacking at least nine people and grabbing what they could, ended with the gang rape and near murder of a twenty-eight-year-old investment banker. After being arrested, one of the attackers admitted hitting the victim with a lead pipe and indicated that it had been fun. As the prosecuting attorney stated, "As she lay screaming for her life, they silenced her with rocks and a rain of punches to her face so they could continue to rape her."

As in other gang rapes, the young men involved in this case also came from middle-class families and, like other gang rapists, they admitted to no remorse. Then, as is usual also, the victim was being blamed for being in the park jogging at ten o'clock at night.

This wilding incident was said to be a motiveless crime. It

was also an attack by blacks against a white upper-class woman, indicating that it was both racially and socioeconomically motivated, all of which tends to absolve the attackers of guilt in this near murder. However, one black was also attacked during the wolf-pack rampage, as were two Hispanics. And though the men showed no remorse, the indictment and conviction of the men involved did point out their guilt.

They depersonalized their victim, left her naked, bound and gagged, seemingly for dead, and then apparently did not care that they had done so, as they indicated in a later videotape during the questioning of five of the six defendants in the case. And these are not boys from the slums, they were not on drugs, and they were not deprived of good family life. And even if they had been, that would have been no excuse.

Each day as the trial progressed, friends and relatives of the accused boys gathered at the courthouse and shouted about the innocence of the boys and guilt of the victim, saying her boyfriend did it, and that she wasn't in the park to jog but to buy drugs. However, after ten days of deliberation the jury brought in verdicts convicting the men of rape, robbery, assault, and riot, though not of attempted murder.

This crime was said to be motiveless, but no crime is motiveless. These boys had beaten other people in the park, but the evening ended with the gang rape of the woman. Everything they did that evening demonstrated that they could exert power over others, but over the woman they exerted the ultimate power.

On August 19, 1990, three of the boys, Yusef Salaam, Raymond Santana, and Antron McCray, all sixteen years old, were convicted of rape and assault and sentenced to five to ten years in juvenile jail. The conviction of these three stopped short of murder charges because, as one of the jurors said, "Youths that age are not well versed in how many blows it takes to kill someone." Does anyone, young or old, know how many blows from a lead pipe it takes to kill someone?

On January 9, 1991, sixteen-year-old Kevin Richardson was sentenced to five to ten years in juvenile jail for his conviction of attempted murder and rape. Kharey Wise, eighteen, was sentenced to five to fifteen years in adult prison for sexual abuse and assault.

In a small New York town of about 4,000 near the Canadian border, a twenty-three-year-old single mother and lab technician drank so much in a bar that she passed out in the ladies restroom with her pants down around her feet. After the bar closed, one of her old-time male friends, the manager of the bar, found her there and maneuvered her to a booth where he and four other young men had sex with her as she lapsed in and out of a drunken stupor and they munched on sandwiches and beer.

Two weeks later, when rumors circulated through the town that the men were bragging about what they had done, the woman realized she had been the victim of a gang rape. She was encouraged by a state trooper to file charges. The men plea-bargained the charge from a felony down to a misdemeanor and were fined $750 each, even though they admitted what they had done. Many in the small town said, "What can you expect of a girl that drunk?"

But from others the outcry over the verdict fueled interest statewide. Governor Mario Cuomo asked for a commission to review the case. On April 26, 1994, a New York supreme court justice ruled that the original indictment was dismissed illegally and he reinstated the case.

Though not categorized as gang rape, fraternity hazing by young men on other young men has some similarities to gang rape. In fraternity hazing, men gang up to humiliate and terrorize new pledges about to join their fraternity. In a spirit of male bonding, the terrorizers as a group think up unusual frightening experiences for the pledges. In the Sigma Nu Chapter of the University of Texas, which has been expelled from the campus because of this atrocity, one pledge was beaten and walked on by members, who then led him around by a sling that encased his genitals. Men are not just violent against women; they can be equally violent against their own gender. There is a major difference between gang rape and hazing. If the young pledge survives the pain and humiliation, especially if he doesn't complain, as in puberty rituals, he will be accepted into the group and will look on himself with pride for having gone through the ordeal. However, in gang rapes of males on females, the victim is further victimized by scorn and often by unceasing harassment.

Serial Rape

Like serial murderers, serial rapists attack often and usually follow a pattern of behavior in the performance of the crime. Newspapers that carry headlines like RAPIST ON CAMPUS or SKI-MASK RAPIST ON THE LOOSE send terror through the hearts of residents. Police warn women to lock their doors, secure their screens, and not to let anyone into their homes unless they are well identified.

The rapist on campus at the University of Southern California in November 1988 had a pattern of approaching women students as they got out of their cars and forcing them at gunpoint back into their cars. He then drove them to an isolated area, raped them, and drove them back to school. To forestall attacks, approximately 5,000 whistles were issued to students, and campus police were instructed to respond to anyone blowing a whistle.

Girls were advised to walk in pairs. However, at California State University at Chico, when a serial rapist was on the attack and the girls were advised not to walk alone, three girls walking to school together were all raped.

The Ski-Mask Rapist, who raped twenty-six women in San Jose, California, was sentenced in June 1989 to 406 years in prison. Twenty-seven-year-old George Sanchez pleaded not guilty to rape and robbery over a three-year period. He stalked his victims, tied them up, raped them, and then stole their jewelry or cash. He attacked in women's homes, in their offices, and raped one woman in a church confessional. In court, the reading of all the crimes took an hour.

Since Sanchez used a pellet gun that resembled a .45-caliber pistol during the rapes, the total years of his sentence were increased over what they would have been if his offense had been rape without a weapon. In exchange for his guilty plea, charges were dropped against Sanchez's twenty-eight-year-old wife, Clara, for receiving stolen property taken during the rapes.

Based on the known pattern of serial rapists, the University of Virginia computer researchers have developed high-tech software that enables police to predict the area of a serial rapist's next attack and even determine where he lives. Classified as either "locals" or "marauders," serial rapists move geographically in somewhat predictable ways.

Miscellaneous

In an effort to understand why men rape, the TV program "The Reporters," May 1989, conducted conversations with convicted rapists. One man said when one of his victims told him she was pregnant, it made her more real. Another man said that after he had tied up a mother and a father and raped their daughter, he untied them and begged their forgiveness. One man had raped his next-door neighbor. He took her clothes off, and the more aggressive she became in fighting him off, the more excited he became. But when she became placid he didn't want to do it anymore. He said he was antagonistic toward women.

Another, who had broken into a home and raped, said the woman should have had bolts on the door, that he got into the house too easily. One nursing home attendant attacked an eighty-one-year-old wheelchair patient. He pushed her wheel-chair down the hall, disrobed, and raped her. When asked what thrill it was to dominate an old woman, he said, "She was not pathetic. She was bossy, telling me what to do. She was a woman."

Sixty-one-year-old former mayor James Blakey of East Palo Alto, California, pleaded no contest in April 1989 to felony charges in the molestation of a thirteen-year-old girl over a period of six months.

When a sixteen-year-old Los Angeles girl was shopping at noon, two men with knives abducted her, held her captive for six days, and raped her repeatedly. She freed herself, flagged down a passing car with three men in it, and asked for help. They drove her to Rose Hill Park in East Los Angeles, where they raped her until she was rescued by two park rangers who heard a commotion in the shrubbery.

In November 1989, San Fernando Superior Court Judge David M. Schacter set aside an award to a paralyzed rape victim who became pregnant as a result of a rape. Judge Schacter said the woman's attorney did not prove she had suffered as a result of the rape. The thirty-eight-year-old woman had lived at the Laurelwood Convalescent Hospital since she suffered brain damage in a car accident when she was nineteen. The girl's parents sued the nursing home for negligence and the jury awarded the victim $7.5 million because of the rape. It was believed that the woman did not know what had happened to her; the attacker is unknown. She had an abortion and was sterilized.

In Lancaster, California, when an eighteen-year-old high school girl attempted to defend herself with a utility knife she had pulled from her purse, her attacker used the knife against her. At 7:00 A.M., when the girl went to an automatic teller machine, a man asked her what time it was. When she looked at her watch he grabbed her and pinned her against the wall, ran his hand under her clothes, and said, "You shouldn't be walking alone. You need someone to protect you." When she reached for the knife he grabbed it and cut her arm twenty times. Fifty-five-year-old John Joseph Scrofani was arrested later when he attempted to attack another woman. He was found guilty of attempted rape and assault with a deadly weapon.

A Los Angeles police officer, Stanley Tanabe, thirty-two, was arrested after allegedly molesting a fourteen-year-old girl. He was accused of stopping the girl on the street and asking where she lived. Then, at three in the morning, her family said he entered her home by telling them he was investigating a call for help. When her parents said there was no call for help, he allegedly forced his way in, woke the girl, and molested her, before her parents could get help.

And in a navy courtroom halfway around the world in Rota, Spain, a navy judge sentenced twenty-seven-year-old Lt. Robin Brown to seven years in prison for raping a female officer onboard the ship *Suribachi*. In addition, Brown was dismissed from the navy and fined.

Rape receives little notice these days by the media. Buried on the bottom of page ten in the *San Francisco Chronicle* is the account of an Alabama woman who, when she arrived in New York to visit a friend, was grabbed and forced into Central Park at gunpoint, where she was raped.

Women cannot be careful enough.

CHAPTER 10

OTHER CRIMES AGAINST WOMEN

The Risks of Being Female

Every minute a woman in this country is raped, every eighteen seconds a woman is beaten, and every day four women are killed by their batterers. It is true that we live in a violent culture, but much of the violence is directed at women, promoted by many things, including pornography that depicts women being whipped or stabbed and popular music that literally calls for the mutilation of women, such as the rap group 2-Live Crew's lyrics about busting someone's "pussy" and then breaking her backbone. As George Will stated in *Newsweek* of July 30, 1990, in a column titled "America's Slide into the Sewer," this country cares more for protecting whales than it does for protecting women. It is not enough that song lyrics tell of assaulting women, they also tell of tearing them up. Will's article makes it clear that in singing about breaking down women's vaginal walls through rape, these lyrics are directed at the destruction of women.

Books, too, vividly describe mutilation of women. In *The Silence of the Lambs*, women are skinned by a serial killer who wants to use their skin for his own purposes. Another book famous for its notorious depiction of mutilation of women's bodies is Bret Easton Ellis's *American Psycho*. In this novel a sated Wall Street yuppie becomes deranged and moonlights as a serial murderer. He rapes, murders, tortures, and dismembers women, and at one point tries to make a meat loaf from the parts of one of his victim's body. He explodes breasts using jumper cables, inserts a starving rat into a vagina, and at one point walks around his apartment naked, sexually connected to a severed head. Peter Plagens in his *Newsweek* review of this book wrote, "The climate of fiction grows steadily darker, its texture much coarser." In considering the anti-woman bent of the book he adds that, unfortunately, "the best that women can do in the cause of literary catharsis is to serve as brutalized bodies in novels, or as boycotting banshees in real life." The "boycotting banshees" he referred to are women from the National Organization for Women who advocated boycotting *American Psycho*.

Tammy Brooks, coordinator of the Los Angeles chapter of the National Organization for Women says, "*American Psycho* is the most misogynistic communication we have ever come across. The book is in effect a how-to novel on the torture and dismemberment of women." George Will connected Ellis's book to the misogynism in the rap music lyrics of 2-Live Crew: "Actually, Ellis is the 2-Live Crew of the literary set, making money from today's depraved appetite for imaginary violence against women."

But other than books like *American Psycho*, pornography, and rap music, there are other suggested causes for the increased violence against women. Some see it as a backlash against the women's movement, some see it as a result of changes in work roles—women working and becoming self-sufficient. Some see violence against women as a result of men's decreasing power over women, and some see it as a result of men's concern that women are a threat to their masculinity. There is also the worry by some men, and some women as well, that feminists are leading us down the wrong path, that the world ought to be left to men. But whatever the reasoning, women suffer the consequences.

For women, fear is a fact of life. If women don't restrict their lives, and if they end up getting beaten or raped, it is seen as their fault. Ask women how they protect themselves, and they will have several answers. Ask men how they protect themselves and, because they do not have the same apprehensions as women, they will only look quizzical.

The testimony at the New York "wilding" trial, the case of the Central Park jogger rape, reveals a disdain for female life. It is said that this was a racist attack, but a black woman would not have fared any better. In court testimony one of the defendants said, "We charged her and we got her on the ground. Everybody started hitting her and stuff, and she's on the ground and everybody's stomping and everything . . . I grabbed one arm, and this other kid grabbed one arm and we grabbed her legs and stuff. And then we took turns getting on her." When asked why they did it, another young man answered, "It was something to do. It was fun."

Fun because it was exciting, illegal, and therefore dangerous. All crimes have those ingredients, but crimes against women have something more. They are crimes to establish power. They are not sexual, though some may think they are. They are crimes to ensure that the weaker sex remains so. Why else would a 250-pound man beat his 125-pound wife regularly, except to establish the hierarchy in his household?

The FBI reports that rape is increasing at four times the rate of other crimes, and so is the battering of women.

According to former U.S. Surgeon General J. Everett Koop, who was speaking at the Conference on Violence in Washington in May 1990, beatings are the most prevalent cause of injuries to women.

Battering

The word *battering* is used to indicate the beating of women. It is not used to indicate attacks on men. When women beat their children, this is referred to as *physical abuse*. As for the battering of women, *Ms.* magazine reports, "1.8 million men beat their wives every year—not including single or divorced men."

Every day four women are killed in domestic violence. Why don't women leave abusive situations? Leaving is a dangerous thing to do. It is when a woman leaves that she is most apt to be killed.

The national attention to the tragedy of O. J. Simpson's ex-wife's death and that of her friend heightens awareness of the depth and scope of domestic violence. Simpson may or may not be convicted of those murders, but it has come to light that he had repeatedly beat his wife. His is a classic case of exerting control over his wife by physical power and then declaring himself the victim as he did in what is now called his suicide note.

After Simpson pleaded no contest to charges of spousal battery in 1989, his attorney said, "I think this has helped bring them closer together." They divorced in 1992 and he was arrested for her murder in 1994. Interviewed after the 1989 charge he said they were both at fault, and, in effect, it was no big deal. He did what they told him to do and they got on with their lives. Some men treat battering lightly.

In the 1989 arrest, Simpson paid a small fine, did some community service, and was required to undergo psychiatric treatment with the therapist of his choice. The psychologist conducted the therapy sessions by telephone, because, as was explained, Simpson was a busy man.

A tape recording of Nicole Simpson's call to 911 in October 1993 clearly projects the terror she was experiencing as she explains that O. J. Simpson had broken down her door to get into her house. One can hear him swearing at her as she pleads with the operator to "send someone." She then calls again, a minute later, begging for help. The cool operator asks, "Is he threatening you or just harassing you?" The operator asks if Nicole has been arguing with O. J., even though O. J.'s voice is roaring in the background. "Is he upset with something that you did?" the operator asks. Then she says the police should be on their way. She continues, "It just seems like a long time because it's kind of busy in that division right now."

If O. J. Simpson is Nicole's murderer it would be understandable that Nicole would not have called 911 on the night of the murder, if she had had the chance. What was the point? She told the police when they came to help her in 1989 that they never "do anything," and the more recent tape of 1993 could hardly have been reassuring that help would come, or if it did, that anything would change. Maybe part of the sadness this country feels about O. J. Simpson is not only about the disappointment of learning that a "hero" is a repetitious wife beater, and may even be a double murderer, but that the community failed Nicole when it seemed, on numerous occasions, she should have been helped.

No one really knows how many women experience similar terror on the same unpredictable schedule as Nicole Simpson. But we do know that the abuse is rampant. More women suffer at the violent hands of batterers than do all the women combined who are victims of rape, automobile accidents, and muggings, according to Karla Digirolamo, the executive director of New York State's Commission on Domestic Violence.

Unlike rape, battering implies a history of repeated physical violence of a man against a woman who are in a live-in relationship. At a study at the University of Rhode Island, Dr. Richard Gelles found that two-thirds of the women who reported an abuse for that year had been abused three or four times in that same year.

The condition of the women matters not to the batterers, including whether or not the women are pregnant at the time of the battering. Of pregnant women, 8 percent are beaten by their male partners, as stated in a March of Dimes Foundation report. In a Houston study of pregnant women, abuse against them ranged from slaps, to punches, to being pushed down stairs. This means that battered women are more apt to deliver low birthweight babies, who are more apt to be born with birth defects than other babies, and who, consequently, increase health care costs. Of low birthweight babies, 40 percent die within the first month.

If a battered woman chooses to leave her mate, she may be signing her own death warrant. At Harvard University's Children's Hospital, where violent families are being counseled, a psychiatric social worker explained, "The man feels vulnerable and that vulnerability infuriates him. He feels a mounting frustration similar to what an angry parent feels when trying to discipline an increasingly 'defiant' child. All the man can understand is that his wife is 'disobeying' him. It becomes a power struggle. If she manages to escape, revenge becomes his motive, and the ultimate revenge for some of these men is to kill."

The women who leave may be signing their own death warrants, since 75 percent who leave are more likely to be killed by their batterers than those who stay, according to an article on battered women in the *Los Angeles Times* by Roberta Ikemi and Susan Berke Ford. The battered wife does not choose a batterer. Often the relationship goes along quite smoothly for some time and then there is a violent attack. This is usually followed by promises that it won't happen again. But when it does, the woman may begin to wonder what she can do so that she won't get beaten again. She hopes to make the relationship work. But the pattern builds of tension, violence, and then reconciliation.

Susan Schecter, who has worked with battered women at Boston Children's Hospital, interviewed by Mary Suh in *Ms.*, April 1989, explained that the man minimizes his battering and blames the woman for what he did. "If you'd only be more loving; if you'd only done dinner right." He not only undermines her self-confidence, he also begins to isolate her from her friends.

It is only in recent history that it has been against the law for a husband to physically abuse his wife. In 1984, a U.S. district court in Washington ruled that "a man is not allowed to physically abuse or endanger a woman merely because he is her husband." In England there was what was known as "the rule of thumb," meaning a man couldn't beat his wife with anything thicker than his thumb. As I said in my book *Women's Roots*, in medieval times, "provided a husband did not kill or cripple his wife, he was free to exercise punishment without the law intervening." Women could not petition the courts because they had no standing in the courts, as they were considered emotionally and intellectually frail. So wife-beating, or what we now call battering, has a long-established history. One which women are attempting to change.

Until a few years ago, police departments considered family fights none of their business. But that all changed with a case brought to court by Tracey Thurman, a Connecticut housewife and mother, who sued and won $2 million from the state police who had not protected her from a vicious attack by her husband. He stabbed her thirteen times and left her crippled for life. Now it is possible for police to make what is known as "warrantless probable cause arrest," because of what is known as the Thurman Law.

Often, battering men return to their women and beg for forgiveness, saying it won't happen again. Sometimes that is true, but often it is not. Sometimes the threat of separation triggers a man's anger. Sometimes, as in the case of Delia Alaniz, from Sedro-Woolley, Washington, a husband will threaten his wife that he is going to rape their daughter.

Because the battered woman suffers low self-esteem and believes somehow the beatings are her fault, she hesitates to get help. Known as "frozen fright," many battered women are immobilized. Some people criticize women who stay in violent situations, yet the women rationalize that if they leave, the children might get hurt, and many know that if they leave they will be pursued. Ellen Pence of the Duluth, Minnesota, Domestic Abuse Intervention Project says, "It's extremely rare that you read about a man who has beaten a women to death while she's living with him. It's when she leaves him that he kills."

Yet one woman, Maria Haines, not only left her battering husband, a former assistant district attorney who made upward of $300,000 a year, she also sued him for assault and battery that she had endured during her six-year marriage.

Putting husbands in jail may not guarantee a woman her safety. Lisa Bianco, twenty-nine, of Mishawaka, Indiana, had her husband convicted of battery and kidnapping, and he was sentenced to seven years. He was able to get an eight-hour pass from prison. During that time he returned to Lisa Bianco's home and beat her to death with an unloaded shotgun. She had not been warned that her estranged husband would be out on a pass.

Because of the murder of Lisa Bianco, prosecutors are now telling endangered wives when their husbands are about to be released from prison. The wives have a little time to relocate themselves and their children. Hiding from husbands who have threatened to get them when they get out, they become victims again, hiding like fugitives.

After filing for divorce, Lois Lende, a thirty-three-year-old airline payroll clerk from Denver, got a restraining order against her husband because of numerous beatings, even during her pregnancy. The restraining order did not prevent her husband from stabbing her to death, after which he then shot himself.

Christy Buzzanco of Connecticut had at least ten restraining orders against her live-in mate, Anthony "Porky" Young, twenty-eight. He was sentenced to a year in prison for beating Christy unconscious and stripping her in front of her four-year-old son. Christy worries about his release from prison because she says he has vowed to kill her while her three children watch.

In Suffolk County in New York, three women who had restraining orders against their battering husbands were killed by them. All did what was deemed to be the "right thing." They left their abusers, they got restraining orders, and yet they were killed. One, April La Salata, thirty-four, received extraordinary protection. The police wired her house with an alarm system and gave her the means to contact them at any time. But in January 1989 she was shot by her husband, who then shot himself. Her husband was free on bail, on charges of attempting to murder his wife the previous year.

The second woman, Lydia Grohoski, twenty-four, was surprised by her husband, Joseph, thirty-four, when he broke down a door and shot her in the face and then killed himself. He was under a restraining order to stay away from his wife. He was out on bail on charges stemming from putting an empty shotgun to his wife's head and pulling the trigger.

The third woman, Elizabeth Croff, thirty, was shot by her husband, William Croff, thirty, when she fell down as he was chasing her. He then shot himself. There had been a warrant for his arrest for beating Elizabeth and for taking their two older children on Christmas Eve, in violation of a court order, but the warrant had not been issued because of a scarcity of clerical help over the holidays.

Restraining orders often do no more than further anger the men. Maria Navarro of Los Angeles had a restraining order against her husband, who sought her out and shot her and three others.

One of the worst mass slayings in New Mexico's history occurred in January 1991, when a sheriff's deputy was serving a restraining order on Ricky Abeyta after his estranged girlfriend told investigators he had shot at her. The deputy serving the restraining order was shot, as was the deputy who came to his assistance. In all, seven were killed. Besides the two deputies, the others killed were the girlfriend, her daughter, her daughter's boyfriend, their five-month-old child, and Abeyta's girlfriend's sister.

For black women, domestic violence is the number one issue, according to Byllye Avera, founder of National Black Women's Health Project, as reported in Evelyn White's *The Black Women's Health Book*. Domestic violence is the number one issue not only because of the high rate of beatings, but because of the high rate of teenage pregnancy caused, not by teenage boyfriendss, but by mothers' boyfriends, brothers, and fathers. Incest is the violence.

In Turners Falls, Massachusetts, where there had not been a murder in 100 years, stress was indicated as the cause for four separate domestic violence murders in less than two years—the most recent in May 1989. A volunteer at the women's shelter in Northampton attributed the domestic violence to hard times. "It's working class, depressed; the factories are all gone. The people have been stripped of dignity in a lot of ways." The women murdered by their boyfriends in Turners Falls are: Vivian Morrisey, thirty, strangled by Gregory Martin, thirty-three; Virginia Ferrer, twenty-seven, stabbed to death by Jose Rayes, thirty-eight, identified as the father of her four children; Catherine Gochinski, sixteen, shot in the apartment she shared with her eighteen-year-old boyfriend, Joseph Demers.

Police departments often don't know how seriously to take threats against women. When twenty-eight-year-old Sylvia

Allen was shot by her ex-husband, the police department in Michigan said it was impossible to know when someone is going to carry out a death threat.

Battered women's shelters do offer great help for many women, but there aren't enough of them. Forty percent of women who run to these shelters for help must be turned away. In many cities there are more animal shelters than there are shelters for battered women.

The name *battered women's shelter* says a lot. Can one even imagine a battered men's shelter? Why is there even a need for a battered women's shelter? In any event, there aren't enough shelters for the women who need to escape the battering and the shelters are underfunded. In California's fifty-eight counties there are forty-six shelters, each costing $250,000 a year to operate but funded by the state at $91,000 each. In San Francisco, 1,000 battered women a year are turned away from shelters for lack of space.

A judge in San Jose, California, Jerome Nadler, has been requiring men convicted of battering to pay fines to battered women's shelters. The county prosecutor stated that the men are creating victims, the shelters need money, and the men causing the expense ought to pay.

Battering cuts across all socioeconomic levels. It usually implies a long-term history, but there are one-time battery charges, too, as in the case of the California Angels outfielder who was arrested for hitting his wife and leaving her on a street. Thirty-five-year-old Claudell Washington was arrested by police in Concord, California, for felony spousal battery.

Where do these male abusers come from? A *Woman's Day* article of October 1989, "Don't Let Yourself Be Abused," examining that subject, stated that many abusers come from abusive homes. As many as 70 percent of men in the Denver program, AMEND, an agency that works with abusive men, had seen their mothers abused, and 90 percent had been abused themselves. The female victims have not necessarily been abused as children. And 60 to 70 percent of wife abusers, says Cortney Pullen, M.A., coordinator of the program, have substance-abuse problems. Both substance abuse and wife abuse, she says, are ways of handling stress. Leslie Katz, former coordinator for the Washington, D.C., women's shelter, Herspace, says, "Some of the most serious abuse happens during drug or drinking episodes." Quoting the *Woman's Day* article, "Being drunk or high sometimes gives a man an 'excuse' to be violent. He can justify hurting his wife because he 'didn't know what he was doing.'"

Batterers are classified into several categories depending on how they handle their emotions, how their personalities change when using alcohol, if they were abused as children, what their feelings are about women, and what their feelings are about their inferiority/superiority status—that is, how much they need to dominate and control a woman in order to feel manly.

There are programs in this country aimed at helping men who batter their wives or girlfriends. Some men enter the programs because they know they have a problem, and others enter because they are ordered to do so by the criminal justice system. Known as violence control programs, these try to help men understand there are other ways to handle their frustration and anger. Violence, they say, is a learned behavior that people resort to when they can't come up with other ways to solve their problems.

Prevention is the best cure for the atrocity of battering. Mary Werner, an assistant district attorney in Suffolk County, New York, says, "We must teach conflict resolution in our schools. We must stop violence on television. We must teach little boys they can be masculine without fighting, without controlling people. And we must teach little girls that it's much more important to be strong than to be nice."

In a February 1991 "48 Hours" program titled "Till Death Do Us Part," another side of the battered-wife syndrome was discussed. With 800 women killing their husbands or boyfriends each year, many women end up in prison with long sentences. The legal justice system is beginning to change the attitude about wives who kill after having been battered for a long time. Previously a woman could not use the defense that she killed her husband because he had beaten her through the years. It is now a permissible defense in several states.

For those women who were convicted of killing men when battering could not be used as a defense, there is a trend toward clemency for women who can prove there was a danger to themselves and/or their children. This has been true in Ohio, where several women were released from prison after receiving clemency from the governor, Richard Celeste.

In Maryland, in February 1991, the governor also commuted prison sentences for women who had killed abusive men, saying he was convinced they had acted in self-defense. Now there is the possibility of legislation being introduced in various states that would automatically permit an expert witness to testify in the defense of a battered woman who has killed her husband or boyfriend. The witness, usually a psychotherapist, can testify to the trauma these women experience, combined with the women's belief that they have no other escape.

On May 12, 1994, the governor of Illinois used the battered woman syndrome to grant clemency to four women who had killed their mates. One had been given a twenty-year sentence; another, who had to be hospitalized many times because of battering by her boyfriend before she stabbed him to death, had been sentenced to fourteen years. Another had stabbed her boyfriend after repeated abuse, and another had shot her boyfriend and was serving a ten-year term. The Illinois Clemency Board had originally requested the release of twelve women, but only four qualified. The district attorney for Cook

County, Illinois, assailed the clemency for these women.

Those protesting the state's commuting of sentences for battered women who killed men object on the grounds that it will then be "open season" for women to kill men. However, those released from prison present evidence of years of deathly abuse by their husbands or boyfriends. If there is not a serious case of long-term battering, there is no commutation.

An Ohio woman, Janet Abbot, who was sentenced to life in prison for hiring someone to kill her husband, was able to prove her case. According to her statements and the testimony from her sons, now grown, beating was a way of life in their family. If she had not had her husband killed, she maintains, her husband would have killed one or more of their children. During her trial, she was not permitted to reveal the battering she and her children sustained. Since having been a battered wife was her only defense, her case was reviewed and, after serving ten years, she is about to receive clemency from the governor of Ohio.

In her book *Terrifying Love: Why Battered Women Kill and How Society Responds*, Lenore Walker explains that battered women come to "believe that nothing they or anyone else does will alter their terrible circumstances." A battered woman who is brought to court for killing her batterer must use the defense of "reasonable perception of imminent bodily danger" at the time she commits the crime.

In spite of the many women who stay in battering situations, many do leave. One woman left her battering husband, to whom she says she was addicted, only when her daughter told her teacher she would rather die than see her mother beat again. Many women stay in a bad situation "because of the children, wanting them to have a father," and many leave "because of the children."

In October 1989, after the San Francisco earthquake, an article appeared in the *San Francisco Chronicle* about the increase of family violence due to stress caused by the earthquake. "Men are lashing out and women are feeling pretty desperate," said a member of Berkeley's Family Violence Law Center. The article states, "According to sociologists, abusive men are more likely to batter their spouses and children whenever they feel they are losing power or control over their lives."

In one family, a husband and wife were picking up glass that had broken and was strewn about their home after the earthquake. When he cut himself he "angrily blamed his wife for the mishap, then picked her up and hurled her against a wall. Fearing an assault on their children, the woman grabbed them and fled."

After Hurricane Andrew in Florida, August 24, 1992, male violence flared against women. Machetes, knives, bats, and fists were used as weapons against women and sometimes against children. Men who had just lost their homes were feeling powerless.

The same reaction follows when the threat of base closures leaves military men fearing for their economic security. *Time* magazine of May 23, 1994, reported an increase in spousal abuse on military bases that may be associated with the end of the cold war and its related reduction of the military.

In 1993 there were almost twice as many reported cases of violence against women by military men than in 1986. The numbers went from 27,783 to 46,287, occurring possibly in one-third of army homes, twice as many as in nonmilitary families. The violence is most pervasive among noncommissioned officers and includes attacks of all kinds, from kicking to shooting. The amount allocated to stem this violence, $80 million, is not enough. The military says it needs $120 million.

The question here, which will be discussed in the concluding chapter of this book, is why stress in men leads to violence. Women in the earthquake, in the hurricane, and in unemployed localities suffer equal stress. Why is women's stress not translated into violence?

Slashing

Maria del Carmen Ochoa, twenty-five, emerged from the witness-protection program of the Los Angeles Police Department after a recovery period to ask the public to help locate her husband, Arturo Ochoa, twenty-nine, who had slashed her face and body. The injuries were so severe she had to be hospitalized for five days. He told her, "I am going to spare your life, but I am going to mark you so you'll never have a husband again." After she was taken back into the protection program, and after her two children, ages three and five, were placed separately in secret homes, Arturo Ochoa made threatening phone calls to Maria's family unsuccessfully trying to learn her whereabouts.

In New York, when model Marla Hanson planned to meet her landlord for the purpose of his returning her security deposit, she was instead met by two men who slashed her face so severely that she needed 100 stitches. She brought suit against her landlord and was later called to testify before the Senate Judiciary Committee studying violence against women. Hanson told the committee that the landlord's attorney told the press, "Before this case is over, I'll have Marla Hanson behind bars." Marla Hanson repeated another statement attributed to that attorney: "This courtroom is a circus. I am the ringmaster, and all I need is a whip to bring this lying bitch to order."

When Viveca Lindfors and two other actresses were talking on a New York sidewalk after an evening theater performance, she was slashed on the face. She described the attack: "In the middle of our discussion, this kid, he grabbed my face. . . . And the next second I found myself down on the pavement." She was slashed on the neck below her ear, an injury that required twenty-seven stitches. Of her attack the actress said, "I'm coming off easily, compared to him. My ear is cut, but his life is going to be hell if he doesn't face something within himself."

Miscellaneous Attacks

Some men use ingenious ways to strike out at women. Enraged that a woman sportswriter could be admitted to men's locker rooms, or possibly that women could be sportswriters, naked members of the New England Patriots, after a practice game, approached the *Boston Herald*'s sportswriter Lisa Olson. "They dared me," she wrote in an article about the incident, "to touch their private parts." The owner of the Patriots, Victor Kiam, was quoted in the October 8, 1990, *Newsweek*: "They can wiggle their waggles in front of her face as far as I'm concerned." After the Gulf War started, with Patriot missiles used to counterattack Scud missiles, Victor Kiam was again quoted in *Newsweek*, "What do the Iraqis have in common with Lisa Olson? They've both seen Patriot missiles up close."

The New York *Daily News* headline DART MAN HITS AGAIN suggests a kind of game where hitting a target may help the perpetrator score points. Yet Dart Man was shooting darts fashioned from pins from a handcrafted blowgun into the buttocks of women on the streets of New York. Though the darts were not lethal, the humiliation for women was genuine. Why isn't Dart Man shooting men in the buttocks?

When women complain about attacks, they may be putting themselves at risk, or they may be putting their husbands' careers at risk. Wives of career armed services men said they feared reporting the sexual harassment by a U.S. military academy gynecologist because they feared their testimony would harm their husbands' chances for promotion. Major Ernest Flores, forty-four, during two weeks of testimony in a judicial hearing at West Point, was accused of sexual misconduct, though several women praised his care. They say he hugged and kissed them as a way of showing he cared and supported them.

In Annapolis, at the U.S. naval academy, Gwen Marie Dryer was handcuffed by two male cadets to a bathroom urinal in a dormitory while other male cadets took pictures of her and applauded. Cadets kept women out of the bathroom as other cadets shouted encouragement to the men who were pretending to urinate on Dryer. Naval academy officials explained the incident as "good-natured high jinx." But Gwen Dryer says, "This was not just a case of hazing at all. It has to do with being a woman." For punishment, two midshipmen were given demerits and loss of leave time. Six received warnings. Academy officials confiscated the photographs, saying they wanted them so that nothing like that would happen again. But as Dryer explains, "Now they're trying to use the pictures against me. They told my father that they have the pictures to prove that I was not under any undue duress that day because I wasn't crying or screaming. They also asked my father just how well he knew me, insinuating that I gladly went along with the whole thing."

Despite ninety identified women victims of indecent sexual assault in what became known as the Tailhook Incident in Las Vegas in 1991, of the 140 naval officers accused, only 30 received some form of administrative action such as a reprimand or a transfer. There were no court martials.

The word *tailhook* refers to the hook that stops jet planes as they land on aircraft carriers. The behavior of accosting women naval personnel as they walked down the hall is known as "butt biting" and "ball walking," which is the groping of genitalia, breasts, and buttocks and stripping off women's clothing. These actions would probably have been punishable in criminal court rather than by the navy itself.

The lieutenant's whistle blowing resulted in her being harassed and maligned to the point where she resigned from the navy. In April 1994 one retired lieutenant colonel, Karen Johnson, writing in *National NOW Times*, says that she sees no change in attitude toward women even after 3,000 interviews. She sees women's degradation in the navy viewed as simply benign behavior.

Admiral Frank Kelso, who was seen on the premises the night of the incident, denied any knowledge of it, though the naval judge ruled otherwise.

For women who have been battered there are numerous unfortunate "side effects," including discrimination against them when they apply for insurance. In New York State, eight of the sixteen largest insurance companies, according to Congressman Charles Schemer, deny health, life, and mortgage insurance to battered women. A State Farm representative on CNN news, May 12, 1994, said, if a woman has a history of repeated abuse it would not be "prudent" for an insurance company to insure that person.

In addition, women who have been encouraged to document attacks on them and report them to their doctors do so at the peril of being uninsurable because this becomes a "preexisting condition."

Many styles of attacks on women are reduced by the media at various times in history to fun words, such as the recent appellation Dart Man and the century-old nickname Jack the Ripper. These light-hearted yet gruesome names serve to give the feeling that not only is the attack a kind of game, but it is commonplace, a fact of life to be expected to continue in one form or another.

To put things in perspective in the media, the term "domestic violence," which sounds rather homey, should be changed to what it actually describes: male violence against women.

CHAPTER 11

CON MEN

Swindlers, looking to take someone else's money, have been around since the beginning of commerce. When the con artist promises his target "a good deal," he really means it's a good deal for himself. When sixty-six-year-old William Sundown, alias Paul Huston and Steven Lance, promised one woman "a good deal" if she would invest in a boat, the woman didn't know that the same boat had already been bought by several other women before her.

In May 1989, six women testified against Sundown in California, and when the case was aired on TV, showing his picture, six additional women came forward to say they had given money to him also, because he told them he was going to make them rich. He appeared helpless, they said, and they wanted to help him. He impressed his women targets with a picture he had taken of himself in a military captain's uniform. After his trial in Northern California, several women in Southern California told authorities that they, too, were this man's victims.

It is difficult to determine how many women and men are

victims of the con artist, because many who are become too embarrassed to admit their vulnerability. It seems surprising that people would give large sums of money to comparative strangers, but it is often with the idea that the money is going to come back doubled or more.

One can fall for the "get rich quick scheme" more easily if the man who offers the riches to a woman is a smooth-talking, apparently generous person. That is the nature of most con men. Because he pulls his victims to him emotionally, his betrayal is a double injury. His victims have not only lost their money and their self-esteem, but quite often they have also lost a romantic interest in their life. When they learn that the con man has used overtures of friendship or romance to rob them, the victims feel foolish and often keep their humiliation to themselves.

One romantic con man, Nicholas Kasemehos, fifty, who has at least six aliases and has been arrested thirty-six times, serving time in prisons in Oregon, Utah, Nevada, Colorado, Washington, and Illinois, is, as of July 1990, at large. Like other con artists, Kasemehos spends money on his victims, convincing them he is generous and wants to help them. They turn over cash to him after knowing him only a few days. He works hard in a short time, taking his women victims to expensive dinners, overtipping, sending the women flowers the next day, and then, when he gets the money for what is going to be "a good deal," he disappears.

Kasemehos persuaded one woman in San Francisco that she needed a new $17,000 Honda, which he could get at a bargain. He said if she gave him $10,750, he would buy some gold and then sell it at a profit, give her the car and $6,000. She gave him the $10,750, and he disappeared. Another woman, who had known Kasemehos only three days, turned over $2,250 so he could buy gold coins and sell them at a profit for her. She never saw him again after she gave him the money.

Giovanni Vigliotto, who has over 100 aliases, claims to have married 105 women. Though he says he was joking that he had married that many women, authorities have confirmed about eighty-two marriages, which have taken place in nine states and Hong Kong. He was known to have proposed to his future wives on his first date and to have left them as soon as he could get his hands on their money. In some cases, when he could get their money before a wedding ceremony, he didn't proceed with the wedding.

Most con artists are known for "ripping off" old women. But con artists are also apt to target males. One man told an unusual story to his victims, who were lawyers. He claimed he was awaiting a multimillion-dollar settlement from a car crash in which his wife was killed and his two children critically injured. He claimed the air bag of his wife's Mercedes failed to inflate and that Lloyd's of London was paying his insurance claim.

When he told his story to one prospective victim, the man recognized the narrative as that of a swindle of another man a few months earlier. This second lawyer alerted the fraud inspector of the San Francisco Police Department, who set up a situation where the con man could repeat his story to an undercover detective. When the con man appeared, he was wearing the $14,000 Piaget watch he had allegedly conned from the first lawyer. He was also wearing the first victim's suit, having told that lawyer he needed the watch and the suit to impress the insurers who were going to offer him a $1.2 million settlement for the death of his wife and the injuries to his children.

When he used the story on the undercover detective who was posing as a lawyer, the con man changed the name of the city where the accident was to have occurred. The fraud officer agreed to give the swindler several hundred dollars so that he could rent a motel room to be close to the hospital where his injured children were. When he began to leave, he was arrested by police officers.

The con man varied his name from victim to victim. When arrested he said his name was Thomas Garza, forty-five. As the *San Francisco Chronicle* reported, he had been convicted of rape in 1983 and was out on parole.

Some men are not content to swindle the same person only once. They return for more. When Jessie Moody, ninety, of Pomona, opened her door to a man dressed in a police uniform, he bilked her out of a lot of money. About a month later he returned to her home dressed in a hospital uniform. When he told her the police had required him to return the money, Jessie Moody once again opened her door to him. Described as a husky man in his fifties, he knocked her down and ransacked her home, fruitlessly searching for more money. Her injuries were serious enough for this elderly woman to require hospital treatment.

More often, con artists persuade gullible people to part with their money or other treasures by persuading them that they will profit in some way. Unscrupulous supposed-construction workers are known to get homeowners to sign contracts for household improvements and then, after a deposit, they disappear and no work is ever done. Senior citizens' retirement groups are often warned about such salesmen.

A usual approach is for a middle-aged man to meet a woman of his age or older, pay her some attention, give her a few favors, and prey on her need for companionship to gain her trust before he gets her to give him her money. This may not be in one sum. It could be in small sums over a period of time, or he may get her to sign over the title of her house to him.

Posing as an attorney, Steven Dony, thirty, agreed to represent elderly women after accepting a retainer fee from them. He was sentenced to five years in state prison and ordered to pay $10,000 to each victim by a municipal court judge in San Diego, California.

Leslie Gall, fifty-six, known as the "Sweetheart Swindler,"

was such a charmer that he is suspected of defrauding at least a dozen elderly women. When he was arrested in Redondo Beach, California, dining with a gray-haired woman, police had been looking for him from Florida to Canada. Meeting grandmotherly women in senior citizen centers, he sent them flowers, candy, and paid them great attention. Police in Canada say he has about eight aliases and has eleven outstanding warrants for his arrest. A worried daughter-in-law began to be suspicious when this man moved in with her mother-in-law, who then began paying for plane tickets to Las Vegas. When they opened a joint savings account, the daughter-in-law called authorities to check up on him. She gave them his car license plate number and was told the car was stolen. At the point when Leslie Gall was arrested, he had two suitcases full of fake identification, stock certificates, blank power-of-attorney forms, and blank checks that tied him to about ten women. The mother-in-law was shocked when she was told the stock certificates belonged to her. In the suitcases were news clippings about the deaths of rich men.

Posing as a medical doctor, Carlo Jaramillo, thirty-three, answered ads from people wanting to sell Rolex watches, valued at about $12,000. Dressed as a doctor, he would meet the prospective seller in the lobby of a hospital, look at the watch, and tell the seller he wanted to show it to his colleague. Then he would disappear. Convicted of grand theft in San Francisco in November 1989, he was sentenced to five years in prison. Though previously convicted in 1984 of credit card fraud, he was unremorseful, saying, "When you have a choice between being a nice guy or $10,000 richer, let's face it, you go for it."

In an art scam, three Sunnyvale men—Anthony Barreiro, thirty-nine, Ernest Ray Parker, Jr., twenty-five, and Jeff Jones, thirty-two—were arrested for selling what they said were drawings and paintings by Van Gogh, Rembrandt, Rubens, Chagall, and Degas. When one person bought $9,000 worth of what he believed were original paintings and later learned they were practically worthless, he reported the fraud to the police. The FBI set up a situation where they posed as potential buyers and then arrested the three men, who had told the agents the art had previously belonged to a sheik in Arabia.

One of the most despicable crimes is the solicitation of money for a charity that is not forwarded to the charity. The Valley Fundraisers of Burbank collected over $2 million over four years and deposited checks written to charities that had not authorized Valley Fundraisers to solicit for them. Valley Fundraisers is licensed to solicit for only three charities. No court has ruled on any limit to the amount of money that can be kept by solicitors, even up to 85 or 90 percent. In 1993 Valley Fundraisers deposited checks totaling $511,911 and sent charities $63,244 (about 12.4 percent).

The president of Valley Fundraisers, Thomas Galambos, admits that "mistakes" have been made, according to the *Los Angeles Times*. Solicitors work as independent contractors over which, Galambos says, he has very little supervision since many solicitors work out of their homes. Checks were received and deposited for Children's Hospice Center and many similar organizations, which the IRS says do not exist as charitable organizations. No charges of fraudulent charitable solicitations have been filed because of the difficulty of linking a victim's check to a misrepresentation over the phone.

How often the con artist is successful is not known because victims are reluctant to report on their own gullibility. Or, in the case of contributing to charities, especially those that send "runners" to pick up the checks, donors may never realize they have been victimized.

DRUGS

The Problem

In trying to curtail the use of drugs in this country, drug enforcement agencies spend enormous sums of tax money to find and prosecute users, dealers, and smugglers. It is estimated that six million Americans are either selling or using drugs, and one in every five babies born in the inner cities is born addicted to drugs. Crack cocaine, the cause of most of the drug problem recently, is so addictive that used only once it captures the user, most often forever. With the increased use of illegal drugs, violent crime also increases, and with needle sharing for drug injections, the AIDS epidemic grows.

In 1991 781,000 people were arrested on drug-related charges, 84 percent male. Every two hours, $6 million is spent on law enforcement against drugs. Of the $14 billion budget for fighting drugs, only $1 billion is allocated for treatment. A leading cause of homicide in this country is drugs, but it is not users who are involved but drug dealers.

The single most important factor for the great rise in the prison population is drug violations. In 1989 77 percent of those convicted for drug violations served prison time. With new mandatory sentencing, 89 percent were sentenced to prison in 1991. Many who are arrested are not convicted.

Heroin used to be the drug of choice, but now it is the derivative of cocaine known as crack, which is cocaine mixed 50-50 with baking soda. This is heated and when it dries it is like Plaster of Paris and is cracked into chunks. Compared to crack, heroin is a sedative. After a quick rush, heroin produces oblivion. In contrast, crack is a stimulant that produces euphoria and sometimes propels a user to commit acts of violence. Heroin has a chemical alternative known as methadone, which, if taken regularly, can keep a heroin addict off heroin. There is as yet no chemical alternative for cocaine.

In June 1985 the police did not make any crack cocaine arrests in New York. From January to November 1988, they made 19,075 arrests related to crack cocaine. Once regarded as a city plague, crack is now easily found in small-town America.

Not only does the drug addict suffer loss of friends, jobs, spouse, and health, but her or his children also suffer. The children of addicts are often cared for by grandparents or are put in tax-supported foster care. Drug-addicted parents are known to neglect their children; they have even been known to rent their children for sexual pleasure in order to get money for drugs.

Another one of the many negative side-effects of drug usage is found in the number of drug-related car accidents. Of the approximately 50,000 fatal car accidents a year, 40,000 involve trucks. Maybe that is because one out of three truckers is said to be buying and selling drugs at truck stops. The drug methamphetamine keeps truckers awake on their long, often boring trips.

Added to the other problems of drug usage is what it has done to this country's court system, which is overflowing with drug offense cases. In 1991, drug cases accounted for more than one-fourth of all criminal cases in district courts, and one-half in appellate courts. Because of the heavy load of drug cases, other court cases, such as those involving the environment and civil rights, are delayed. In Washington, D.C., there were 40,000 felony arrests in 1990, but the court system is set up to handle only 16,000 cases. Most court systems in this country cannot handle such an overwhelming number of drug cases.

Suggestions have been made that there should be more cops on the beat, that many drug crimes could be reduced to misdemeanor crimes, and anti-loitering laws should be reinstated to curtail the neighborhood drug problem before it becomes unmanageable. Sending young offenders to prison often teaches them to become more adept at crime. With a 70 percent recidivism rate, the offenders return to the same environment that sent them to prison in the first place. They return to their crime, and then back to prison again.

The Rand Corporation reported on June 13, 1994, that the get-tough policy on jailing drug users had no effect on the drug problem in this country. The report indicated that while the number of cocaine users had decreased, the actual amount of cocaine consumed had increased. What works? The Rand Corporation stressed that treatment works in getting people off drugs and reducing drug consumption, whereas prison does not. When a drug user is arrested, the Rand Corporation advised, he could be coerced into accepting treatment instead of jail time—treatment being more effective and also cheaper than jail time.

Fewer than 10 percent of those arrested for drugs go to prison, yet everyone who does costs taxpayers from $20,000 to $40,000 a year depending on the state and the type of incarceration. In some cities, like Miami, almost all crime is related to drugs. People working in the criminal justice system often have a sense they are wasting their time because their work does not appear to affect the using or dealing of drugs.

Housing projects particularly feel the scourge of drug dealing. Despite numerous arrests of drug dealers, the dealing continues. Residents who complain to the police are often victimized by the dealers or their children are harmed. Most prefer to say nothing, to keep their children inside, and to venture outside only for necessities. While residents are encouraged to take control of their housing project or neighborhood, they often do so at great expense to themselves. There are some notable exceptions, however, where residents have driven the drug dealers from their areas. Police say the best success they have in cleaning up a neighborhood is in areas where local citizens take an active part in driving drug dealers out. This means that the drug dealers move into a new neighborhood, which is usually another gang's territory. This may cause gang fights and even death for the newcomers.

Who is causing all this drug crime? While it is true that women are users of drugs, and some are dealers, most dealers, traffickers, or smugglers are men.

Numerous murders occur as a result of a drug deal gone bad. When a dealer does not receive his money from a seller, he cannot go to the police. Therefore he often takes the underground law into his own hands. "Drugs were a possible motive" frequently describes what would otherwise be a motiveless crime.

When Jack Reilly, thirty-eight, was found with his throat cut and stab wounds in his chest, Donald Dacus, twenty-two, was arraigned for his murder in February 1990, in Napa, California. Reilly, a computer store owner, allegedly became involved in a drug deal with Dacus in an attempt to solve some of his financial problems. As with many drug murders, this one probably resulted from a drug deal that had gone bad.

In another instance, a Compton, California, man allegedly murdered a man and woman while the woman's two small children slept in another room in the house. The police noted the usual "drugs were a possible motive."

Drug Agents Who Become Criminals

When an arrest is made and the money seized must be used as evidence, it is easy and tempting for some Federal Drug Enforcement Agency officers or state and local narcotics officers to pocket the money, often in collusion with other officers. In recent convictions of drug officers accused of such crimes, all are veteran officers and many have distinguished themselves in the past with various service awards and honors. All over the country, drug agents are having to arrest other drug agents.

Smuggling through the Miami area became very profitable not only for drug smugglers and their South American suppliers, but also for some members of the U.S. Coast Guard and the Miami police force. When Miami was hard-pressed to hire enough police to deal with the growing drug problem, many men were hired who had police records. As reported on an August 1989 "60 Minutes," seventy-five members of the Miami police had been under investigation for drug smuggling. Of the seventy-five, twenty-one were arrested and convicted.

NBC's TV program "Exposé" reported in May 1990 that members of the coast guard working on Islamorada Island in the Florida Keys were involved with cocaine smugglers. As Lt. Commander Jeff Karonis of the coast guard's Southeastern division said after watching the show, "The coast guard people involved were brought to justice and are in jail right now."

In Brockton, Massachusetts, the chief of police, Richard Sprole, who was known as a drug fighter and who had organized crime-watch teams, was arrested in October 1989 and pleaded guilty to cocaine use. According to the reports, he had been a cocaine user for three years before he was made chief of police. With a key to the evidence room that was filled with cocaine, he had access to drugs for his own use. By the time he was arrested he had been an addict for five years. In addition, at least $70,000 taken during drug raids was unaccounted for.

It is difficult to know where the money went. The chief apologized to everyone. Because he pleaded guilty there was no trial. He was sentenced to seven to ten years in state prison.

Not even the Drug Enforcement Agency headquarters in Washington, D.C., is immune from inside corruption. With the arrest in August 1989 of Edward O'Brien, forty-four, a highly decorated official who had access to sensitive investigative information, the Drug Enforcement Agency said it was "extremely concerned." O'Brien's brother, thirty-nine-year-old John O'Brien, was allegedly a messenger in a cocaine ring and was also arrested. A younger brother, thirty-four-year-old Paul O'Brien, was arrested and released on bail, though Edward and John were initially denied bail. The arrests came after three weeks of a sting operation in which Edward O'Brien allegedly agreed to deliver a certain amount of cocaine to a DEA officer posing as a drug dealer, whereupon O'Brien was arrested.

In another case, six veteran members of an elite drug-enforcement team of the Los Angeles Sheriff's Department were convicted of stealing cash and laundering money seized when they arrested drug traffickers. In a federal agents' sting operation, the men were videotaped taking drug money. The money the men gathered in their drug enforcement duties was used to buy cars, jewelry, vacation homes, and boats. The total stolen by these officers was estimated to be $1.4 million.

Once known as the best and the brightest of the Sheriff's Department, the men convicted were Eufrasio Cortez, thirty-nine, once honored as a top drug officer; Ronald Daub, thirty-nine, a seventeen-year officer; Daniel Garner, forty-four, a nineteen-year officer; James Bauder, thirty-two, whose father had retired as a narcotics officer; Terrell Amers, forty-seven, a twenty-three-year officer; John Dickerson, thirty-two, winner of the Medal of Valor and an eleven-year officer; and Macerio Duran, forty-four, a fourteen-year veteran. Except for Duran, all of the men were convicted on one count of taking money from a drug trafficker (who was actually a federal agent). In the days that followed the sting operation, the men's houses were searched and marked money was found by federal agents.

One former sheriff's sergeant, Robert Sobel, agreed to testify to other charges against the men in exchange for a reduced sentence. All except one of the men had worked in the sheriff's office for Sobel. Sobel testified how he and his men beat their drug suspects, skimmed money, and wrote fictitious reports.

Even while James Bauder and Daniel Garner were on trial, they allegedly posed as agents and searched an apartment for cash, though no indictment was issued against them.

The effect of this scandal seriously curtailed drug enforcement proceedings in Los Angeles County. A letter from Captain Waldie of the Narcotics Bureau indicated: "Bureau productivity plummeted. Arrests and cocaine and asset seizures dwindled. Little or no major narcotic trafficking investigations went on for a full year and a half. . . . Numerous cases of major drug dealers were lost due to suspensions and/or indictments."

The Quandary

With the high cost of trying to keep drug use down, with the increase in crime related to drugs, with the growing number of addicted babies, and with the AIDS risk of sharing needles, there is talk of legalizing drugs. Former U.S. Surgeon General Jocelyn Elders suggested that the idea of legalizing some drugs in order to curtail the crime rate should be studied. President Clinton made it clear that her remark did not represent the view of his administration.

The argument is that legalization would cut down on the number of prisoners, and therefore cut down on the need for more prisons. It would also cut down on the cost of adjudicating drug cases in the courts and cut down on the number of violent crimes committed by drug traffickers.

The idea is that federally controlled stores would sell what are now illegal drugs at federally controlled prices, thereby taking the profit motive away. Accordingly, there would be no need for smuggling, nor any more need for Coast Guard surveillance, nor any more Mafia or gang-connected drug rings. As with alcohol, it would be illegal to sell drugs to minors, and those who did would receive severe prison sentences. Money that is being used now on the war on drugs would be used for educating against the use of drugs and for drug treatment centers.

There have been several forums to discuss the legalization of drugs, with forceful arguments for legalization and forceful arguments against. The fear about legalization is that drugs would be readily available, even to children, though illegal. The argument against that argument is that drugs are already readily available to children. Some argue that drugs should be made extremely difficult to obtain, not made easier. The answer to that is that the war on drugs, which costs billions of dollars, has not made drugs any more difficult to obtain. The cost of drugs has steadily decreased over the past few years, which means the supply has increased in spite of the Coast Guard surveillance.

Whether drugs are legalized or not will be a political decision, and it appears politically impossible to introduce legislation for the legalization of drugs at this time. In addition to the many arguments against legalization, there are vested interests in keeping drugs illegal. On one side are the Mafia, the gangs, and the drug traffickers who make fortunes on drugs. On the other side is the huge infrastructure of the drug enforcement agencies, federal, state, and local, made up of people who earn their living because drugs are illegal.

There are those who say there should be more prisons and that people arrested for drug-related crimes should be incarcerated longer. Currently the largest budget item on any state's budget is the item for building prisons. Incarceration, say the experts, does no good, except it gets that particular man off the street for a while. But when his sentence is finished he almost invariably goes back to doing what he was doing that got him into prison in the first place—the revolving-door syndrome. Drug trafficking is so lucrative that the risk of a short prison sentence is negligible.

Treatment for drug addicts, available to only 15 percent of those who need it, and which has about a 30 percent success rate, would be less expensive than prison. Most prisons have no drug treatment programs. Intensive drug treatment costs about $10,000 per addict per year, compared with prison, which costs about $20,000 per prisoner per year. But because money for treatment centers is scarce, there is a waiting period for addicts, who are then sent into the revolving-door prison process. There are those who say that building treatment centers would be too costly and take too long. Yet during the Gulf War, the navy built a 500-bed hospital in Saudi Arabia in three weeks—proof that drug treatment centers could be set up quickly if the administration had a mind to do it.

How effective has the war on drugs been? In the past two years admissions to Los Angeles County emergency rooms for cocaine crises have doubled. In California, felony drug arrests have doubled in the last five years. Los Angeles County Sheriff Sherman Block reports that 75 percent of prisoners are there because of drug-related crimes. The Los Angeles Police Department reports that 61 percent of murders and 80 percent of robberies are drug-related. These figures are probably similar to figures for other cities around the country.

Dr. Mitchell Rosenthal, president of Phoenix House, a private, nonprofit drug rehabilitation institution that has treatment centers in California, New York, and New Jersey, recently said, "We are still no closer to bringing on line desperately needed new treatment facilities than we were almost two years ago, when the national strategy was first announced. My fear is that as more middle-class Americans continue to reject casual drug use, the public will come to ignore the heavy-using and high-risk users who are responsible for most of the drug-related violence, crime and social disorder in this country."

For the time being, a war on drugs will continue—and so will the crime connected with drug dealing.

CHAPTER 13

GANGS

The Extent of the Problem

Forming into gangs had a romantic beginning, as in *West Side Story* where neighborhood youths joined together for mutual protection or for just plain fun. Now the main purpose of gangs is to deal drugs and take revenge against other gangs. The ritual for joining a gang is for a "wannabe," a grade-school boy who wants to join the gang, to be "jumped in" or "courted in," which means he is beat up by gang members. If he shows he can take it, he has passed the initiation test and can from then on administer beatings to other wannabes.

The law enforcement definition of a gang is any group that organizes, takes a name, and commits crimes. One of the first signs of gang activity in a neighborhood is graffiti. Known as the newspapers of the streets, graffiti sends hostile messages to rival gangs and expresses respect for any gang member who has been killed. It also marks the territory and strength of the gang. If a rival gang member's name is written in the graffiti with a line drawn through it, that means he is to be blown away.

In Los Angeles County there are about 800 gangs, the most notorious being the Bloods and the Crips. The gangs are more like loose confederations, or "sets" and "subsets," groups from neighborhoods with memberships of about twenty to thirty boys between fourteen and seventeen years of age. The Bloods, an African-American Southern California–based gang, wear red pants or underwear and are known to be loyal to each other. The Crips wear blue, fight each other, and are even known to kill each other. The Crips, also African-American, have about 225 sets, outnumbering the Bloods by about seven to one. Crips is short for kryptonite, the substance strong enough to kill even Superman. Other sets that are known to the police have names such as Payback Crips, the 165th Denver Lane Bloods, the Broadway Gangster Crips, and the Bounty Hunters. The Surenos, a Latino gang, wear red.

Originally gangs fought each other over turf, but now they engage in a kind of guerrilla warfare over revenge and drugs. "There's absolutely no question," Lorne Kramer, the assistant commanding officer of the Los Angeles Police Department's gang-drug section, said in November 1988, "that street gangs have made a metamorphosis into drug dealing." Drug trafficking is important to gangs, and gangs are important to drug suppliers because gangs keep drugs moving into the inner cities and then into the suburbs. The Drug Enforcement Agency reported in 1988 that 80 percent of the cocaine recovered at the Los Angeles Airport involved gangs.

Gangs as a Form of Terrorism

In gangs, young men are assassinated if they try to compete with established leaders or if they do not follow through on a job to which they were assigned. Five to ten percent of young men in Los Angeles belong to gangs, with deaths among and by gang members rising each year. In 1989 there was a 16 percent rise in gang-related murders over the previous year.

Fewer people have been killed in the past twenty years in the war in Northern Ireland than in gang killings in Los Angeles in the past ten years. There have been more killings from gang-bangers in the last five years than in terrorism around the world. When compared to the Al Capone gangsters of the Prohibition period, police say there is a major difference: today's teenage gangs are more violent than Capone's gangsters. On an NBC special, "Gangs, Cops and Drugs," a veteran police officer was asked how gangs have changed in the past eighteen years. The answer was that gang members now do not value human life. Asked how much time a gang member spends in jail, the officer replied that, because of crowded jails, a gang member is booked and processed and then "he's out the door." The Los Angeles jail capacity is 12,600, but at any one time there are over 23,000 inmates.

In 1986 there were 328 gang-related murders in Los Angeles; in 1987 there were 387 gang-related murders; in 1990 there were 1,000 such murders, most connected with drugs. Angry and resentful gang members are armed with sub-machine guns and will kill anyone who gets in their way or who in any way offends a fellow gang member. One first-grade girl was killed because her brother wore the wrong color baseball cap. Innocent bystanders killed in crossfire or in drive-by shootings are referred to by gang members as "mushrooms." Of those killed in gang violence between the years 1986 and 1988, more than half were not part of any gang, but were the so-called mushrooms. In Los Angeles alone, a teenager or a child is killed every day in a drive-by shooting. As a result of the outrage at this kind of killing, an initiative passed on the June 1994 California ballot that imposes harsher sentences on killings resulting from drive-by shootings.

When patients are brought into the emergency room at Martin Luther King, Jr.–Drew Medical Center, Dr. Syani Atturi said in the *San Francisco Examiner*, "You can tell when emergency patients are gang members. Then our hallways are full.

Half may be there because he's one of theirs; the other to make sure he's really dead."

When one gang member invades the territory of another, this is a call to murder. When the profit in drugs decreases because of the oversupply and consequent low price of cocaine, gang members move out into other cities and other states, exporting their drugs and accompanying terrorism. The Bloods and the Crips have fanned out across the country, opening up new drug markets in Seattle, Kansas City, and Baltimore, among other cities. They recruit children to look out for police and pay them about $100 a day.

The gang's business tactics are a kind of franchising. One gang member can hire thirty to thirty-five grade-school or junior high school children in a short time. The new recruits graduate to runners, bringing cocaine to dealers for about $300 a day. The next step, as the young boys grow up, is to become full-fledged gang members—dealers, with the supplier offering a commission. Success is measured in the kind of clothes the boys wear, the cars they drive, or the jewelry they have.

Part of the problem in the new communities where gangs move is that the residents and law enforcement don't recognize the symptoms of gang activity, such as increased graffiti displaying the name of gangs or specific turfs and young men hanging around on corners. New communities don't start attacking the problem until it has become entrenched. On the TV program "48 Hours" it was estimated that when gangs moved into Seattle there were 225 drive-by shootings in the first year.

Residents in gang areas live in fear. It isn't only that young boys growing up in gang neighborhoods might become gang members, it is gunfire from gang members. More and more children are being killed by bullets aimed at gang members. Small children must learn early to scatter when a gang shooting is threatened. When one gang member was told about a youngster being shot in a drive-by shooting, he was said to have remarked that the mothers should keep their children inside because they know the boys are "gangbanging." One elementary school in Los Angeles has erected a six-foot concrete wall around its playground to protect the children from gunfire by rival gangs.

A typical drive-by shooting occurs somewhat as this one did in Orange County, California, in September 1989. With an automatic weapon, a group of young men in a pickup truck opened fire on a family as they were getting into their cars to go to a movie. The men shot at about a dozen people, killing seventeen-year-old Miguel Navarro, a known gang member, who had thrown himself across his girlfriend's body when the shooting started. The girlfriend said she would have died if Navarro had not covered her with his body.

In that shooting, four-year-old Frank Fernandez was also killed. His father had told him to get down when the shooting started, but the little boy remained standing in the back of the car parked in the family driveway. His father said, "I tried pulling everybody down, but my little boy was standing up in the back and he got shot in the chest."

In San Francisco, a superior court judge sentenced twenty-five-year-old Anthony Walker to five years for killing another person who parked in what was a sacred shrine for a dead gang member. The sentence included three years for voluntary manslaughter and two years for being an ex-felon in possession of a firearm.

From California to New York gangs practice violence. In the infamous subway stabbing of the Utah man visiting New York with his family, the perpetrators were gang members who not only wanted money to go to a dance, but also were allegedly participating in an initiation ritual that required new members to complete a mugging or to beat up someone. The eight gang members ranged in age from seventeen to twenty.

When gangs determined that Portland, Oregon, was soft on crime, they moved there in large numbers to set up new markets for their drugs. When they moved to Tacoma, Washington, two Crips murdered a girl who waved at them. They thought she was giving them a rival gang sign.

Revenge is the major motive in gang warfare, more so than fighting over drug turf. Sometimes the gangs are fighting each other over things that happened six or seven years ago, or for things they can't remember. Even in jail, violence continues between gangs, and members of gangs fight each other.

Gang violence, according to the executive director of Community Youth Gang Services, is rising. South Central Los Angeles is held hostage by street gangs. Gang murders account for approximately 3 percent of murders in the country, but for Los Angeles, gang murders account for approximately 40 percent, mostly because of the proliferation of guns, which have replaced fist fights as the response to avenge insults.

A mere gathering of young people may be an incentive for a gang to invade the group, as happened at a park near Los Angeles Memorial Coliseum. On April 8, 1994, gang members arrived and fired on the first group, sending three to the hospital.

In Gardena, California, an eighteen-year-old high school student attending a party was sought out by a noninvited gang member and shot in the back, dying immediately. His basketball coach said, "He was one of the nicest kids I've ever coached."

In the carjacking murder of two Marymount College students from Japan, a reputed gang member, Raymond Butler, was arrested in April 1994. His alleged accomplice, Alberto Raygoza, accused of receiving items stolen from the victims' car, is also charged.

At another party in Los Angeles, gunfire lasted twenty minutes when rival gang members drove up and began firing at party-goers. At 12:30 A.M., people in the otherwise quiet neighborhood rolled out of their beds and onto the floor for safety. Even when one twenty-five-year-old woman was killed, the two groups kept firing at each other. Though ten men were wounded, neighbors refused to talk to reporters for fear of reprisal from gang members.

Ethnic gang rivalry among Cambodians and Latinos resulted in a 1920s gangster-style shoot-out. Young Latino men were leaving a dance party in the Long Beach area on May 15, 1994, when the Cambodians opened fire on six, killing three. This, it was assumed, was in retaliation for a killing a week previous. The victims, however, ages fifteen and nineteen, were not part of any gang.

This was an unusual drive-by in that it was well organized, was not done on the run, but done methodically with numerous witnesses. The attackers, according to witnesses, appeared to be boys between fifteen and twenty years old.

The Purpose of Gangs

Gangs serve many purposes, such as security in belonging to a group and as a source for drug money. When the Drug Enforcement Agency raided a South Central Los Angeles neighborhood in May 1989, they arrested the alleged leader of a $1 million-a-month cocaine business operated by a gang known as the Five Deuce Hoover Gangster Crips, which has about a thousand members. A spokesman for the DEA described this particular gang as "one of the most vicious and violent in terms of number of drive-by shootings, armed robbery, rapes, and armed assaults."

Who Joins Gangs?

African Americans make up 55 percent of the gangs nationally, according to the American Psychological Association, and Hispanics make up about 33 percent, with Asian membership rising. The male-female ratio is 20:1, with females resorting to more and more violence because "they need to commit the violent acts to make themselves credible to their male counterparts," says Stanford social psychologist Fernando Soriano.

Children need rules and security. Many have poor academic ability and get no praise from anyone. Gangs have rules, colors, guidelines, and security in the sense that the group "hangs together" against all others. Because children have to walk through gang turf to get to school, mothers wait nervously for their children to come home. Some children can't resist the gang appeal. Most gang members are nonreaders who have little reasoning skill and little ability to make good choices. Life is hard for children who have to walk through gang turf and get jumped on every day. There is security and also opportunity for making money in joining a gang.

Gangs provide a power base for young people who otherwise feel powerless. The typical hard-core gang member, according to Lucy Quarry of the California Youth Authority (as quoted in the University of California, Davis, newspaper, *Cal Aggie*, in April 1989), is "a member of an underrepresented ethnic group, comes from a single-parent family, receives government financial assistance, and lacks a male authority figure. . . . In addition, one or both parents may have been gang members who encouraged their children to join. This is known as the 'assembly-line production' of gang members. In East Los Angeles there is a strong tradition of gang membership that results in third- and fourth-generation members."

There are, Quarry says, three types of gang members: "shot callers" are the ones who commit the crimes; "associates" or "wannabes" are those who just hang around the gang members. The third group is made up of "peripherals." In this group are most of the gang-related females, who stay around the gang members for protection and live in the same gang neighborhood. When gangs move into new territories, they recruit children with school problems or family problems, or children from families with employment problems. The children bring home their gang-related drug money to their families, who are grateful for the income but who may be fearful of its source.

Gangsta Rap

Gang rap songs have made their way onto the airwaves. One group that brings the message is a group that calls itself Niggas with Attitudes, who do a song, "Gangsta, Gangstas," that describes the ghetto gang life and the casualness of taking a life. Some disc jockeys and radio stations have refused to play this song, as well as their song "F—— tha Police." But there are radio stations that do play these songs and songs from Guns N' Roses, 2-Live Crew, Ice-T, and Snoop Doggy Dogg and say that refusing to do so is censorship.

As Jon Pareles wrote for the New York Times News Service on December 12, 1994, "Gangster rap offers listeners the vicarious thrills of brutally pure self-interest, perfect male bonding, defiance of authority (including the almost obligatory cop-killing scenarios) and increasingly rigorous 'realness.'" The rappers apparently believe in the brutality of their songs. Pareles reminds us that Tupac Shakur, gangsta rapper, was recently convicted of felony sex abuse and that Slick Rick has been in jail for three years for attempted second-degree murder. Snoop Doggy Dogg, the multimillion-selling rapper, will be tried for murder in January 1995.

The songwriters say they are simply reflecting ghetto life and that young men who see no future for themselves in mainstream America are the ones who join gangs.

Women's groups such as the National Organization for Women and the National Political Congress of Black Women have joined together to try to get these anti-women songs off the radio and TV, saying the songs glorify violence against women. The beat of the music camouflages words that refer to women as bitches and whores.

Girls in Gangs

Gangs offer girls the same things that they offer boys, a sense of identity and structure. It is estimated that 10 percent of gangs are girl gangs, according to Anne Campbell's *The Girl in the Gang*. There are an estimated 7,000 girl gang members in Los Angeles and around the country. In an ABC News report of February 1990, several girls explained that they joined gangs mainly because they were tired of being victimized. They broke away from the male gangs, staked out their own territory, dealt drugs, and got power from doing so. "Soft people don't make it," one said.

Most girls in gangs receive little love. Their own lives, as they admit, are meaningless. Many have parents who were also gang members. "What do you want for your daughter?" one was asked. "A better life," she replied. "I don't want her to be in a gang."

The girls refer to themselves as "homegirls," like the boys' use of "homeboys." Michael Genlin, chief of the hard-core gangs division of the Los Angeles district attorney's office said in the *San Francisco Chronicle* of February 11, 1990, that of all the violent gang-related crimes, women were involved in few serious crimes. "Violent aggression seems to be almost entirely a male prerogative."

The Hope for Elimination of Gangs

In September 1990, the Los Angeles district attorney, declaring gangs as "a new and dangerous form of organized crime," maintained that his office will not plea bargain with gang criminals but will prosecute to keep them off the streets as long as possible. In Los Angeles, an average of two people die in gang-related killings every thirty-six hours. Many are not gang members. Many are children.

As with the Mafia, extortion is another part of gang-related crime. Reporting against this gang activity can be dangerous. But that did not deter an Asian market owner in Sacramento from turning in the names of three men, which enabled the police to make arrests. Demanding up to $100 a day from Southeast Asian–owned businesses, three Southeast Asian immigrant men were arrested for extortion and possession of a deadly weapon. When they beat a jeweler who refused to give them $2,000, the businessman called police saying he worked too hard to give his money away. An immigrant himself, he said, "This is America. I'm going to do what is right."

When young men attempt to steer young boys away from joining gangs or to warn neighborhoods that a gangbang will be happening in their area, they put themselves in jeopardy. Nineteen-year-old Anthony Gardner, an exemplary student and leader who had graduated from a Los Angeles County Sheriff's program that helps young people understand the work of law enforcement, was shot and killed by men driving by his home.

Even so, many efforts are being made to try to prevent young boys from joining gangs. Gang members who have dropped out of gangs have given talks at schools to tell children the dead-end kind of life they face if they join a gang. One such organization is Right Way Youth Activities, Inc., which tries to steer young boys in Los Angeles away from gangs by providing a variety of activities.

Some mothers of gang members have joined together to support one another and to try to find ways to keep their younger sons out of gangs. Trying to keep their children in school is one way these mothers are trying. Though 30 percent of students cut class every day in the Watts area of Los Angeles, the mothers are hopeful they can keep their younger sons in school. Since most gang members are illiterate dropouts, efforts to keep susceptible youngsters in school would seem to be a most positive effort.

Painting out graffiti is one way, some suggest, to cut down

on gang activity. Graffiti is a warning. It says your home is in gang territory. When a rival gang member crosses out the graffiti, the gang that is claiming the territory comes back to seek revenge on the gang that crossed it out.

Periodic police crackdowns sweep gang members into jail for questioning and identification. In Los Angeles, the police department's Operation Hammer, an anti-gang task force, arrested over 120 suspected gang members on one night in September 1989. Forty suspected gang members were arrested for narcotics violations, but because of jail overcrowding, they were released. Many in law enforcement believe they cannot control gang activity. Their only hope is to keep it down a little.

With police sweeps come complaints that police are brutalizing suspected gang members and indiscriminately bringing nongang members into their nets. Teenage black or Hispanic males are seen as targets of the police, and several nongang members have filed complaints against the Los Angeles Police Department for being denied their civil rights when they were roughly handled by policemen cracking down on gangs.

A November 1990 Associated Press release reported that a "decade of police crackdowns has failed to stop gang violence. . . . Despite toughened laws and the city's mass-arrest Operation Hammer, gangs are larger and deadlier than ever."

Some gangs have recently taken it upon themselves to police their activities. At a funeral in San Francisco, the rival gangs of Hunters Point and Sunnydale housing projects came together after the funeral of a member of the Sunnydale gang. The Sunnydale gang crossed into the Hunters Point territory and asked for peace. Overcome with emotion from the funeral, the Sunnydale gang of about 1,100 approached the Hunters Point gang. There were hugs and tears. Then both gangs got into about twenty cars, toured the streets, honked, and shouted, "Stop the violence!" When it was over, about 200 youths proclaimed they would communicate with each other over conflicts and would police themselves to curb the violence.

Besieged with complaints about gang violence, the California legislature passed two bills last September, known as the Street Terrorism Enforcement Act, that makes it illegal for anyone to participate in a criminal gang, knowing that the gang has participated in a "pattern of criminal activity." A "criminal street gang" is one that is an "ongoing organization or association of three or more persons who adopt a common identifying symbol or name and whose primary goal is to commit certain criminal acts." The new law makes it possible for the judicial system to add one or two more years to a sentence if the defendant is a gang member.

"The answer is jobs," says Jim Johnson, director of the University of California Los Angeles urban poverty center. Yet it is difficult for a ten-year-old who makes $100 a day as a lookout to be enticed to stay in school or later to take a job at minimum wage. But even as the problem of what to do about gangs was debated, a five-year-old girl was gunned down and killed in South Central Los Angeles and two teenage boys were being sought. At the same time, a marine sergeant was stabbed by gang members, a fifteen-year-old boy nearby died after he was beaten in a gang fight, and an eighteen-year-old was critically injured from nine stab wounds in a fight with rival gang members. As Sheriff Sherman Block said, "We need social programs. The message to be made clear to average citizens is that putting more dollars into law enforcement is not going to enhance their safety. As long as gang cultures exist, we are chasing our tails."

Yet administrators for an anti-gang project in Los Angeles called Hope in Youth, when asking for $5 million to continue its program, met opposition from city councilmen who claimed that the program could not prove it had been effective after its one-year operation. The plan was to send into gang areas $30,000-a-year social workers who would find wholesome activities for pre-gang-age children and work with parents and schools. Councilmen objected that the program had no track record and was requesting too much money, compared to the many other programs that also needed money.

A promising truce in Los Angeles County among twenty-four gang groups surfaced on May 18, 1994. After lengthy negotiations, ex-gang leaders of the Crips and Bloods, now in their early thirties, came together to discuss raising money to start legitimate businesses for young black men and to discuss laying down their arms. Police are skeptical, saying that when there have been truces before, the crime rate has not fallen. However, now that the boys are older, maybe their maturity will lend weight to a long-term determination.

CHAPTER 14

BURGLARY AND ROBBERY

Burglary

The people most susceptible to burglary are those who can afford it the least. Black urban apartment residents with low incomes are the main targets of burglars. According to U.S. Justice Department statistics, in 42 percent of such burglaries, the burglar was a friend, an acquaintance, or a relative. Thirteen percent of burglaries occur when someone is home.

One burglary occurs every ten seconds in this country. There were 410,000 residential burglaries in California alone in 1990. Does crime pay? It seems so. In San Francisco in 1990, of the 10,618 residential and commercial burglaries, only 1,442 criminals were arrested. In other words, 87 percent were successful.

A burglary, as distinguished from a robbery, is the forcible entry into a building, especially a dwelling, with the intent to steal. A robbery is the theft of something from a person by use of violence or threat.

Stealing a car is most often a weaponless crime, with approximately 300,000 cars in California stolen each year, almost all by young men. Over the past five years, auto theft nearly doubled in Southern California. In San Gabriel Valley, auto theft rose 96 percent in five years. In 1990 statistics from the Justice Department, auto thefts rose by 19 percent, or 1.4 million completed thefts of cars, vans, and trucks, and 770,000 attempted thefts.

Whether anti-theft devices on cars are deterrents to auto theft remains to be seen. But in one case such a device would not have done any good. When a car thief wanted a brand new Mercedes-Benz, he simply sat in the new car in the showroom, revved the motor, and drove it through the plate-glass window of Downtown L.A. Motors. He was last seen heading toward Harbor Boulevard.

Thieves work in many areas and gear their thefts to items that are in demand. Keith Lawson, thirty-two, pleaded guilty to four office break-ins in San Francisco in a six-month crime wave of stealing money and computer equipment. He is suspected of committing as many as 100 such burglaries.

In another computer business theft, $321,000 of computer microchips were stolen by two men who intended to sell them to buyers out of the country. The chips, known as Simm chips, boost the memory capacity of a computer. One of the men arrested, in July 1990, Bernard Pornaras of Hollister, California, was confronted as he tried to sell the chips in Honolulu to an FBI undercover agent. His accomplice, Raymond Reynolds of Sunnyvale, was arrested later near his home.

An extortion that is referred to as an attempted burglary was committed by a former San Francisco police officer who pleaded guilty to demanding $50,000 from a woman, saying he would harm her two children if she didn't pay. He was arrested at the arranged pickup point. And in another theft, more like a white-collar crime, James McGrail, fifty-two, was extradited from Australia to be charged with raising the $125 figure on an insurance check for his son's medical bills to $125,000. He deposited this check in the bank, together with another check stolen from a bank in England, and then fled to Australia.

Two Air Force security officers were arrested when the FBI set up a fictitious company in Utah near Hill Air Force Base to buy stolen military equipment. The two men brought in jet engines and other supplies to sell. Members of the FBI said other items brought in for sale were clothing, small firearms, and ammunition. "Many of the participants are military policemen," they said.

Even in death one is not safe from robbery. A deputy coroner was arrested in December 1989 in San Francisco, charged with stealing $3,200 from the home of an eighty-three-year-old deceased woman. Allen Jeffries, forty-nine, who had worked for the coroner's office for eleven years, admitted he had taken the money.

A specialty robber is someone like Harold Huddleston, fifty-one, arrested in Portland, Oregon, May 1994, for burglarizing cars in campgrounds as their owners slept in their campers. Considered to be a one-man crime wave, Huddleston, who was paroled in 1991 on a burglary charge, may be the burglar in over a thousand robberies in cars. He was arrested when marked items were found in his apartment that police had planted in cars used to pull vacation trailers.

Stealing air bags from cars in auto dealerships and parked cars is reaching epidemic proportions. The air bags are sold to unscrupulous auto repairmen. The repairman pays the thief probably $150 and installs it in another car whose air bag has been stolen, billing the insurance company about $1,000.

Robbery

A car theft occurs in the United States every nineteen seconds, according to NBC's "Dateline" of June 9, 1994. Asked by a reporter how best to protect one's car from being stolen, a convicted car thief now serving time in jail answered with a smile, "Hire an armed guard."

In the United States a robbery other than car theft occurs every forty-six seconds. The most dangerous places to work in terms of chances of being robbed are gas stations or convenience stores at night.

The chief of the FBI's Violent Crime Unit in Washington says of the increase in bank robberies, "It's in part related to the increasing drug problem." Of identified bank robbers, approximately half are known drug users.

They start young! Accused of robbing two banks in California, one in Newberry Park and one in Camarillo, Andrew Carrillo, twenty-two, was indicted in May 1990.

When two men robbed a Brink's armored truck, killing the driver and wounding two others in San Francisco, September 1989, they did not get any money. The bag they stole contained only certified mail. The two men escaped on ten-speed bicycles, which were found later with the serial numbers filed off.

In another armored truck robbery, two men wearing Halloween masks stole a sack of money intended for a Fast Cash store in the business district of San Francisco in October 1989. The men abandoned their stolen car and escaped by running behind buildings.

Sometimes robberies end in the death of the robbers. Two of the three men who attempted to rob a grocery store armed with a MAC-10, were shot dead by the owner of Chico's Mini Market in Compton, California. When the would-be robbers demanded money and threatened the owner's six-year-old son, his other son, fourteen years old, went to protect his little brother. The assailant then shot the fourteen-year-old and the owner shot the two men. Though wounded severely, the fourteen-year-old survived.

Another case of would-be robbers getting shot involved an off-duty Los Angeles Police Department rookie. He was walking to a friend's house at 1:00 A.M. to get help because he had run out of gas when two men approached him, one with a .38-caliber handgun. They demanded his money, which he gave them. Then they demanded that he empty his pockets, and when the officer hesitated for fear they'd see the police badge, one man yelled, "Shoot him." One of the men aimed the gun at him, and the officer grabbed it, took his own gun from his waistband, and shot the man identified as Eric Johnson, twenty. The second would-be robber escaped.

Sometimes the police officer *is* the robber. Such was the case in Louisiana in May 1994, when two New Orleans policemen, Bruce Douglas and Fred Russell, who, while on duty, robbed various people. In New York, twelve policemen were charged April 15, 1994, for stealing money from drug dealers, stopping cars, searching them illegally, and taking what they wanted, and accepting bribes for nonarrest. In searching an apartment crime scene, two of the officers divided the $100,000 that was found. Three officers immediately pleaded guilty.

In San Jose, a gunman suspected of robbing at least ten restaurants using a sawed-off shotgun was arrested after a 100-mile-per-hour chase. The men arrested were James McColloch, twenty-five, Chris Caldwell, thirty-five, and Robert Deets, twenty-five.

No place is safe, not even the Department of Motor Vehicles in Bellflower, California, where four men in ski masks bound six employees after the bandits demanded cash.

Another group vulnerable to robbery are Asians, especially new immigrants. Would-be robbers know that most immigrant Asians do not use credit cards and have large amounts of cash. Also, since they are seen as obedient to commands, Asians are especially vulnerable to being robbed in the subways of New York, where there are few police, and they are also charged excessive cab and limousine fares. The total overall subway robberies in New York increased 56 percent from 1987 to 1989, when the number of subway robberies was 8,264. But for

Asians it was three times that number, or probably much more, because Asians do not generally report robberies to the police. This may be because police in their homelands were hostile police or because it is difficult to find an interpreter in a robbery emergency. Asian police decoys acting as tourists arrested twenty suspects, of whom eighteen were indicted in just three months in 1990.

Thirty-two-year-old convicted bank robber Laving Hayes had a difficult fight on his hands when he entered a copy shop and asked a woman employee for the use of a restroom. When he came out he had an ax he had found in the restroom. He held it to the woman's neck, but her daughter rushed him to get the ax, and Hayes hit her several times. Even with blood all over her face, holding her eye, the daughter swung at him. He then hit her in the head again with the ax. When he demanded money, the mother opened the cash drawer and he took the money—less than $35. The daughter's wounds required 143 stitches, but she suffered no brain or skull damage. Hayes was arrested at his home, identified by fingerprints he had left on the ax handle.

When people withdraw their bank money from automatic teller machines, they run a serious risk of robbery and even of being murdered. One man in Sacramento, withdrawing $100 at 11:00 A.M. on a Sunday, was startled by a man demanding the money. He refused to give the robber the money and was stabbed to death.

Some robbers make a career out of watching ATMs and taking the money at gunpoint from their victims. Probably the most prolific ATM robber in the country was thirty-four-year-old Curtis Taylor, a drug addict and ex-convict who, in a plea bargain, pleaded guilty to thirty-seven robberies and attempted robberies at ATMs in Southern California. He would approach his victims as they were giving the ATM their code numbers and tell them, "Punch $200 or I'll blow you away." Though he indicated he had a gun, he apparently was using only a toy pistol. "I'm sorry, I need the money for drugs," he would tell his victims as he left. Because he used the threat of a gun, he was sentenced to twenty-eight years, but he could be released from prison in eleven years.

Elderly people are especially vulnerable to robberies. In the Tenderloin District of San Francisco, a group of young men act as escorts, walking with old people to stores or other places where they need to go, to prevent robberies.

Crimes against the elderly have become a national disgrace. Unable to defend themselves, old people are prey for young men who knock them down, grab their purses or wallets, and dash away. This represents the same disregard for human life evident in other crimes, but because of the age and the frailty of the victims, crimes against old people seem especially unfair. It was for that reason a law was passed in the California legislature that permits extra years to be attached to the prison sentence of a person convicted of a crime against anyone over sixty.

When Marshall and Roby Goodloe, both seventy years old, answered their doorbell at about 10:00 P.M. in January 1989 in Napa, California, they were beaten and knocked to the floor even after they gave the robbers their money. Both victims required stitches, and Marshall Goodloe required dental repairs. Eighteen-year-olds Clifford Threat and Paul Myers were later arrested.

Las Vegas casinos would seem to be easy targets for robberies. But three men were arrested May 2, 1994, right after the robbery of Harrah's Hotel, taking about $100,000. Two days earlier $158,000 was taken from the Flamingo Hotel. The men, two of whom were nineteen and one twenty, were arrested and jailed pending $100,000 bond. Two seventeen-year-old juveniles were placed in custody of juvenile authorities. Since there is still $100,000 missing, the judge ordered that he approve any further bail in order for him to determine the source of the money. Though five males were apprehended and no money has been recovered, the police believe it was handed to some-one else who is still at large.

In a schoolroom, a twelve-year-old boy brandished a .375-caliber gun at his teacher on May 11, 1994, after the other students had left. The teacher had been collecting prom money and was robbed of $4,000. The boy was arrested soon afterward.

It is often said that young men become criminals because they foresee no future for themselves, having dropped out of school and with job opportunities slim. Yet there are those who have potential and still turn to crime. That was the case for a promising Hispanic man who had been an altar boy, a star athlete, an honor student in high school, and received a scholarship to Harvard. In August 1989, that man, twenty-two-year-old Jose Luis Razo, Jr., was convicted of six robberies in Orange County, California, and of attempting to escape from police. The sentencing judge said that because Razo's crimes involved multiple victims, premeditation, and were not just "temporary aberrant misconduct," he would get the maximum sentence of fifteen years. Witnesses testified that Razo told them if anything went wrong in the course of the robbery, he would kill them. He confessed to police that he needed the money and was high on drugs when he robbed. On the witness stand he confessed that he had used marijuana during his junior and senior high school years.

Hijacking

We're familiar with airplanes being hijacked and trucks being hijacked, but seldom do we hear of buses being commandeered by strangers. But it happened when two young men boarded a shuttle bus leaving Miami Airport. The men robbed the tourists, many foreigners, at gunpoint, taking money, jewelry, luggage, and passports. One of the men ordered the driver to make a wrong turn while the other man did the robbing.

Carjacking

"Carjacking" is a term that originated in 1992. Because anti-theft devices have made it more difficult to enter locked vehicles, thieves have resorted to lying in wait for a person to return to his or her car and then demanding the keys on the threat of the owner's life.

International attention was focused on the March 25, 1994, carjacking of two students from Japan who were attending Marymount College in San Pedro, California. Even though this carjacking was only one of 300 that Los Angeles reported in that same month, this incident inflamed the public. At about 11:00 P.M., Takumo Ito and Go Matsura were shot execution style at a supermarket by two young men who then stole their Honda. The governor of California, the U.S. ambassador to Japan, and the mayor of Los Angeles issued condolences to the victims' parents, who arrived from Japan to collect the bodies.

In Venice, California, on April 30, 1994, three teenagers carjacked three cars within ten minutes of each other. As they said, they did it "for the fun of it." One carried a handgun and another a shotgun.

Increasingly, murder is part of carjacking. The special circumstance of "lying in wait," for which an assailant can now receive the death sentence, is often added to the sentence for the crime. When a twenty-nine-year-old father of three dropped off groceries to a friend in Gardena, California, on May 15, 1994, he was shot and his car stolen by two men. An anonymous tip led police to the suspected murderer, thirty-one-year-old Leland Chambers. Chambers will be tried under the Three Strikes law because he has been convicted of two previous felonies.

Fencing

It was simply a little tire store operation on Whittier Boulevard in East Los Angeles until a customer walked in to buy a new tire and discovered numerous boxes of electronic equipment. He alerted the sheriff's department in Los Angeles, which then arrested the owner, forty-one-year-old Antonio Coronel, and five other men, who were booked on suspicion of grand theft. Their success was their own undoing. With a trailer full of equipment from a Circuit City store in Hollywood, they found themselves with so many boxes that they couldn't hide them all in the store. When sheriff's deputies arrived, the men were trying to load them onto their own trucks to be stored elsewhere. Ordinarily the equipment would be stored in the tire store until it could be fenced. The sheriff's department said they would be returning with search warrants for the houses in the neighborhood, where goods like these are often stored. Several merchants and residents said they were surprised that the tire store was a haven for stolen goods right in their midst.

CHAPTER 15

TREASON

Robert Lindsay's book *The Falcon and the Snowman* made famous a young spy named Christopher Boyce from Palo Verdes, California. His father was an FBI agent, and in high school, Chris always wanted to outdo others. In college he joined protestors and drug dealers, then dropped out and began working at TRW at twenty-one years of age.

At TRW he transmitted and received classified FBI information. His friend sold information to the KGB and persuaded Chris to do the same. When the friend was arrested, he turned in Chris. At twenty-four, Chris was sentenced to forty years in prison because the government said the information he'd sold was the most important since the trial of the Rosenbergs. It was information that the Russians already knew, but it told them what this country knew about them.

In January 1980, after only two years in prison, Chris escaped. He then became a bank robber, and by August 1981, he had allegedly robbed sixteen banks. In continuing to evade the law he has become a kind of folk hero, even though he committed treason against his country.

Being in the armed services, earning relatively low salaries, and having high security clearances makes it tempting for men to obtain important secret information to sell to whoever is this country's enemy. In 1989, an army warrant officer, James W. Hall III, was court-martialed for treason. Hall is said to have severely damaged electronic eavesdropping operations that the United States had aimed at the Soviet Union and Eastern Europe. This action occurred when Hall was on duty in Berlin as an enlisted man. The devastation caused in this army case was thought to be comparable to the navy's case of a Soviet spy ring led by navy warrant officer John Walker, Jr.

James Hall's investigation revealed that he not only passed on data about eavesdropping, but he also provided the Soviet Union with information about plans in case of a European war. During a six-year period, Hall received about $300,000 for the secrets he sold. He is now serving forty years in prison, but the army remains concerned about the vulnerability of some of its most secret technology, especially since it is managed by lower-paid personnel who can be more easily tempted to sell vital information.

In another army case, twenty-eight-year-old former sergeant Roderick Ramsay was arrested in June 1990 on charges of conspiracy to sell intelligence information to Czechoslovakia and Hungary. For $20,000, Ramsay is said to have given a retired army sergeant important material. Ramsay's duties, with a top secret clearance, was to safeguard all classified and military papers. In 1985, it is charged that he videotaped hundreds of papers and turned them over to a retired sergeant, Clyde Conrad, who reportedly sold information from 1975 to 1985 for about $1.2 million, which, according to the trial judge, "endangered the entire defense capability of the West." Though the information went to Czechoslovakia and Hungary, it is assumed that that was simply the route to the Soviet Union.

Twenty-one-year-old Airman Recruit James Wilmoth was sentenced in October 1989 to thirty-five years for trying to pass on classified information to a Soviet agent. He worked in the food service department of the aircraft carrier *Midway* and did not have a security clearance. Just what he was trying to pass or how he obtained it, the navy is not saying.

In another navy case, two radar operators were arrested in December 1989 on charges they were trying to commit espionage. They were allegedly caught with secret documents, but the documents were not passed on to Soviet agents. The two sailors were identified as Petty Officer 3rd Class Charles Edward Schoof, twenty, and Petty Officer 3rd Class John Joseph Haeger, nineteen. One of the men apparently tried to pass the information to a Soviet agent, had talked with the agent by telephone, but had not made it to Washington where they were to meet.

The only FBI agent ever convicted of espionage, Richard W. Miller, was given a twenty-year term for spying. Though sentenced to twenty years, he could be free soon because he becomes eligible for parole after serving one-third of his time. Miller had an affair with a Soviet spy, Svetlana Ogorodnikova, who lured Miller into giving her important information, and thereby betraying his country. Ogorodnikova is also in prison, serving an eighteen-year sentence. The prosecuting attorney had wanted a longer prison sentence for Miller, because, as he said, Miller was an agent entrusted with guarding against espionage.

The most recent case of treason against the United States involves a fifty-two-year-old CIA agent, Aldrich Ames, who had worked for the CIA for thirty-one years and who had sold information to the former Soviet Union for $2.5 million. Arrested in February 1994, he confessed to an eight-year spy operation in which he gave the Soviets the names of about a dozen of their men who were secretly working for the United States. All of those men were executed by the Soviets. Ames cooperated with U.S. officials in return for his wife's receiving no more than five years in prison for her part. Rosario Ames claimed she knew nothing of her husband's activities. Ames is serving a life sentence, and his wife was sentenced in October 1994 to five years.

While espionage cases are few, their severity is great. People who spy against their own country are despised. The man is left without a country, and his country is weakened by his actions to increase his own personal gain.

CHAPTER 16

CRIMES AGAINST CHILDREN

The Extent of the Crimes

Every year two million children are abused, either physically or sexually. That means one child is abused every two minutes. When they are adults, these victims are most often dysfunctional, putting huge burdens on taxpayers by their substance abuse and unemployment. Who are their abusers?

Physical Abuse

One of the most brutal abusers was Charles Rothenburg, who poured kerosene on the bed of his six-year-old son and lit the fluid as the boy lay sleeping in a motel room the father had rented for his visitation day. Then he phoned his ex-wife from a booth across the street. Later, confronted with the crime, he said he wanted to get even with his ex-wife, that he wanted to "shut Maria's mouth."

The boy was burned to the point that his bones were sticking out of his body. His mother wondered how he could ever recover. Over the past six years he has had 150 skin grafts at the University of California–Irvine burn center. The skin grafts do not expand as he grows, so consequently he is continually growing out of his skin and will need many more operations.

For this crime, Charles Rothenburg spent six years in prison. Though he says he loves his son and wants to see him, his son, now in his early teens, successfully appealed to his father's parole board to keep his father away from him. On parole, Rothenburg is required to wear an electronic device that notifies his parole board where he is at all times.

Many children do not survive the physical abuse inflicted by their parents. In New York, Lisa Steinberg, six, was beaten to death by the man who had illegally adopted her. Joel Steinberg said she had choked on vomit, but the prosecutor presented evidence of permanent brain damage. Though some jurors at first believed it was Hedda Nussbaum, Steinberg's live-in companion, who had beaten the child, medical experts convinced the jury that Nussbaum, who herself suffered repetitious beatings, was not capable of inflicting such a ferocious attack as to throw a forty-five-pound girl against a wall. Steinberg was convicted of first-degree manslaughter in January 1989.

Lisa had been beaten often, but as *Time* magazine reported in 1989, "her plight only once came to the attention of city officials. Neighbors and adults at school who noticed her bruises never reported their suspicions." Interfering in family quarrels or reporting suspicious family abuse flies in the face of what is considered the sacredness of the family.

In another beating case, Joshua de Shaney of Wisconsin is permanently paralyzed and retarded as a result of his father's continual abuse when Joshua was four years old. Though Joshua was hospitalized many times for severe injuries and was often observed by a county caseworker to have bruises, he was not removed from his divorced father's custody. This case went to the U.S. Supreme Court, where it was ruled in March 1989 that Winnebago County, Wisconsin, was not responsible for Joshua's paralysis or retardation. His father spent two years in prison, convicted of child abuse.

In Santa Rosa, California, Robert Mills, twenty-eight, was convicted of murdering his two-year-old stepdaughter in June 1989. The court said the 275-pound man had beaten the toddler, Kari Mills, during a period of several months. Testimony of witnesses described how Mills beat the youngster for minor infractions of his rules—for instance, if she looked up from her plate when eating or did not sit with her hands on top of her head for hours without making noise. The Sonoma County Child Protective Services took two weeks to investigate a doctor's report that Kari was probably being beaten. By the time they got around to the case, she was dead.

An attack on a four-year-old girl took place inside a movie theater on August 6, 1990. The father had brought his two girls to a movie, and when one girl went to get a drink of water, a man followed her and dragged her into the men's restroom where he hit her and tried to strangle her. When he was interrupted he ran out of the theater. Witnesses said that before the theater had opened, the man had been seen pacing back and forth outside and had watched other little girls. The following night a TV newscaster reported that a man had been arrested and charged with the attack. He was described as a parolee with two prior convictions on false imprisonment.

In June 1989, a seven-year-old rode his bicycle on the forest trails near his home in Tacoma, Washington, when a man joined him. Police believe that the man raped and stabbed the boy and then sexually mutilated him. Police arrested ex-convict Earl Shriner, thirty-nine, and charged him with assault and attempted murder. The accused had been charged and/or convicted of assaults on children since 1966, when he was accused of killing a fifteen-year-old classmate. For that crime he was sent to a home for the mentally ill until he was twenty-one. In 1977 he served a ten-year term for attacking two ten-year-old girls and in 1987 and 1988 he received minimal sentences for attacking two boys.

Because of this attack, citizens of Tacoma were outraged, not only by the record of the attacker, but because there had been so many attacks against children in Tacoma recently. FBI figures show that 2,000 attacks against children were reported there in 1988, 25 percent over the previous year.

In one case against the accused in the Tacoma attack, children decided not to testify against Shriner. As one mother explained, she could understand why children wouldn't go to court. One reason is that they are fearful of seeing their attacker again, and the other reason is that courts often do not believe children. When her son was abused, the mother said, he told his story in court and the judge indicated that one could not believe a nine-year-old.

In states that require teachers and others employed in child-care situations to report any evidence of child abuse to Child Protective Services, many employees say they have problems with this requirement. Often they become the targets of the adults upon whom they have cast suspicion. Also, they say, they are not trained to make judgments on whether a child has been abused. But in spite of the difficulties, in San Francisco alone, there were about 425 reports of child abuse each week in 1989 to the San Francisco Department of Social Welfare. Most reports, however, come from grandparents and neighbors.

Sexual Abuse

"At least 22 percent of Americans have been victims of child sexual abuse, although one-third of them told no one at the time." That was reported in the *Los Angeles Times*, August 1985. It is estimated that before they are eighteen years old, about eight million girls and five million boys are sexually abused. That means that one in four girls and one in eight boys are sexually abused before they are eighteen. The *Times* reported that sexual abuse among whites is about the same as among blacks. But a different statistic, from *The Black Women's Health Book*, is that black females nine to twelve years of age are more likely to be victims of sexual abuse than white females.

Who are the perpetrators of this crime against children? Most often they are members of the child's family, a mother's boyfriend, an uncle, an older brother, a friend of the family, a neighbor, or men who are in trusted guidance positions. Almost always, they are men.

Child sex offenders often refer to themselves as being virtually incorrigible. One, Larry McQuay, who writes from a Texas prison and was quoted in *The Washington Monthly*, projects a dismal prospect for rehabilitation. He says he will never change, that prison just keeps him well fed and gives him a place to sleep until he can get out and search for more children to molest. In prison he has child pornography and he can fantasize about the children he sees on TV. He believes the best thing for him would be castration, but no state permits it. He says he has inflicted terrible pain on his victims and, it seems, would wish he did not have the compulsion to continue. His parole date is June 1995.

SEXUAL ABUSE BY TEACHERS

A few male teachers use their position of influence to molest innocent children. In February 1989, Paul Wad Price admitted on a videotape played to a U.S. Senate panel that as a teacher he had been molesting young boys for fourteen years on the Cherokee Indian Reservation in North Carolina. Though administrators at the school were warned of Price's behavior, they took no action against him. His prison sentence was for ten years.

In Corona del Mar, a physical education teacher and track

coach at the private Harbor Day School—the father of two boys, one and nine years old—was arrested in 1987 for bringing fifth- and sixth-grade boys into a boys' club by showing pornographic material and then luring them into doing sexual acts with him and with each other. At the time of his arrest he had been employed about a year at the school.

Though evidence was collected against him, Alan Thomas Rigby denied his guilt and was sentenced to nineteen years in prison for molesting nineteen boys. During his May 1989 sentencing, the judge referred to Rigby's "cruelty, viciousness, and callousness." Rigby, however, referred to his acts as "locker-room frivolity." One father had written to the judge, "Once he had the children and the parents in his web of deception, he unleashed his sick scheme of games, clubs, secrets, and devices with the sole purpose of satisfying his sordid desires."

Evidence revealed that Rigby molested the boys on field trips and sometimes in their homes. In his home, pornographic materials were seized, including an issue of the *North American Man-Boy Lovers' Association* magazine. Rigby had been arrested two times previously for child molestation but was never convicted.

In another private school molestation case, a chess teacher, Randall Feliciano, forty, was arrested in May 1989, charged with molesting twelve boys in two schools. Unlike the charge against Rigby, who was accused of sodomizing some of the boys, in this case there was no skin-to-skin touching, and the acts never occurred in backrooms or in hidden areas. The police investigator said just because there was no skin-to-skin touching, "that does not lessen what was done." Like Rigby, Feliciano had been teaching in the schools for about a year. He was accused of molesting about forty boys.

After a thirteen-year-old girl became pregnant and the teacher's aide admitted having sex with her over a period of time at a middle school in Compton, California, the aide was sentenced to six years in prison on April 12, 1994. When allegations against the aide had been brought up from time to time before, he denied the accusations. Girls who had accused him were in turn accused of lying by school officials. The girl who became pregnant had been kicked and humiliated by other students before the aide admitted the abuse.

In another case, a thirty-five-year-old elementary school teacher, Keith Culhane, allegedly lured a seventeen-year-old into a motel, ostensibly to help her with her college work and, according to the charges against him, then raped her.

At the University of Maryland, the head of the nuclear engineering program, fifty-four-year-old Frank Munno, was indicted in January 1990 on charges that he sexually molested his daughter from the third grade on. The daughter said she made the charge to help others in her situation. Munno was charged with perverted sex practices, incest, and unlawful carnal knowledge.

SEXUAL ABUSE BY SCOUTMASTERS

Scout's Honor: Sexual Abuse in America's Most Trusted Institution, a book by Patrick Boyle, describes how scout troops offer great opportunities for pedophiles to exploit boys because they are away from home on camping trips and dependent on the leader. For instance, Carl Bittenbender was a convicted child molester who had been discharged from the navy and had been fired as a teacher because he molested children. But parents in the scout troop didn't know his history when he took over to lead their boys. He was eventually sent to prison.

After an ex-Boy Scout leader was indicted in the spring of 1989, six former Boy Scouts sued Steven Kabeary, thirty-five, for civil damages in Oakland, California. The abuse was said to have occurred in the leader's home, on boys ages ten to fourteen. Kabeary is serving eight years in prison. Also being sued are the Boy Scouts of America and the school district that hired Kabeary as a school assistant.

When another Boy Scout leader, thirty-two-year-old Charles

Lawrence, requested leave from prison in Napa, California, in May 1990, the request was denied. Lawrence is charged with molesting a friend's son in his Boy Scout troop, and in the process, using force.

In Berkeley, a seventy-year-old Boy Scout leader pleaded guilty on two counts of molesting a boy in his troop. As part of the plea bargain, the charges against him for molesting two other boys were dropped, and he was required to register as a sex offender.

In Galt, California, a small farming town in the Sacramento Valley, Allen Lee Trueman, another scoutmaster and Galt's 1988 Citizen of the Year, was sentenced to ten years in prison. He pleaded guilty to nine counts of molesting children.

In October 1990, a Boy Scout leader in Barstow, California, pleaded guilty to molesting fifteen boys in his troop. His guilty plea spared the community a difficult trial. Forty-three-year-old James Buxton was originally charged with thirty-two counts of committing lewd acts and three counts of sodomy on children under fourteen years of age. He faces forty-two years in prison.

A spokesman for the Boy Scouts said more incidents have been reported lately of abuse by scoutmasters. He said they have been encouraging boys to "yell and tell." A Berkeley police lieutenant said the best way to avoid problems of molestation in a Boy Scout troop is having a parent go on outings.

SEXUAL ABUSE BY PARENTS

When pictures of naked boys got processed in a photo shop in September 1989, the police in Redwood City, California, were alerted. They searched the home of the man who had sent the film for processing and found thousands of pornographic slides, at least 800 involving adolescent boys. The slides included the names of the boys and dated back to 1959. The man, an Austrian, was identified by photos that police took to the principal of the local high school. The man's step-son, after first denying everything, admitted his stepfather had molested him for about a year. His stepfather had been in this country about that long.

Another stepfather, this one in Ohio, was acquitted on a sexual abuse charge in May 1989. He explained that he only wanted to learn if his fourteen-year-old stepdaughter was a virgin, that he received "no sexual gratification" from molest-ing her.

Divorced fathers with visitation rights are sometimes accused of sexual abuse. Since this kind of abuse on very young children is difficult to prove, mothers who seek help or bring ex-husbands to court are told, as Karen Newson of Mis-sissippi was told by Judge Sebe Dale, Jr., that the trial "had shades of Old Salem,"—in other words, a witch hunt against husbands.

With more physical evidence that her daughter was being abused on visitation, Karen Newson refused to give visitation rights to her husband and she was jailed. She eventually gave in and told the court where her children were, and her ex-hus-band now has custody of her daughter and her son.

In another Mississippi case, Dorrie Singley's case came up in the same court of Judge Sebe Dale, Jr. He awarded custody of her daughter to Singley's ex-husband. When Dorrie Singley took her daughter, Chrissy, to Children's Hospital in New Orleans and acquired evidence that the little girl had been repeatedly molested, the judge would not allow a new trial. Singley fled with her daughter, but died later from a massive brain hemorrhage.

Helpful women arranged for the San Francisco Juvenile Court to gain jurisdiction over Chrissy, and Judge Dale in Mis-sissippi appeared willing to cooperate and open up the case for review. But once Chrissy was back in Mississippi, the case was closed and Judge Dale forbade anyone connected with the case to talk to anyone in California about the case. Singley's ex-husband was awarded custody of Chrissy. Chrissy's paternal grandfather made sworn statements that when he was living with his son, contrary to custody restrictions, his son had spent time alone with Chrissy and had, as the report in *Ms.* magazine said, "insisted on sleeping in the same bed."

In numerous cases, women, after divorce, bring charges of sexual abuse of their daughters against ex-husbands, and in numerous instances the courts continue fathers' visitation rights and sometimes give these fathers custody in spite of medical evidence of abuse. In Susan Howard's case, the appeals court ruled that her husband, who had previously been able to choose the visitation supervisor, could visit his daughter only with severely restricted supervision. Since that time he has seldom visited his daughter.

Other cases of women going to jail rather than reveal their daughters' whereabouts, or going into hiding with their daughters rather than allow what they claim are sexually abusive ex-husbands' visitation rights, include Janice Wilhie of California who has been in hiding for over two years, and Valerie Marcus of Ohio, who went to jail.

In cases like these, of sexual abuse and of violence against women, "there's an underlying presupposition that a man has a 'right' to his wife and children," says Lucy Berliner, director of research at Harborview Sexual Assault Center in Seattle, in *Ms.* magazine. This idea comes down through history through early Judaic practices that gave fathers life and death power over their children. In addition, all property belonged to men until recent times, and this property included women and their children.

SEXUAL ABUSE BY OTHERS

In September 1989 a millionaire from Stockton, California, real estate developer Eckhard Schmitz, forty-four, was seized in Germany, where he had fled to escape prison for child molestation. Because he was so popular in Stockton, all the superior court judges disqualified themselves to hear his case. An out-of-town judge sentenced him to thirteen years in prison on nine molestation charges, but the sentence was suspended. He was allowed a work-furlough, spending nights and weekends in the county jail. When he was caught violating his parole by visiting two fifteen-year-old boys, he posted all his assets so that he would not leave the country. But then he did leave, after he learned that a thirteen-year-old had gone to the police accusing him of paying him for sex. In skipping bail he forefeited his more than $8 million fortune, his home, and other valuables.

One prominent businessman in San Francisco was indicted on twenty-one counts in August 1989 for soliciting sex with underage female prostitutes—girls as young as thirteen. According to the indictment, sixty-three-year-old Donald Werby, owner of numerous hotels and properties in the San Francisco Bay Area, allegedly gave the girls drugs in exchange for sex, between 1984 and 1987. A month after his indictment, Werby was arrested again on the charge that he attempted to bribe a teenage witness. A prepared statement by the district attorney stated, "It is alleged that Donald Werby promised he would support the witness and her unborn baby for the rest of their lives, if she would change her story from that testified to before the grand jury."

Sentenced to eighteen years in prison, thirty-three-year-old Joseph Mosqueda infected his seven- and three-year-old stepdaughters with the venereal disease chlamydia. Three other children, an eight-year-old niece, a seven-year-old neighbor, and another seven-year-old girl were molested but not exposed to the venereal disease. Mosqueda had never had a criminal record before.

COMMENTS

A *Ms.* article "Custody Wars: Moms Held Hostage" reports that sexual abuse by men has historically been blamed on women because, it was alleged, wives were neglectful or frigid, which made it necessary for husbands to use other members of the family for sex.

Richard Gardner of Columbia University claims that women are manipulative and that they "brainwash" their children. Arthur Green, psychologist, claims that 50 percent of sexual abuse charges are false allegations, with wives wanting to get even with ex-husbands. The Association of Family and Conciliation Courts claims that 50 percent is not accurate, that false allegations amount to probably no more than 14 percent.

Several groups have formed on both sides of the controversy. VOCAL is an organization to protect parents who are Victims of Child Abuse Laws, which was set up mostly to help accused fathers. In response to that group, Mothers Against Raping Children, MARC, was organized to help those who make charges. MARC helps to hide children they feel are in danger. For many judges it is easier to believe that the children lie, says attorney Garnett Harrison in *Ms.*, "than that fathers would do these unspeakable acts."

LEGISLATION

For years sexual abuse was to be endured and tolerated because children and/or mothers were not believed, or if they were, they were told to keep quiet for fear of destroying the family. For the child there was no one to turn to.

California legislation passed in September 1989 now allows allegations to be brought against an accuser even if the child cannot remember the exact dates or places where the abuse occurred. This legislation was the result of an acquittal of an accused county supervisor who was charged by his daughter of sexual abuse over the years but could not remember the dates of the molestations. This bill is designed to protect children under fourteen. It is aimed at those adults who live in the same house for at least three months and have access to the child over that time.

In Connecticut, the state supreme court ruled that only a "fair preponderance of evidence," against a parent need be presented. The state of Washington is the first to allow hearsay evidence of what a child has said to another person about abuse, so the child does not have to face the accused.

In the state of Virginia, a camp has been set up for abused children. Most of the children feel valueless because, as they say, if they had been worthy they wouldn't have been treated as trash. The camp was the subject of a TV documentary, *A Bridge for the Children*.

The great problem in parental sexual abuse is that these cases stun those who would prefer to see the family as the primary protector of children. Allegations of such abuse fly in the face of "sacred family values." Yet protecting the individual child is more important than protecting an illusion about families.

LONG-TERM EFFECTS OF CHILD ABUSE

Young children abused over a period of time lose interest in exploring their environment, according to child psychologist Byron Egeland of the University of Minnesota. At age one, children not neglected score about 120 on what is known as a Bayle scale. For those who were neglected, the scores were about 80 when they were two years old. The study, reported in the February 17, 1991, *Los Angeles Times*, included about two dozen children who had been abused in their early school years. Since being in a low-income group is known to make abuse more likely, that variable was separated out. Egeland's conclusions were that those who were abused were more likely to be held back in school, to achieve less, to be unable to follow directions or work by themselves. They also feel helpless, not accepted by their peers, and, especially for the boys, were prone to act out aggression.

Other studies, like those of Roy Herronkohl of Lehigh University and Cata Spatz Widom of the State University of New

York, agreed with Egeland in that the more severe the punishment in childhood, the more dysfunctional that person became in adulthood. All three researchers agreed that childhood abuse results in lowered intelligence and lowered reading scores, that the abused are more likely to be addicted to alcohol or drugs, to be depressed, to be unemployed, and to be arrested as children and also as adults.

Two long-held beliefs were put to rest by studies that proved that temperamental children are not more likely to be abused than others, and that girls who are abused do not necessarily turn to prostitution.

Long-term childhood sexual abuse of a man who rose to the position of president of American University eventually resulted in his professional downfall. Dr. Richard Berendzen confessed on Ted Koppel's "Nightline" that he had been making obscene phone calls and that his behavior was the result of having been sexually abused when he was a child. He made the confession in the hope that other children who were being sexually abused would try to get help for themselves. He resigned his prestigious position after the investigation led to his admission of guilt.

SEXUAL ABUSE AND MURDER

There are times when the sexual abuser, fearful of being identified, murders his small victim. Such was the fate of thirteen-year-old Jennifer Moore, April 1989, in Novato, California. Jennifer went to the store a few blocks from her home for an ice-cream cone. She was a pleasant, popular eighth-grader. She never returned home.

At first the town paid little attention to the news of a missing child. That news could not compete with the horrendous news from nearby Boyes Hot Springs and Cotati where Ramon Salcido had, the day after Jennifer disappeared, left a trail of dead bodies. But gradually the townspeople in Novato realized that Jennifer's disappearance was not the act of an unhappy teenager staying away from home a few days. Maybe, they thought, she had been kidnapped.

Her mother appeared on TV and, just in case she had run away, begged Jennifer to come home. And in case she was kidnapped, she begged the kidnapper to return her daughter. Other parents with missing children came from the Bay Area to give support to Jennifer's mother. They helped the community print up flyers showing Jennifer's full, innocent smile with braces.

So many people helped—Jennifer's schoolmates, teachers, neighbors, and strangers, including a deacon from the Bethel Baptist Church named Scott Williams, a twenty-nine-year-old man who put up a missing person poster at the Chevron Food Mart that he managed. Williams was also a groundskeeper at the church in Novato, where he taught Sunday school.

Dumped in a ravine and inside a garbage bag, Jennifer's nude body was found only two miles from her home four days after she disappeared. Books from the Bethel Baptist Church were found in the discarded garbage bag. The church books led police to discover Jennifer's blood on a rug in the church reading room. Scott Williams was arrested for her murder.

After being advised of his rights, Williams confessed that he had lured Jennifer into the church library, raped her, then strangled her and bludgeoned her on the head with a baseball bat to prevent her from identifying him. He steadfastly maintained that he was not under the influence of drugs or alcohol. Williams was a mild-mannered, respected man in Novato. His wife, Heather, who washed his pants that evening when he returned home, went into hiding. Williams had one prior arrest, for the possession of a billy club, but was not convicted.

According to the defense attorney, Williams was addicted to pornography. In the months before Jennifer's murder he had spent several hundred dollars on "969" telephone calls. In a plea bargain, he received a life sentence without possibility of parole. He could have received the death penalty because his crime included sexual assault. After the sentencing, Jennifer's grandmother told the court, "To lose your only child or grandchild is to lose your future. For the rest of our lives we will be deprived of the opportunity to love Jennifer, to hug her, to enjoy her company on visits and trips, to watch her mature, learn, marry, and have her own children. . . . If there is a God, he is cruel and capricious and I want nothing to do with him and certainly nothing to do with any church. A God who permits a child to be raped and murdered in a church by a deacon exhibits a strange kind of irony.

"She was treated as garbage. Shoved in a garbage bag and dumped in a gully."

Just one month earlier, another girl, nine-year-old Nadia Puente, had been abducted, raped, murdered, and then thrown in a garbage dumpster in Santa Ana, California. On her way home from school she was approached by a man in his early thirties, driving a small gray sedan. Nadia got in the car, school friends said, and the man drove away. Eleven hours later a transient searching for recyclable cans found her body.

Eight-year-old Eileen Franklin, whose father took her and her eight-year-old friend Susan Nasson for a ride in his van in 1969, repressed the knowledge of the molestation and murder of her friend until twenty years later, when she was an adult with a daughter of her own. Susan Nasson's skeletal remains had been found, dumped in a ravine near a reservoir three months after she disappeared.

Eileen Franklin, whose name is now Franklin-Lipsker, told the court that she remembered her father molesting Susan in the back of the van, then using a big rock to smash her head. She said that when she tried to help her friend, her father stopped her. He told her he would kill her if she ever told anyone what had happened. The memory of this event apparently faded and lodged in her subconscious for twenty years until one day she looked into the eyes of her own child and began to remember. Under hypnosis, she was able eventually to reconstruct the action and went to the police.

Her father, fifty-one-year-old George Franklin, Sr., a former firefighter for the city of San Mateo, California, and later a real estate investor, was arrested and brought to trial. While there was considerable effort on the part of the defense to discredit Franklin-Lipsker's testimony, there was enough evidence to convince the jury that what she told the court had happened. Her description of her friend's crushed ring, which had been stored in the sheriff's department's evidence room for over twenty years, was important to the case.

The investigator at the time of Susan's disappearance says, in retrospect, that he should have interviewed each child in the neighborhood. That might have caused Eileen to break down and tell what happened to her friend. At that time, family members, friends, and neighbors were not as likely to be suspected, as they are today. Since that time it has been learned that most abused and murdered children know their attackers.

A probation report presented at George Franklin's sentencing portrayed him as a man who brutalized and sexually abused children, including his own. At one time he held a gun to his ex-wife's head. In January 1992, he was sentenced to life in prison but will be eligible for parole in seven years. He escaped the death penalty because capital punishment at the time of the murder was considered unconstitutional.

Eileen Franklin-Lipsker's testimony was attacked, not only on the grounds that it was from repressed memory, but because, as defense lawyers said, she was motivated by lucrative book contracts for her story. She countered that accusation by revealing that she had received $60,000, of which $55,000 went to charities for homeless children and teenage prostitutes and $5,000 for attorneys' fees.

A few of the other children who were sexually abused and then murdered include six-year-old Jeremy Stoner, found four days after he disappeared in February 1987. He had been molested and then strangled. Five-year-old Angela Bugay was taken from her front steps and raped and murdered in Antioch, California. Five-year-old Adam Walsh was abducted and murdered. His plight became a TV story that spurred national legislation to help find missing children.

When an eight-year-old girl's body was found in November 1993 in the closet of Hooman Ashkan Panah of Woodland Hills, California, he was charged with kidnapping, sexual assault, and murder. Special circumstances, which include murder plus sexual assault, make Panah eligible for the death penalty. His attorney claims Panah is retarded.

The Polly Klaas kidnapping and murder, October 1, 1993, in the peaceful Northern California town of Petaluma, shocked the nation because the twelve-year-old was taken from her bedroom where she was having a slumber party with two girl-friends. The fear of crime escalated. How could anyone be safe, even in their own homes? The man who had abducted Polly with a knife, Richard Allen Davis, thirty-nine, is charged with the crime. He allegedly entered the bedroom and took Polly while the other terrified girls watched. Polly's mother and another sibling were asleep in a nearby room. Davis, who has a criminal record going back twelve years, was paroled shortly before Polly's disappearance. Polly's badly decomposed body was found two months later.

Child Abduction

There is nothing worse for parents than not to know where their kidnapped children are, not to know if they are all right, not to know if they are even alive. How many parents live with this kind of twenty-four-hour nightmare? Just think of the fear the child feels as she is being stolen from her front porch, or even from the security of her own bedroom! And the horrible terror as she is abused or, if not killed, later required to perform sexual acts with other children or adults in front of a camera for a pedophile who will make money off of his abominable cruelty. What of the audacity of these men who steal children from their parents, inflicting deep, lifelong suffering, not only on the children, if they are kept alive, but also on their parents, grandparents, brothers, sisters, and other loving relatives.

The National Crime Information Center does not know how many missing children there are, but it estimates about 28,000. Many states have records on how many cars are stolen each year, but not on how many children are stolen. Most children are abducted by members of their own families, usually in custody fights, but those abducted by strangers are in life-threatening situations. After the passage of the Missing Children's Assistance Act of 1984, there is now a National Center for Missing and Exploited Children.

As of May 1989, there were thirty-one California children missing. It is possible that about 1,000 children a year in California are abducted, abused, and released before reports are made or posters can be printed. Therefore these abductions are not included in statistics. This was true for a six-year-old in LaVerne, California, in November 1989, who was grabbed in front of her home, where she was playing with her two brothers, ages nine and ten. She was grabbed from behind by a man who covered her mouth and carried her to a truck nearby. He drove for three blocks, molested her, and then released her. She described her attacker as a white male about thirty years old.

The list of those who are missing in California include Michaela Garecht, then age nine, who was kidnapped when she went with her friend on their scooters to get a soda two blocks away. When they came out of the store, one scooter had been moved to a position near a van. When Michaela went to get it, a man grabbed her, threw her in the van, and drove off. Her friend ran into the store, yelling for help. Police were called, and since that day, November 19, 1988, millions of flyers have been sent across the country. The FBI, volunteers, and police have worked tirelessly. Though they have a good description of the van and the kidnapper, and have offered money as a reward for the kidnapper's arrest, as of this writing there are no leads.

As with the efforts made for recovering Michaela, there also have been massive efforts made to recover the following missing children. As of this writing, they are still missing.

- Ilene Misheloff was abducted after school in Dublin, California, in May 1989.
- Amber Swartz-Garcia was eight when she was playing in her yard and abducted.
- Three-year-old Clark Honda was kidnapped from his Fairfield, California home, August 1984.
- Mitchell Owens, four years old, was taken by the man who raped his mother in February 1983, from their Menlo Park, California, home.
- Kevin Collins was ten when he was kidnapped from a San Francisco street corner in 1984.
- Michael Masgoay, sixteen, has been missing since January 1989 from San Francisco.

It is estimated that in the past four years more than 500 children have disappeared in the United States. One hundred have been found dead, and the rest are missing. Ninety percent of missing juveniles are runaways, but the news of the other 10 percent galvanizes a community into action and strikes fear into every parent's heart. David Collins, father of missing Kevin Collins, said, "It's an easy crime, kidnapping children."

Other parents have advised that the best thing parents can do is to let their children know in every way that they are loved. In case of abduction, this assurance of parental love fortifies the children against brainwashing by a kidnapper. In any event, in the homes of missing children there is always someone there to answer the phone in case the child can get to a telephone and call home.

Missing children cases are difficult to solve. Kidnapping for money is easier to solve. But abductions that are not for money, according to Bill Grijalva, an officer with the Oakland Police Department who specializes in cases dealing with child pornography and pedophiles, would most likely be cases of sexual perversion. For that reason he keeps pictures of the missing children on his desk, because occasionally pictures of missing children come to his attention as subjects of pornographic photography. If missing children are alive, he would probably say they are in the hands of a pedophile, a person who sexually abuses and/or exploits children. That would be a mixed blessing for the child and parents, but if true, the child would be alive and might at some time in the future be reunited with the parents.

Who are these pedophiles who are harboring these missing children? A Hayward, California, police officer suggests that someone knows. Steven Stayner, a boy who had been kidnapped for seven years, told police that several people he knew during that time either knew he was a kidnap victim or suspected it but didn't do anything about it. There is the hope, then, that someone who knows will do something about these and other missing children across the country.

Pedophiles

Kidnapping of children, which used to be primarily for ransom, is now more likely to be for sexual exploitation. The child is used either for gratification of the kidnapper or for pornographic photographers who sell these pictures around the world. Investigators carefully study the profiles of men who have kidnapped children and held them against their will until rescued. Investigators have learned that child molesters or pedophiles operate a lot like con artists. They almost always work alone, and they use various schemes to win over their victims. They bring the child toys and they get their favorite food for them. They often tell the child their parents don't want them, don't love them, or can't afford to raise them. In public, the pedophile is meek and mild, rather pathetic. Many were abused as children and when asked about their crime they say they couldn't help it.

When Steven Stayner was kidnapped at age seven from his Fremont, California, home by Kenneth Parnell and taken to Oregon, where he was held for seven years until he escaped, he was told that his parents had given Parnell legal custody. Parnell even faked phone calls to Steven's parents, relaying the information to Steven that they didn't want him. Steven was used regularly for Parnell's sexual pleasure. Seven years later, when Parnell kidnapped another boy, five-year-old Timmy White, Steven did not want the little boy to go through what he had. Secretly, Timmy asked Steven to take him home to his mother and father. When Steven could make his escape he took the boy into town to the police department where he, then, was also identified. He said he never tried to get away before because he believed what Parnell had told him. Parnell was tried and sent to prison for three years. He is now out of prison and registered as a sex offender.

Pedophiles make the children feel guilty about the sex they are having with their captors. They tell their victims if they don't do what is wanted they will show the sexually explicit photographs they have to their parents, which would make the parents hate their children. This assists in keeping the children from running away, because the children are ashamed of what they have done. Some organizations that were created specifically for the exploitation of children include the Rene Guyon Society—with a motto, "Sex before eight or it's too late"—and NAMBLA (North American Man-Boy Love Association).

Tara Burke was abducted from her parents' car when she was two and a half years old. She was found about a year later, nude, in the van of the two men who had kidnapped her. They were teaching Tara about sex. When she was found she did not know how to speak, but she did offer sex.

Like Timmy White and Steven Stayner, Tara Burke was rescued because another child was brought into the group. Mac Lin was able to escape and bring police back to the van. One of her kidnappers, Tree Frog Johnson, was sentenced to 464 years in prison; the other, Alex Cabarga, was sentenced to 208 years.

Candi Talarico, kidnapped in June 1988, was rescued after forty-five days when her abductor was caught as he was trying to kidnap another girl. Her kidnapper, a deaf mute, had imprisoned her under the church where he worked as a janitor. All the time the parish was praying for Candi's safety, she was actually hidden away under the church floor, where her abductor had been sexually molesting her.

Pornography

This chapter concerns crimes against children. But it is difficult to separate information about child pornography and information about adult pornography. This section will therefore include both.

The Supreme Court's test for defining obscenity is whether an average person, using the standards set by the community, would consider that the work, whether it be art, music, acting, or any entertainment, appeals to the prurient interest of the listener or viewer. Difficult as this may seem, one U.S. Supreme Court Justice said, "I know it when I see it."

Pornography is classified as hard-core penetration, depicting women and children in forced sex or sadistic bondage; soft-core titillation, depicting sexual consent from women and children; and child porn that is used in both soft- and hard-core porn, that is, children in forced sex pictures and also in pictures with other children consenting to have sex with an adult. Soft-core porn also depicts children engaged in consensual sexual acts with other children. The Greek definition of pornography is the graphic depiction of sexual slaves or prostitutes.

But who are the people who own industries engaged in these activities? As reported in the *Los Angeles Times* of February 17, 1991, it is men like Mark Curtis, who has reduced the price of X-rated videocassettes from $100 to $5. Arrested on charges of tax evasion, Mark Curtis was said to have an annual income from pornography of well over the $2.96 million that he reported to the government. Most hard-core pornography is manufactured in downtown Los Angeles and the San Fernando Valley. Though women perform in hard-core porn, they are not known to have a financial interest in the companies producing the material.

Another major player in the porn business is sixty-six-year-old Reuben Sturman, who ran 300 companies, controlling bookstores across the country and in foreign countries, and owned theaters, video companies, and distributors of porn magazines. He owned one company that made sex toys and another that made peep machines and is said to have built the pornography industry into a multibillion-dollar international business.

The Mafia has long been considered a major player in the pornography business, though how much they are involved is impossible to determine.

In her book *Child Pornography and Sex Rings*, Dr. Ann Burgess says pornography is used to induce children to engage in the sex acts they see pictured. Syndicated pedophile rings use hundreds of thousands of children in this country, photographing them in various sex acts with other children or with adults. The photographs are then sold to pedophiles or others in a market estimated to be about $5 million a month. Pornography employs about 165,000 people and is a $10 billion industry annually.

In March 1988, the U.S. Customs Service put into practice Operation Borderline in an effort to stem the tide of child pornography coming into this country. It was this operation that caught twenty-seven-year-old Michael Bardy, a scoutmaster dressed in his scout uniform, when a package of pornographic pictures arrived. When the officers searched his apartment in Springfield, Illinois, they found pictures of Boy Scouts in their underwear and hundreds of child pornography magazines. Arresting the many men buying pornographic material has led to the arrest of at least twenty-four child molesters in Operation Borderline.

In another sting operation, law enforcement agents printed and mailed child-porn postcards to a list of suspected child-porn buyers they had been unable to arrest. These pictures had an order coupon for the receiver to send for more such pictures. When orders were received by the agents, who had set up a fictitious company, the recipients were arrested. It is illegal to purchase child-pornography, but, in most states, possession is not illegal.

Following up on each man who had bought the pictures, the agents were able to learn if the men had jobs where they were in contact with children or if they had records as sex offenders. David McNutt of Conneaut, Ohio, had purchased pictures in June 1987. When the agents went to his home they found his three-year-old daughter and two-year-old son locked in their filthy rooms. McNutt admitted to having had sex with his children from their infancy. Locked in their rooms, the children could come out for food or for his sexual pleasures. David McNutt was convicted of child rape and sentenced to ten to twenty-five years. His wife says she knew what was going on but couldn't say anything for fear he would beat her. She is charged with child endangerment.

In a most extreme child-porn venture, three San Jose undercover police broke up a plot to kidnap a young boy. The plan was to videotape him in pornographic acts, hold him as a prisoner for a week, and then videotape his murder. The undercover police officers were contacted by thirty-four-year-old

Dean Lambey from Richmond, Virginia, who told the officers he was interested in finding a white boy not quite in his teens, for sexual interest. Lambey then brought his partner, thirty-four-year-old Daniel Depew of Alexandria, Virginia, to a meeting with the undercover officers for the purchase of a young boy. The purpose of the pornographic scheme was to sell the so-called snuff video to pedophiles and other buyers of child porn. Before the men were actually arrested, over 100 FBI agents had been involved in the case.

The FBI and the Canadian Justice Ministry conducted a study of men who had been convicted of sex-related crimes, such as rape, child molestation, murder, and incest, and learned that often the men used pornography to stimulate themselves before committing their crime.

Dr. William Marshall, a psychologist at Queens University in Toronto, interviewed rapists at the penitentiary at Kingston and learned that over 19 percent used hard-core pornography and 38 percent used soft-core immediately before committing their crimes.

Dr. John Zillan of Indiana University, in his studies of pornography, reported that exposure to violent pornography appeared to desensitize the viewers and caused them to be insensitive to victims.

Neil Malamuth, professor of psychology at the University of California, Los Angeles, studied viewers' attitudes after they had seen sexual images. He learned that the men who were exposed to images of sexual violence were "more accepting of violence against women."

"Dial-a-porn" amounts to a $2 billion business. Who's listening? Unless parents exercise strict control over the telephone, their children have easy access to sexually explicit suggestions simply by dialing the number.

Mark Curtis, whose name comes up in any conversation about video pornographers, is referred to in the February 17, 1991, *Los Angeles Times* article "Into the Valley of Sleaze" by

John Johnson. When Curtis is asked about the performers he hires, he answers, "My mother used to tell me, 'All women are whores and sluts.' And she was right."

Almost all pornography has some violence in it, in that it is a male subjugating or dominating a female. Pornography teaches that violence is necessary for sexual arousal and more violence is necessary for continual arousal. The people in pornographic pictures are not all acting. In these pictures there are women and children who are gagged, bound, whipped, raped, and mutilated, all for the sake of selling pictures of them in these conditions. Annie Laurie Gaylor, as quoted in *The Humanist* (August 1985), tells the extent of pornography in this country:

> Pornography is probably the largest entertainment industry in America. It is larger than both Hollywood and the record industries combined. It is raking in seven billion dollars a year. Six of the ten best-selling monthly magazines on the market are what is called "male entertainment." Some of them are what we consider more soft-core. But it gives an indication of the kind of money that is being made by pornography. The combined circulation of *Playboy* and *Penthouse* is greater than that of *Time* and *Newsweek*. We all know that in any metropolitan area there are at least two or three or four or five twenty-four-hour-a-day bookstores. They have to be open twenty-four hours a day. The only other things we need open twenty-four hours a day are grocery stores. That's how big the business is. There are four times as many sex emporiums as there are McDonald's franchises in this country.
>
> So we are talking about a huge commercial industry in which money is being made by the sale of women, the sale of women's bodies, or the sale of images of women for the profit of men, for the entertainment of men, at the expense of women. It is probably the most pervasive image of women that we have in this society.

It is also probably the most pervasive image of children. There are two hundred fifty kiddy-porn magazines now available despite a Supreme Court decision that was unfavorable to the production and use of child pornography. The FBI estimated in 1977 that 1.2 million children a year are involved in commercial sex, which includes both prostitution and pornography. The two tend to go hand in hand. . . . The major themes in pornography are . . . domination . . . torture . . . slavery . . . and the enjoyment by women of being raped. Nobody enjoys being hurt. But pornography tells us over and over again that women do enjoy being hurt.

The child pornography law signed by President Bush in November 1990 will not become law because several groups have convinced the U.S. District Court that the law may be unconstitutional, denying First Amendment rights to artists. The law requires that anyone distributing videos, films, or photos depicting nudity or sexual activity must keep records of the names, addresses, and ages of models. It also requires that the book, film, or video contain the name of the person who maintains the names of the models. Failure to keep records is a felony. The law refers to "actual" sexual activity, but the argument is that it is difficult to know from a film which is actual sex and which is faked. Those who sponsored the bill are disappointed because they felt it was a way to curb at least some child pornography.

Is it any wonder that women and children are sexual victims?

Failure to Pay Child Support

For a child, the failure of his or her father to meet a financial obligation is one thing, but usually that also means the father does not see his child. Nearly half of all children between eleven and sixteen living with their mothers had not seen their fathers in the past year, according to a *Newsweek* article of December 18, 1988. The child is left without an important support, emotionally as well as financially.

Abandoned women with children whose husbands pay no child support often become welfare recipients, dependent on others, until, and if, they can become self- and child-supporting. A federal report based on U.S. Census figures states that fewer men are paying child support. Of the 4.4 million mothers who should be receiving court-ordered child support, only half received what was ordered, 25 percent received a part of what was ordered, and the other 25 percent received none at all. Of the 5.6 million children under fifteen who live in homes without fathers, only one-third receive financial support from their fathers.

Because a father can usually escape child support payments by moving to another state, Washington committees are exploring elimination of the state boundary escape route. If nonpayment of child support becomes a federal crime instead of a state crime, as it is now, wherever the father lives in this country he will still be liable for supporting his children. Nonpayment of child support affects a child's education, health, and self-esteem.

In a divorce or separation, it is usually the major wage earner who moves out of the house. In a study of divorced women, sociologist Lenore Weitzman of California learned that a year after a divorce the women and children suffer a 27 percent drop in their standard of living while the father's standard of living rises on average 42 percent.

Not all nonpayers are men. Many women are obligated for child support, and many do not pay. But the total number of defaulting women is miniscule, because in cases of separation, children are almost always placed in the custody of their mothers. In divorces where there is joint custody there is a higher percentage of parents who pay support.

WHY FATHERS DON'T PAY

If there is little conflict in the relationship between the mother and father, the chances are better that fathers will make their support payments. But hostile postmarriage relationships decrease the chances for child support. The fathers then become known as "deadbeat dads" who may skip town, hide assets, or quit work to avoid payments. Holding back on money may give an ex-husband a sense of power over someone who has rejected him. Often, too, ex-husbands do not think of support money as that which is supporting his children. They often think of it as money being given to ex-wives, whom they see using it for their own desires.

The reason most often cited for withholding child support payments is because the mother has denied the father visitation rights. When the father then quits payment, she further refuses him his visitation rights. This all leads to a no-win situation for all parties and can be especially harmful to children, who then seldom see their fathers.

Another reason for nonpayment of child support is the remarriage of the father, when his expenses are likely increased. He supports another home, may have additional children, and his loyalties may change.

When fathers don't pay child support, the taxpayer takes on this responsibility. More than half of the parents not receiving child support in Napa County, California, were on welfare in 1989. That means that 2,800 families in one small county were supported by the county taxpayers. The cost of processing claims for welfare payments, before any money is actually paid out, is high. This involves paying social workers, attorneys, and local court expenses. Society pays not only the money that the father should pay for support, but it also pays for the collection of support money.

GETTING MEN TO PAY CHILD SUPPORT

In the past it was not of much concern to governmental agencies that fathers did not pay child support. But since 1975, when it was evident that tax-supported agencies needed to support women and children when fathers could not or did not pay, several support systems were created. The all-encompassing federal Child Support Enforcement Amendments Act of 1984 gives agencies the right to garnish wages from a parent thirty days late in child-support payments, to collect from state income tax refunds for late payments, and to put liens on property owned by nonpaying parents.

Census figures revealed that in 1985 $11 billion was owed in child support but only $4 billion was paid. Taxpayers and others either picked up the slack, or the mother and children slid into poverty. In Los Angeles County there are 300,000 active cases where the county is trying to help mothers collect child support. According to the chief deputy district attorney, the county receives 6,000 new cases a month. Los Angeles County was considering contracting for outside help to try to locate deadbeat dads.

In Ventura County, California, there is an annual roundup of deadbeat dads, who are put in jail on Father's Day. In June 1989, twenty-three men were jailed, one who owed $44,000 in back child-support payments. Most, however, owed about $6,000 and were at least three months late in their payments.

In the state of Maine, as of June 27, 1994, deadbeat dads will be required to forfeit their driver's licenses should they not pay their child support. One man quickly paid the $140,000 he owed to preserve his driving privileges.

In California, the governor signed a bill in July 1991 that could prohibit anyone who is delinquent in child support payments from getting a driver's license or registering a vehicle. It also would require the suspension of professional licenses from licensed professionals who are delinquent in child-support payments. Unpaid child-support payments amount to about $2 billion a year in California. Enforcing this new law will require considerable taxpayer money.

One can only guess what the impact is on the children whose fathers do not support them. It is bound to be harmful. As Congresswoman Marge Roukema, the primary sponsor of the Child Enforcement Support Act, says, "Child support is not a voluntary commitment, but a legal as well as a moral obligation."

Out-of-Wedlock Children

The *San Francisco Chronicle* of June 22, 1989, reported that of unmarried women under thirty who gave birth in San Francisco County in 1988, 28 percent were black, 30 percent were white, and 42 percent were Hispanic. The reason given for men not wanting to marry and start families is that there are not enough jobs, and those there are don't pay enough for a man to raise children. The women raise the children without child support from the fathers. But the women are not getting pregnant by themselves. These men are having families; they're just not supporting them.

CONCLUSION

Not all men are criminals, but almost all criminals are men. By a ratio of 94 to 6, men outnumber women in prison, a fact that raises the question of why crime is a masculine statement.

Male Susceptibility to Crime

"Boys will be boys!"

This excuse for male crime—that males will do what males must do—might be an explanation for childish mischief, but not for murder or other serious crimes.

REWARDS AND PUNISHMENTS

In crime, the rewards for boys are great and the punishments are weak. Boys are programmed to win, even at robbery. Scaling a two-story home to steal rubies from a bedroom safe while the occupants are eating dinner downstairs creates excitement for a boy. The action is considered courageous, and if he succeeds, he wins more than the jewels. He wins self-esteem for himself and praise from his friends. The girl, on the other hand, is not programmed for daring adventure. She is programmed to be good. She wins by being considerate, by doing favors for the family members, and by making herself attractive.

Crime is action, and boys learn to crave action because that is what men do in the schoolbooks they read and it is what men do in TV and movies. Avoiding the police in an auto chase would be stimulating and thrilling to a boy but would frighten a girl. A girl in the car would beg her boyfriend to pull over—to give up. But for boys, giving up is shameful, disgraceful. When little boys pile on top of each other, wrestling, one constantly asks the other, "You give? You give?" The victor puffs himself up with one more conquest. Life is for winning. This is foreign territory to a girl.

But what happens to the concept of right and wrong? Does the fledgling criminal know that it is wrong to steal the rubies? Of course he does, and knowing that it is wrong and knowing he is breaking the law is part of the excitement. It is the opportunity to get away with something, to get the better of someone. Will his conscience bother him if he succeeds in his burglary? Probably not, because the rewards for success are greater than the punishment for failure. If he is caught, his family might be embarrassed and he may go to a juvenile detention facility for a short period of time. There he will also have free room and board, TV entertainment, physical exercise equipment, and he can continue his academic education as he refines his criminal skills learning from his fellow inmates.

James Q. Wilson, author of *Crime and Human Nature*, says, "Criminality requires that a person with certain personality traits be in an environment in which crime appears to be rewarding." Males have certain personality traits different from those of females, which make males more susceptible to crime. Even when both males and females live or work in the same environment, as in poverty areas, crime appears to be more appealing and/or rewarding to males than to females, according to Wilson. It is the expectation of rewards or the desire to avoid punishments that drive us in our actions.

Lawrence Kohlberg, in his stages of moral development, refers to three levels of moral development, with their concurrent rewards and punishments. From childhood to early puberty, actions are based on a desire not to be punished and to satisfy personal needs. At this level the little boy is seldom punished for his rambunctiousness but the little girl is scolded if she gets too boisterous. The girl is rewarded for pleasing others, especially Daddy, and so she continues to do so. The little girl is rewarded for being nice; the boy is rewarded for being brave.

In Kohlberg's second level of moral development, adolescence to adulthood, both boys and girls feel rewarded if they are approved by their peers. In this level there is peer pressure to wear certain clothes, to get into specific groups, to speak and act in a certain style. At this level there is more peer pressure on boys than on girls to be aggressive, not to back down, to excel in physical sports. Girls continue to try to please, though this now includes the desire to please boyfriends. The girls laugh when the boys expect it, listen to the boys attentively, cheer them on from the sidelines to win at sports, and, in a sense, are co-dependents in man's addiction to being superior. Girls depend on a male who is a winner, in control, self-sufficient, and physically strong. Boys depend on girls to approve of their being that way.

The third level of Kohlberg's theory of moral development occurs in adulthood and involves an adult's perception of a social contract. What do we owe our community? Being a part of the community, men and women generally become concerned with obeying the law and maintaining social order. The difference in the way girls and boys are brought up affects their attitude about their community and how they approach the moral duty of maintaining social order.

Women, brought up to feel a sense of connectedness to the family, wanting to please others, and, as primary caretakers of children, are generally more concerned than men with preserving social order. In frontier days, it was the women who established schools, churches, and hospitals. The men acted out their rambunctiousness, frequenting brothels and saloons, and riding off to capture horse thieves. Today, women, or at least those people who are exercising the feminine principle, legislate for safe child care, health care, safe nursing homes for the elderly, and environmental protection, while those people embodying the masculine principle expand the military and industry.

The highest stage of moral development is in exercising one's own conscience. Few people, according to Kohlberg, achieve this stage, where conscience dictates the rightness and the wrongness of an act. Several generations ago there was a more public sense of acting according to the dictates of one's conscience. It was stressed that wrongful acts would weigh heavily on one's conscience. The reward for doing the right thing was in having a clear conscience and feeling good about one's self. The punishment for doing wrong was in suffering the pangs of conscience.

Not being tormented by conscience after committing a crime means that moral punishment is nonexistent. In felony crimes, what is left is societal punishment—imprisonment. But is prison really much of a punishment? Admittedly, there is a loss of freedom and no one wants to be in prison, but it does provide warmth, food, recreation, and companionship. With a few exceptions, the results of get-tough policies and longer incarcerations are not as successful as law enforcement would wish. Prisons become overcrowded, which means that inmates are often released before their sentences are completed to relieve that overcrowding. Early release and the basic lack of funds to keep prisoners incarcerated for long periods of time have a practical effect on how tough we can be on crime. As a consequence, in crime the rewards for men are great and punishments are weak.

POOR SCHOOL PERFORMANCE

In addition to the demise of high moral standards, another reason for the escalating crime rate is the school dropout rate and the high rate of illiteracy. Crime is an available alternative to both boredom and economic deprivation for men with no preparation for jobs and no reading skills to fill out an employment application. In Japan a prison inmate cannot be released from prison until he has achieved a minimum reading level. If, in this country, the amount of time spent on developing reading skills for inner city children were increased, both the reading handicap and the propensity to crime could be reduced. If prisons in this country adopted the Japanese method, it might reduce recidivism as well. Another qualification for prison release could be passing the high school equivalency test, since a diploma is a requirement for most jobs. One way of judicially setting up such a parole arrangement might be for sentencing to include an assessment of damages that the inmate could work off by getting an education or learning a trade, leading to a productive incarceration.

UNEMPLOYMENT AND POVERTY

Another reason given for the high male crime rate is the high unemployment rate, which especially affects those with little education, brought up in poverty areas. Poverty itself is not a cause. Not all males brought up in poverty commit crimes. An April 1991 study on poverty by the Brookings Institute placed an emphasis on individual behavior as a determinant of who stays poor and who doesn't. Not all poverty is the result of insufficient good jobs, nor is all poverty a cause of crime. A comparison can be made with countries in Western Europe that curtailed crime without increasing employment, providing better housing, or instating longer prison terms or capital punishment.

Family economics is not a predicter of crime. In the S&L

scandal, most criminals were men raised in middle- or upper-middle-class environments with college educations and high-paying jobs. The S&L situation presented an opportunity for thievery and particular male traits of competitiveness and making more money than others as a show of power.

Females brought up in the same poverty areas with little education and no jobs commit few crimes, almost none violent, and most related to drugs.

ABUSED AS ABUSERS

Another reason given for the high crime rate is that many convicted physical and sexual abusers were themselves victims of child abuse. More females are sexually victimized than are males, with an estimated eight million girls and five million boys sexually abused before they are eighteen years old. Though more girls are abused, almost all sexual abusers are men. It would appear that sexual abuse has to do with a history of previous abuse and that it refers primarily to men.

FAMILY BREAKUP

Frequently, people will refer to the disintegration of the family as a cause of crime. The single-mother home, in which the father is absent, is pointed to as a factor in not giving a boy a solid footing in life. The fact is, the family is not disintegrating: it is simply changing. True, there are many more single-mother homes now than ever before in our culture, and that often makes life difficult for both mother and children. Without a man to help support children, there is financial hardship. But financial hardship does not necessarily lead to crime. There are many poor cultures where the crime rate is low.

What is needed in any good family situation is a good relationship between whichever parent is available and the child. Single mothers are often overworked, fatigued, and worried. So are mothers in two-parent families. This is not to minimize the problems of single motherhood but to stress that there are no studies indicating that families headed by women are any more crime-prone than other families. The absence of a father is not necessarily a crime-inducing factor. To say that being a single mother increases her children's chance for crime is to blame a woman for having a child out of wedlock, or to blame women for getting a divorce, or to blame women in every case in which the man leaves the home for whatever reason.

The myth of the superiority of the two-parent family as being the best for raising children is just that—a myth. In my book *The Two-Parent Family Is Not the Best*, a study compared children raised by single mothers with children raised by single fathers, by two biological parents, and by a stepparent. The results of this scientifically controlled study indicated that there is no one family configuration better than another for raising children. What matters is the relationship between family members. Are the children respected, nurtured, encouraged, and loved? The study showed that single mothers had a more difficult time because of finances, since their mates no longer provided income or had not paid child support, but there was no difference from other families in other characteristics. It is important not to lose sight of the fact that the criminals most highly rewarded for their crimes, those in the S&L scandal, were almost all from two-parent families.

TESTOSTERONE

Another reason given for male crime is the aggressiveness attributed to the male hormone testosterone. In a Norwegian study of boys who are bullies, Dan Olweus, a professor of psychology at the University of Bergen, found that the higher the level of testosterone, the higher the intolerance for frustration, which then led to a provocation. In a 1973 study of male hormones in rats by G. Raisman and P. M. Field, male rats who were castrated at birth and female rats who were treated with testosterone at birth exhibited aggression equally when they were adults. Also, female monkeys who had been in utero with male monkeys exhibit more tumultuous play after their birth than female monkeys who had not been in utero with males.

A further question would be: Of the females who were said to acquire testosterone in utero, was their aggression violent and destructive, or was it aggression directed at protecting their young or building a strong nest? Testosterone may cause aggression, but aggression need not equal violence.

In *Male and Female*, Margaret Mead wrote about male aggression and concluded, "In every known society, homicidal violence, whether spontaneous and outlawed or organized and sanctioned for military purposes, is committed overwhelmingly by men." Wondering about the effect of environment on gender differences, she asked the question, If boys and girls were raised in exactly the same environment, would they be different? In the *New York Times Magazine*, August 14, 1990, in an article titled "The Aggressors," Melvin Konner, M.D., answers her question by drawing on Professor Olweus's conclusions: "The boy would hit, kick, wrestle, scratch, grab, shove and bite more than the girl and be more likely to commit a violent crime later in life." However, there is disagreement as to whether this behavior is testosterone-driven, or whether the boy's aggressive actions are driven by the approval of society as being the way boys should be.

Is testosterone actually a source of aggression? Or is it that society transforms biological indicators into certain behavior to serve society. In the hierarchy of oppression, people tend to act out their part because they feel it is the right thing to do. Boys will be boys because that's what they have been taught and that's what society expects. Girls do not learn to be nice simply because they have less testosterone, and boys do not learn to be aggressive simply because they do. The psychologically healthy personality includes both feminine and masculine characteristics. Having androgynous personalities, men are not overmasculinized; that is, they are sensitive and caring as well as responsible and strong. The women are self-sufficient and adventurous as well as nurturing and conciliatory.

There is a tendency these days to attribute the maleness of crime to testosterone and to throw up one's hands, as if testosterone is a given and therefore male aggressiveness and subsequent crime is also. But males have always had testosterone. Testosterone is no explanation for the massive crime wave this country is experiencing.

STRESS

Stress is also often cited as a cause of criminal violence. After the San Francisco earthquake of October 1989, complaints of domestic violence increased. Women were beaten by their husbands, and their lives were at risk. It was said by a director at a women's shelter that this was happening because men were feeling angry and frustrated with loss of their homes and their jobs. Yet women were also under stress and they were not battering others. The increase of domestic violence in Turners Falls, Massachusetts, was described earlier as being caused by stress. As someone at the battered women's shelter said, "Turners Falls is working class, depressed. The factories are all gone. The people have been stripped of dignity in a lot of ways." Again, women were stripped of their dignity, too, yet they did not strike out at their mates. Attempting to keep the social order, they fought their fear. Stress-driven violence does appear to require some particular male trait.

When Steven Imler, married and the father of three children, was arrested in March 1991 for allegedly making over 500 obscene phone calls to women, terrorizing them by saying their husbands were being held, bound and gagged, he excused his action by saying he was driven to make these phone calls because of stress on the job. Imler worked for ten years as a telemarketing manager for a firm in Compton, California.

When he turned himself in because he was aware the police were getting closer to locating the obscene caller, he said the phone calls were a way of relieving his anxiety. The victims of these phone calls reported that the caller asked many of the women to disrobe and perform sexual acts on themselves as they talked, insisting that the women call him "sir." This, Imler said later, relieved his stress.

FBI agents at the National Center for the Analysis of Violent Crime, after lengthy questionnaires of prisoners, determined "the organized offender [one who systematically preys on victims] to be of at least average intelligence, and socially and sexually competent. . . . He commonly commits his crime after some stressful event."

Stress often builds up within a person's psyche. A man in a difficult situation will take a drink to relieve his tension, the drink will release his inhibitions, and he will let his temper fly. There are studies in process attempting to learn why alcohol triggers violence in some people and silliness in others.

While stress can cause men to lash out in anger, women are apt to turn their stress inward, even to repress hostility. This repression may have its own cost. Though it does not usually cause crime, it can cause anxiety and inner turmoil. In a recent study of heart attack victims, those men who suffered more recurrent heart attacks than other men were those who were the most aggressive and the most angry. Among females, those who had the most recurrent heart attacks were the women who suffered from anxiety.

From the world of their mothers, girls learn to comfort, and as adults they comfort their women friends. Men under stress do not usually have nor do they seek out other males who will comfort them. Women rejected by their mates tend to seek other women friends to help them through the painful process. Rejected males often suffer their pain in solitude because to seek help for anything would be to admit weakness, which is not considered masculine. Or men lash out at the women who rejected or humiliated them, sometimes in a murderous rage that involves others. Rape of an unknown woman is often seen as a symbolic payback to a specific woman who humiliated the man when he was younger. To be humiliated by a person who is considered weaker or inferior to one's self is a great insult to masculine pride.

Stress may cause criminal behavior—in men. It is not likely to do so in women. For many men, murder is a way of relieving stress.

ANGER

Generally, women turn their anger inward; men turn their anger outward. It has been said that it is psychologically healthy to vent one's anger, to get rid of it. But studies have proved otherwise. In her book *Anger: The Misunderstood Emotion*, Carol Tarvis explains that venting one's anger does not get rid of it. On the contrary, anger causes more anger. When one is angry one wants to do something about it. What one does about it often depends on whether the angry person is male or female.

Rock star Billy Idol, possibly under stress as a performer, let his anger out while he was on a vacation in September 1989 by destroying his Bangkok hotel room. When the hotel officials wanted to stop him, his friends told them to just leave Billy alone, he would pay for everything. The bill came to $11,200. He had previously torn up rooms in two other hotels in Thailand at a combined cost to him of $9,200.

In Westwood, California, in March 1991, angered that they could not get in to see the movie *New Jack City*, which is about a Harlem drug king, 1,500 youths, both black and white, let their anger out by starting a riot that cost merchants thousands of dollars. The young men broke windows, stole stereos and bicycles, and roamed around destroying what they could before police riot squads arrived.

Destroying property is akin to the little boy kicking over his sister's dollhouse in jealous anger. Little brothers are known to be a menace to their sisters, often wrecking their sisters' possessions.

Property damage and property crime may be a forerunner to bodily crime when men take action in the midst of anger. What is it but unbridled anger when thirty-six-year-old Gregory Calvin Smith stabs a twenty-four-year-old college student, Nancy Cheek, over and over with both a knife and a screwdriver? Charged with thirty-seven crimes against twenty victims, Smith, a security alarm technician, was arrested in San Jose, California, in August 1989. He is married and the father of two-year-old twin girls.

At the University of Oregon Graduate School of Professional Psychology, Dr. Mary Kay Biaggio studied the cause of anger for ten years. She concluded that men were angered by people who annoyed them, while women were angered by people who criticized or rejected them. The reactions to anger were that women had feelings of being emotionally wounded, but men experienced strong feelings of hate.

Boys learn to be angry; in fact, they are taught to be angry. Engaging in contact sports does not teach them sportsmanship so much as it teaches them to be at least temporarily angry and to beat their opponent. Anger will give them an adrenaline surge, which will help them achieve victory. During the Gulf War, soldiers were told by their Commander-in-Chief George Bush to get angry—to "kick butt." Many of those who returned from the war lamented that while they were glad the war ended quickly, they were disappointed they hadn't had a chance to get into a fight—hadn't had a chance to *kick butt*. This war was said to have remasculinized our country, which will make it more difficult to change the current acceptance of violence as a way to solve problems.

Is it necessary to whip up anger in soldiers if they are to defeat an enemy? How else would military leaders get well-mannered, respectful young men to kill people? By relying on the technique of repetitiously portraying the enemy as less than human, military commanders make it easier for soldiers to kill. The enemy then becomes the institutionalized bad guy—the target of the soldier's aggressive, whipped-up anger. The soldier proudly claims he is doing his duty, fighting for his country.

But anger is not all bad. If enough people could get aggressively angry at the amount of pollution in the air or the amount of toxins in the earth, the environment might be cleaned up sooner. Constructive anger is often necessary to right a perceived wrong—for instance, when a school is about to close for lack of funds while money is available for building new roadways to an unfinished subdivision. As Aristotle said, "Anybody can become angry—that is easy; but to be angry with the right person, and to the right degree, and at the right time, and for the right purpose, and in the right way—that is not within everybody's power and is not easy."

Anger quickens the senses. The German monk Martin Luther wrote in 1835 that when he was angry he could preach better, and "my whole temperament is quickened, my understanding sharpened, all mundane vexations and temptations depart." In reports of mass murderers, as they walked the floors of businesses gunning down their victims or methodically murdering all their relatives, the men were all described as acting "matter-of-factly." Their anger quickened their senses. Their actions were wrong-headed, but they were clear-headed and purposeful in committing them.

The sum total of the effects of poor school performance, unemployment, poverty, childhood abuse, single mothers, stress, and anger is that these factors do not necessarily cause crime. Girls grow up under the same conditions as boys, and girls are relatively crime-free. What we should look at is *the way* boys are raised.

THE RULING GENDER

From the day he is born, the little boy knows he is special, that he has a kind of symbolic privilege. In several studies, both boys and girls indicated that they believed boys were more important than girls. In school, it is the boy who gets most of the attention. Myra Sadker, dean of American University's School of Education, says that teachers pay more attention to boys, give them more counseling, ask them more questions, and give them more direction.

In school the boy learns almost exclusively about men and what men have done. For thirteen years, grades K–12, both boys and girls are required to read about the history of men. In high schools in California, 90 percent of the history teachers are men and most of those are also sports coaches. Most have neither the inclination nor the time to learn and teach about women in history, though women have been teaching men's history for centuries. Even with affirmative action and Title IX requirements to increase gender equity in instructional materials, recent reports reveal, for example, that in a 700-page required United States history text, only seventeen pages are about women. This overemphasis on male accomplishments tends to elevate man's importance in society, and vicariously the boy's importance in his world and the girl's unimportance.

And what does the boy learn in these history classes? He learns about wars and generals and conquering territory. He learns about Napoleon, Caesar, Hannibal, Alexander the Great, and the Vikings, all of whom conquered other people, destroyed property, plundered, and brought the spoils home. This gives the boy an understanding of his own privilege. The plunderer gets into history books.

What does the girl learn? She learns about Joan of Arc who was burned at the stake for speaking her mind, no matter that she had led the country's armies to victory. She learns about Cleopatra, the great beauty, who killed herself when her lover,

Marc Antony, was defeated. The girl learns that she will never be in the history books, and that she is to admire boys for what their gender has accomplished historically. She learns that she is expected to hold up the symbolic privilege of men. Both boys and girls learn something, and it doesn't serve them well.

In classes where reading is taught, both boys and girls will read books in which the main character is a boy or a male animal. The wise author knows that both boys and girls will read a book about a boy, but only girls will read about girls. That is also true, for the most part, for adults. Men and women read books about men, but only women read books about women. No wonder men say they can't understand women! No wonder Freud asked the question, "What do women want?" It would seem to be virtually impossible to know much about women if all one does is learn about men.

If girls want to learn about their own history, they have to wait until they get to college, where they can enroll in Women's Studies classes, populated entirely by females. One cannot even imagine a course entitled Men's Studies. School *is* Men's Studies.

A boy in school reading about girls would be considered a sissy. Girls learn to accept their position in the hierarchy. They learn to stand back, to cheer the boys on. Girls come to believe—in spite of statistical evidence to the contrary, which says that most women work about thirty-five years during their life—that they have a choice of either having a career or getting married and being supported by a husband.

It used to be that only boys were educated, because they were the only ones expected to make a living for a family. However, with women now making up 50 percent of the work force, this points to the need for educating girls as completely as boys. The U.S. Census figures for single mothers now measure nine million and growing. Women are and will continue to be the sole support of millions of families in this country.

Boys learn to accept their position in the social hierarchy, realizing that even though much is expected of them because they are male and considered more important, they are more deserving. As the boy comes to believe his own importance both at home and in school, for him there's never enough of what he feels he should get. The criminals of the S&L scandal are the epitome of this expectation. As many incidents in this book demonstrate, males are easily frustrated and quick to anger when they don't get what they want, and they are constantly feeling deprived.

In addition to the S&L criminals who are examples of males who were well off and yet felt they deserved more, the Menendez brothers, who killed their wealthy parents with shotguns. They are examples of men who were brought up extravagantly and yet wanted more, even if they had to kill their parents to get it.

LACK OF MALE EMPATHY

Having no feeling for others makes it easy for criminals to attack. In almost all male crime, violent and nonviolent, there is a lack of sympathy for the victim, a lack of empathy. Often the victim is faceless. The S&L criminal robs taxpayers. Burglars and robbers rob unknowns. Rapists rape women. There is no sense of the personhood of the victim. This lack of empathy is absolutely essential to criminal victimization, whether the victim is known or unknown. The only time a rapist is persuaded by a victim to discontinue his attack is when he sees her as a human being. One attacker ceased raping a woman when she told him she was pregnant.

Boys are not brought up to be aware of other people to the extent that girls are. Girls are brought up in the world of their mothers, caring for others, understanding, listening—in short, girls are generally trained to be empathetic, concerned for others, a characteristic foreign to criminal behavior. Girls are brought up related more to the home, boys to the outside world, where there is more opportunity for crime.

People would not be able to commit crimes if they were sympathetic. Generally, men are trained to stifle their feelings. This is a necessary component of war. If men had feelings for the people they were killing, they could not be sent into battle. In factories where they build bombs, men have to train themselves not to think about where those bombs are going. When the soldiers came back from the Gulf War, victorious and jubilant that less than 400 of their countrymen had been killed, they blocked out feelings about the thousands of people *they* had killed. As the poet Robert Bly suggests, there appears to be among men an inability to express grief. He might also suggest that instead of the Gulf War victory celebrations with marching bands, we should be grieving for the dead and dying in Iraq. Denying grief is like denying an illness that doesn't cure itself.

The psychiatrist Alice Miller explains that men who commit heinous crimes have been able psychodynamically to split off a part of themselves. They have closed off feelings of weakness such as shedding tears, or being emotional, showing pity for others, or having feelings of helplessness. The vicious criminal was very likely mistreated as a child and did not have anyone who treated him empathetically. So how could he learn to be empathetic? Unable to express his own hurt feelings to another human being, he closes that part of himself off and cannot empathize with his own suffering as a child. He may have an unconscious preoccupation with pain, inflicting the same pain on others as was inflicted on him. Some men go so far as to attempt to destroy themselves in destroying their victim.

Not only must men block out sympathetic feelings, but, as mentioned earlier, they must develop a propensity to anger if they are to be useful in war. These are characteristics for good soldiering and for criminality. Aggressive anger is necessary for violent crime and for some nonviolent crime. Understanding why males are more prone to destructive anger than females will help understand male violence and male susceptibility to crime.

But we need to start at the beginning—at the beginning of life, a boy's life.

Causes of Male Anger

BETRAYAL AND REJECTION

At birth or shortly after, a baby boy is usually circumcised, though there is rising evidence that there is no medical reason for this practice. As Ashley Montagu has said, "You find cultures where the foreskin is regarded as female, and has to be cut off to make the male a complete male." This is purposefully inflicted pain—a pain that can't be consciously remembered, but which nevertheless is part of a boy's subconscious psyche. Psychiatrist Alice Miller writes in her book, *For Your Own Good: Hidden Cruelty in Child-Rearing and the Roots of Violence,* that if childhood cruelty happened too early to be part of conscious memory, then that person must commit cruelty.

Not every circumcised male is cruel, largely because there are ameliorating factors as he grows up, such as being able to express himself and his anger or frustration and being listened to by an adult who cares about him. Nevertheless, circumcision is the first attack on a male, and if his life is a series of attacks and humiliations without compensation, and without being able to express his resentment or feelings, then society will likely eventually feel the sting of his anger.

After the baby boy is circumcised, he is then gathered up and almost always nursed at his mother's breast, held close to her warm body, nestled and softly spoken to in loving tones. Though there are some men who are now sharing parenting, almost always the principal care giver for the first several years of a boy's life is a woman.

As a toddler, the boy is still considered a baby and as such is treated with hands-on affection, mostly by his mother. But, as with millions of others between the ages of about two and four years old, the male child is subjected to a ritual that takes him out of his babyhood and into the world of little boys. This is the occasion of his first haircut. Struggling against the unknown, the fearful child is perched on a wooden board that straddles the arms of a huge chair where a man he has not seen before approaches his head with a pair of scissors. This is the second attack.

What does the boy feel as he sees his mother standing by, not only allowing, but promoting someone to abuse him? No wonder he screams! The mother thinks of *her* sadness, braces herself against the sense of loss as she sees the boy's curls fall to the floor, when her baby becomes a boy.

The mother returns home where she presents her boy to her husband who beams with the joy that his son, having gone through this important rite of passage, now looks like a little man. That which had made him look similar to his sisters has been removed. That which had been feminine, which might make him appear a sissy and therefore weak, has been cut off.

This ritual, played out across the country, with variations in barbershops, kitchens, or backyards, is similar to puberty rituals in tribal societies. Boys are removed from their mothers and ritualistically indoctrinated into the male society. Their elders inflict wounds on the boys' bodies, letting a few drops of blood fall to the ground, symbolically removing woman's blood, getting rid of that which is weak. Those tribal boys and our little boy with his new haircut will forever after deny anything about themselves that is feminine or weak. (This does not take into consideration those boys who grow up to be homosexual. In our culture homosexuals are ridiculed and even attacked. In some tribal societies, especially among American Indian tribes, homosexuals are protected and given special consideration.)

After their puberty rituals, the boys henceforth in many tribes worldwide live in "the men's house," forbidden to return to their mothers' huts for fear of being contaminated by anything feminine.

Our little boy will continue to live with his mother. He will go to school when he is about five years old, will play with groups of boys, will learn to say that girls have "cooties," and call girls derogatory names to let his peers know that he is one of them. In many homes in the next few years, his father, or another male, may take the boy fishing, or to a ball game, or on a short backpacking or hunting trip. He will start the process of leaving the world of his mother and begin the task of becoming a man.

Many children, both boys and girls, grow up with absent fathers, either divorced or separated, fathers too busy to spend much time at home, or fathers who are at home but who spend little time with their children. Boys born to single mothers are often introduced into the world of men by uncles, older brothers, grandfathers, neighbors, and male friends of the boys' mothers. In tribal societies it is the mother's brother who is the important man in a boy's life. A woman may have several husbands who may come and go in her children's life, but an uncle is always an uncle and he takes his family responsibility to his sister's children seriously.

In this country, boys without fathers do not usually receive physical affection from any man. Men who come into their lives, if there are any, are generally not involved in the early stage of the boy's life. They usually make their appearance when a boy is beyond the baby years and is old enough to explore the adult male world. The man who helps the boy to manhood may serve as a protector of the youth and as the person educating him about the man's world. In some localities, a boy with or without a father, looking for a male protector, will join a gang looking for what represents a strong male authoritarian figure who will protect him in a crime area. Gangs serve this purpose because they are a sex-segregated society with strict behavior rules.

In two-parent families when the boys are past eight or nine, mothers more or less turn their sons over to the fathers and then are reluctant to interfere in the father-son relationship. In her book *Mothers and Sons: Toward an Understanding of Responsibility*, Linda Forcey says that women have been conditioned to believe they should raise sons who are stereotypically masculine, yet women have ambivalent feelings about what are considered masculine values. According to longstanding custom, women persist in raising manly boys and in maintaining the system of symbolic privilege for their sons. Regardless of who raises the children, they are raised according to society's expectations of what a boy should be and what a girl should be. Mothers work just as hard at masculinizing boys as do fathers.

A mother will be somewhat aware that her son will join in pranks with other boys as he moves from childhood to his teenage years. These pranks represent the third rite of passage in which the boy must not be afraid to try things like dumping over garbage cans or throwing rocks at street signs. These "boys will be boys" pranks, participated in by groups of peers, are forerunners to the older male group acts, such as mailbox bashing and college hazing, which is now banned in several colleges because of the consequences of male violence.

Childhood pranks are also the forerunners of the more extreme male group acts, such as gay bashing, or even gang rape—acts that the boy would probably not commit if he were by himself. Refusal to participate in a gang rape might lead a boy's friends to question his masculinity. But these group acts prove that the boy has separated from the female world and is part of the male world.

All-male pranks are also forerunners of a male cohesiveness that is very important during wartime. The will to do it together helps men overcome the enemy. In their book *America Can Win*, Gary Hart and William Lind state that being part of a group binds men together in war. A soldier cares what other men think about him, so he fights. The pranks of his child-

hood, carried out with his male peers, help to build the sense
of cohesiveness with the male world. Incorporating women
into the military is seen by many as intruding into the last all-
male bastion.

Or *is* the military the last bastion? More likely it is sports
with national media attention. Women's sports now get about
3 percent of sports coverage. According to *The Stronger Women
Get, the More Men Love Football*, by Mariah Burton Nelson, each
weekend men escape into a fantasy world where only men
play. Giving them national coverage is like letting undesirables
move into the neighborhood. Sure, women are permitted to
cheer and admire the plays, but they can hardly fantasize carrying that ball to a touchdown. That's reserved territory.

For the boy, separation from the female world is vital to
make the transition from baby to boy to man. The boy's father
does his part in this separation process by taking him on sex-
segregated outings. His mother not only helps but often must
be aggressive in pushing him away from her. She must "cut
him from her apron strings." She must curtail her "mothering"
impulses, not kiss or hug him as often as she did or wants to,
may even change her tone of voice when she talks to him, not
sound as sweet but more matter-of-fact and less emotional.
From all of this the boy will learn to be less emotional. He
must learn not to cry, out of fear of being called a baby, a sissy,
and therefore considered weak.

While he is experiencing acceptance into the world of his
father, he is experiencing a gradual rejection from the world of
his mother. He misses being able to go to his mother for physical comfort, for hugs and kisses that his sisters still enjoy. Over
a period of a few years, he is cut loose from those physically
loving ties and, without knowing why, feels gradually abandoned. But he must be strong, must not cry for what he wants.
It has been said that grown men are afraid that if they start to
cry, they will cry forever.

In this separation process, the father, who used to hold his little boy on his lap and even used to kiss him good night, begins to play roughly with him on the living room floor, often in competitive play where he may ridicule his son if he does not try hard enough to win. When his father leaves for work in the morning, or on a trip, he warmly embraces his daughters and wife in farewell. He will hold himself back from embracing his son, but rather, puts his arm around his son's shoulder as he tells him to take care of the family. The boy no longer has the physical affection of his mother, nor does he have it from his father.

In this transition period much is lost. The little boy cannot nuzzle up to his parents as he used to, nor can he talk to them as he used to, because discussing things that might make him cry are, without being said, not acceptable anymore. So he doesn't discuss his feelings or ponder out loud about what bothers him. Bruno Bettelheim said that in "good enough families" there is enough talking among family members. Talking lets off steam. But talking gets to be something that his sisters and his mother do together. Since he's not included, he ridicules them for "gabbing." His mother's task at this time is to get out of the way.

Sooner or later, as Olga Silverstein and Beth Rashbaum say in *The Courage to Raise Good Men*, "usually by the end of their teen years, this incessant denial will spell the death of feeling." Mothers, in turn, to protect themselves, learn the art of a cool detachment. Then they wonder why, in later years, sons don't write or phone. Having suffered "mother-loss," these sons seek wives who will mother them. Silverstein and Rashbaum point out that no matter what Robert Bly and others say about men looking for their fathers, it is at time of crisis and at near death that men cry for their mothers.

In one of the many televised homecomings from the Gulf War, there was a poignant scene where a mother and her son, about eight years old, rush to a soldier with outstretched arms. The soldier takes his wife in an embrace while their son circles them several times, trying to get in. He eventually settles for burying his face between their two bodies at hip level, one arm on each of them, while they, obliviously, continue their embrace.

Most boys, with or without fathers, grow up knowing their mothers love them and also knowing that it is not socially acceptable for their mothers to be physically demonstrative with them as they get older. But knowing something intellectually and accepting it emotionally are two different things. Rejection is rejection, and it hurts. Rejection and betrayal can cause great anger. More so than girls, boys lash out, spit, throw rocks, shoot 22-caliber guns at road signs, are disruptive in school, punch, set fires, and hurt animals, as they might want to hurt the one who has hurt them if they only knew what it was that was bothering them. Boys are not so much interested in picking up their fathers' traits as they are in denying their mothers'.

Riane Eisler, in her popular book *The Chalice and the Blade*, writes that violence in men is caused by what she calls "the dominator model of society." In ancient historical periods, one sex was not dominant over another. Her thesis is that as long as one sex needs to feel dominant, that sex, which is male, will equate masculinity with dominance, which necessarily entails violence.

The second great betrayal in boys' lives is the trick that is played on them, having to keep quiet about the reality of death when ordered into battle. They hear a lot about the glory, but underneath the surface of their understanding is the grimness of their gender's fate. Every boy is born at risk because he is expendable in time of war. The country talks up the glamour of the high-tech war equipment, but the country does not talk about the subject of the death of young men. That talk is taboo. That silence creates an unconscious rage at a possibly uncontrollable situation.

But boys learn to cope. Generally speaking, most boys learn to accommodate the difficult mother-son rearrangement without even knowing it. Eventually they find a woman who pleases them, as women have been trained to do, and the man becomes dependent on her for clean clothes, food, and sex, though he will frequently complain that he does not get enough of the latter. But here again is a problem for men. In knowing that they are dependent on women, they dislike themselves because dependency is a sign of weakness and few men permit themselves to be weak. The man will marry the woman, but he will go to great lengths to show that he is not going to be dependent on her.

Dependent-independent ambivalence is played out in the marriage. The man loves his wife, wants to be married, but must control his dependency. He's much more dependent on what the other men think of him. The theory of symbolic privilege is evident in his marriage. Carried to extremes, this fear of dependency is evident in a man not wanting to ask directions, not seeking medical help, not wanting to go into therapy. Men generally dislike any dependency, but they especially dislike being dependent upon women, on those they consider weak. One can't be dependent and also be the superior gender. The hierarchy must be maintained. In disliking their dependency on women, many men turn this dislike of their dependency into disdain for the gender on which they are dependent.

Unable to handle rejection triggers underlying anger. "He is the last person I thought would do anything like that," is said of men who murder wives and girlfriends who have rejected them. In the everyday world, these men appear kind and calm, but what goes on in the family is often the darker side of the picture.

What of the majority of men, who have also grown up with this arrangement of rejection and betrayal, who have not committed crimes? The suggestion is that mothers were more gentle in their rejection, fathers were more nurturing, that both parents permitted both the maleness and the femaleness of their personalities to evolve. In healthy families stereotyping is mitigated. Boys do dishes as readily as girls mow the lawn. Humor and conversation take precedence over punching and humiliation. And the boys themselves, without knowing it, work through their rejection. They face their hurt and anger and talk about it, bringing their feelings into their consciousness, unlike a counterpart whose anger is repressed until he is able to take it out on someone else. Then, too, other factors come into play. For a boy to engage in criminal activity there must be the opportunity for crime, as well as the means to commit the crime.

Simplified, the propensity toward male anger is caused by many things: anger at mother for rejecting the son, though neither are consciously aware of this rejection; frustration when one cannot do what one wants, have what one wants, dominate whom one wants. If those are a man's needs, the outlet for this stress and frustration is violence. O. J. Simpson could not dominate his wife. His frustration over this turned to rage and resulted in his beating her on many occasions. In his previous glorious pursuits he could never be seen as needy, nor could he appeal for help or express his feelings, even to his best friends, of whom he had many. Kings are not meant to cry. For then, what would peasants do?

Children who are not allowed to express their feelings need to find an outlet for revenge. The child who is brought up free to let his feelings be known, does not need to humiliate anyone. But for others whose opinions and ideas are throttled, anger builds up. It may lay dormant for years, or it may burst into violence directed at anyone or anything or no one in particular. This male anger can erupt into the torching of homes, it can manifest itself in the irresponsible discharge of one's duty so that an oil tanker ruins wildlife and fishing villages, it can erupt into mass murder of unknown persons, it can cause the alcoholic driving home from a bar to destroy a family in a station wagon.

When children cannot talk about their own suffering they

may need to split it off: that is, project the very same suffering onto someone else. As there are many more male criminals than female criminals it could be surmised that little boys are not only more likely to be repressed in expressing their feelings than little girls, but they may also be more likely to be scolded and humiliated than the little girls who are coached to be nice. There is possibly more for the little boy to get even about than there is for his sister.

There is a direct correlation between criminal acts and early childhood. Alice Miller says that any act of cruelty has antecedents in the perpetrator's past. The way children are raised has a direct bearing on whether they will become criminals. Is regular discipline a system of humiliation and mistreatment at the same time that the child is not allowed to complain? Do the parents take out their own disappointments and their impotence on their child? Does the child have one single human being in whom he can confide his innermost fears and true feelings?

THE MYTH OF THE ALL-POWERFUL MOTHER

In the child's infancy the power of the mother is a fearsome power. It is she who has the power to give the infant food and to withhold it. No one else has such power. She is the boy's first love. She feeds him, rocks him, keeps him warm. Her power is an awesome, total power, exerted at the most dependent time in one's life. As the child grows, the mother can humble, humiliate, or thwart him as easily as she can praise him.

When he becomes even slightly socially aware, he can see that the important people in the outside world, like those who hire others for work, those who preach in churches or synagogues, those he reads about in school, like presidents, are mostly men. The important people are the same gender he is. Being a member of the ruling gender he feels a separation from his mother. Loving and loyal to her, he recognizes that his mother's power, which was awesome to him when he was very young, is, outside the home, extremely limited. She is relatively powerless. The myth of the all-powerful mother is just that—a myth.

In his infancy he was nurtured close to his mother's body, which held the mysteries of life which she had given him. Yet she is not like him, and the boy sees that he can never be like her. He turns his disappointment at his separateness to a dislike of that which is different from him. He must develop an intolerance for femininity, experiencing an additional sense of betrayal in learning that his mother, who had meant so much to him is, after all, in worldly terms, unimportant.

In order for him to develop fully, the boy must escape his mother's domination. If he does not use his will over her eventually, he cannot grow. To make his own decisions is one thing, but he must also make decisions that demonstrate he is not part of his mother's world—that is, not part of the feminine world. He must prove his masculinity, not allow himself to develop traits considered feminine.

It is said that all men have to overcome their mothers. Girls, too, are under the domination of their mothers, and they, too, must overcome their mothers. But they do not share their brothers' trauma in this development. Between girls and their mothers there is often friction, and girls must also eventually exert their own will. But mothers do not need to reject girls as they need to reject boys in order for boys to enter the male world. And because girls' bodies are like their mothers', girls do not have that sense of separateness. For girls to grow up to be women, their mothers do not need to reject them.

In her book *In a Different Voice*, Carol Gilligan writes that because of the way girls and boys are raised, boys fear intimacy and girls fear isolation. Because girls belong to their mothers' world and are connected in ways boys are not, girls generally absorb their mothers' nurturing characteristics, empathize in ways that women do, learn to take care of others, unselfishly share for the sake of their family, and, in nurturing infants, learn compassion for others.

Yet girls, too, need to overcome their mothers. The need for patriarchy, or male domination, in governments and other institutions is seen as the result of both sexes needing to overcome mothers. Nations, all male dominated, exhibit masculine traits of power, domination, and the need for territorial rights, because citizens need to escape what they consider to be the weakness of their mothers as they seek protection. We all want to be free to exercise our own will, but we also want to be taken care of. As a consequence, both sexes revert to a form of infantilism in the need for a male-dominated society.

Much of male criminal violence is the symbolic destruction of the early power of mother. Derogatory expressions related to destroying "mother" crop up, even in wartime. During the Gulf War when Iraqi tanks in Kuwait tricked the allied forces by turning their turrets backward in a show of surrender, enabling them to get closer to open fire, the men in the U.S. forces were understandably angry. One, according to a *Los Angeles Times* article of February 2, 1991, was reported as saying, "From now on, I say 'screw it.' All those mothers die." This "mothers" is a derivative of the expression for the lowliest of low men, a motherfucker. However, the only word that now remains to describe the lowliest of the low is the word "mother."

Larry Singleton's crime of raping a fifteen-year-old girl and cutting off her hands was described by Amanda Spake in her article in *Mother Jones* magazine, "The End of the Ride: Analyzing a Sex Crime," as male rage and fear of being dominated by a woman. To be dominated by a sex considered weaker than his own is a man's humiliation.

Male violence against women, representing the need to dominate the gender that dominated them, rejected them, and then turned out to be unimportant after all, can be seen in the rapist, the murderer, the batterer, the arsonist, the con man, the toxic waste dumper. But it is most clearly seen in the serial murder or mass murder. An example is the story of Roy Anderson.

Shortly after a breakup and an unsettled reconciliation with his wife, thirty-nine-year-old Roy Anderson shot to death his wife and two teenage daughters, stabbed to death another daughter, aged twenty, and then shot himself on February 25, 1991. One shocked neighbor in Lancaster, California, said the family was "a typical all-American family." Another described the father, saying he "ran the household like a military guy, like a platoon leader." The oldest girl's boyfriend said at one time he had to take his girlfriend home to his house because her father was so angry with her he would have killed her then. "He would yell, scream, hit," the boyfriend said.

Anderson's wife was a secretary at an elementary school and his daughters were popular, attractive, athletic girls. They were all getting ready for school or work when the killings occurred. A colleague of Anderson's wife said that when his wife and daughters left him, "he was just a fish out of water." She added that his wife, Deborah, had told her that any argument over the least little thing would lead to Anderson's question, "You're not going to leave me again, are you?" The school coach said the family traveled virtually every weekend to volleyball tournaments, which was expensive. The colleague said that the family was heavily in debt, having just bought a home and two new cars. The stress of the debt and the anxiety that he might have to suffer the pain of rejection again was apparently more than Roy Anderson could tolerate. When women are killed as these women were, they will have no further opportunity to reject their husband and father. As the school coach said, "I just think he wanted to keep them all with him." He did that.

Curtailing Crime

CRIME AS A PUBLIC HEALTH ISSUE

As long as this country declares war on crime, we will simply have violence against violence. There will be no more success in reducing crime than the war on drugs has displayed in reducing drug use. Crime must be seen as a public health issue.

If this crime epidemic were a medical epidemic the government would be hiring microbiologists to examine the causes and prevent the spread of the disease. The government would not simply resort to bankrupting state treasuries in order to build more hospitals and hire more nurses to care for the sick, which is the equivalent of building more prisons and hiring more police to fight crime.

In the United States, 50,000 people a year are infected with the AIDS virus, and scientists are frantically looking for a cure. Yet 25,000 people a year are murdered and thousands more are victims of other crimes, and all we are doing is relieving the symptoms—by incarceration in burgeoning prison systems. Yes, dangerous people need to be removed from society, but if that is all we are doing, the desease will spread until we are all afflicted.

If this crime epidemic is going to be stopped, our country needs a different mindset. But as is often true, there are vested interests in keeping the epidemic flourishing. There are prison guards, police, drug enforcement personnel, a whole criminal justice system thriving on the disease. Not that we don't need them. For this virulent epidemic, most are needed. But when other remedies are suggested, those with vested interests and those whose sole focus is punishment are prone to shrug aside suggestions for prevention. No healthy society should live in fear from its people within. It is time to change our focus.

Bringing in Father

Because mothers reject their sons in order to raise boys to fit society's expectations, they could be seen as the principal culprits causing male anger. This pushing away of sons does have serious consequences for many boys, but another major problem is the absence of fathers during infant care. With few exceptions, fathers have little to do with caring for infants. The whole experience of infancy is left to women.

As a general rule, when men get involved in child care, beginning with infant care, there will finally be solid hope for curtailing male anger. Both boys and girls need a male mother as much as they need a female mother. If at least 50 percent of the time males would nurture newborns until they are grown, there would be no rejection by the principal caregiver, because there would be no principal caregiver. If the father's warm, loving body were as readily available to the small boy as his mother's, the boy would not see that his body is different from that of his principal caregiver. There would be no sense of betrayal. He would not be rejected from the wholly female world because his infant world would include a male. The boy would not see himself as needing to separate from the one he most loves.

As it is now, male anger, easily aroused, leaves the wife as the conciliator between her children and her husband. The family getting ready to leave on a vacation, packing the car under father's direction, treats father with great care trying not to irritate him because they know that when he is under stress he is apt to explode over trifles. A boy who goes with his father on fishing trips soon learns that his father will be good-natured for just so long. If the son snares his line too often, or, worse yet, loses a fish, he is apt to feel his father's anger when he yells at his son for being so clumsy.

The power of mother in a child's infancy is too powerful to be concentrated in one sex. It must be diluted and shared with fathers. The eventual realization that mother is actually societally weak leads to a craving for dominance as well as disgust and rage against women. With a male mother, children would still have a male authority figure, but, as one who cuddled infants, he would be a compassionate male authority figure, a male figure his boys could emulate.

Boys growing up in single-mother homes where there is no male to show them the outer world, will possibly absorb more of the stereotypical feminine characteristics of listening, caring, empathy, and understanding. This is not to say that the boy will necessarily be better off without a father, but without a father who only teaches him to be competitive, dominant, and aggressive, his chances for a balanced, androgynous personality are greater. Even without a father he will have access to "the male point of view" everywhere he looks—on TV, in his schoolbooks, at the movies.

There is no physiological or psychological reason why women should be the only ones to nurture infants and children. In a recent family living research project in which women were asked what things a mother could do that a father couldn't, almost all women said that except for breast-feeding, "nothing." The infant does not know whether a man or a woman has given it birth. It is the female caregiver who has forced this dependency on the infant.

There is, however, a societal, economic, and political reason for maintaining women as the principal caregivers. As long as it is said that women are the ones who should raise the children, then they are the ones who will do it. Being told that she should do it, for them to turn this task over to others, even for brief periods, makes mothers feel guilty, makes them feel they are abandoning their societal responsibility, abandoning their children, and denying what they have been told is their major role in life. The combined need for caring for their children and the need for employment helps to keep women moving in and out of the labor market, which limits their earning capacity, their retirement security, and maintains a pool of cheap labor for industry. Political parties that lean toward supporting business interests over human interests invariably stress the importance of what they call "family values," which means keeping women at home or at least employable only at minimum wage.

But what if the national psyche were changed? What if it were considered noble and manly for men to be equally responsible for raising children from birth? In Sweden the parliament passed legislation in June 1994 that requires fathers to take the one-month government-paid child-care leave or lose that time. This was done in an effort to get fathers more involved in raising their children so that mothers would not have to do it all.

If men in this country were 50 percent involved in infant and child care, how much more legislation would there then be for decent child care? For employee family-leave policies during birth, illness, or death? And with women having time and training to take a more meaningful role in the outside world, how much more respect would they earn from their children, especially their sons? With increased respect for women, how much less violence would there be against women? How different would the world be if women shared equally in deciding legislation that governs them and their children?

A different boy would grow up in that world. With males playing a significant role in raising children, boys would have the opportunity to learn to be nurturing, caring, compassionate, empathetic, and understanding. These would not be considered stereotypical female qualities because they would be fathers' traits as well as mothers'. Though it is a fear that if men nurture they would do so at the risk of losing their stereotypical male characteristics, there is nothing to say that this would be so, though that would not be disastrous if it happened. In fact, in a recent study of father-raised children, most said their fathers were not only good mothers, but also had the characteristically masculine personality traits as well.

Some have asked, "How can men raise children when they are lacking in empathy and nurturing skills?" The answer to that question is, "The job makes the man." What man, no matter how hard-crusted, can hold a newborn infant in his arms, knowing he is responsible for that baby's life, without softening, without wanting to keep it warm and fed? There is no training for fatherhood, but then there is none for motherhood, either. We all learned from the first child on.

At the idea of raising boys differently, some say, "We'd be raising a nation of wimps. Other countries would conquer us." Just because a man is kind, caring, and does not lose his temper when he doesn't get what he wants, doesn't mean he couldn't defend his country.

In the musical *My Fair Lady*, Henry Higgins sings the song, "Why Can't a Woman Be More Like a Man?" To reverse that, if men could be more like women, a thought that no doubt repels men, they would be empathetic and be more apt to see human beings as people with human needs and less apt to see them as those with whom they must compete. They would learn to listen, to negotiate, and not to hit first. They would know that conquering territory is not as important as taking care of the people within the territory they now have.

REDUCING MEDIA VIOLENCE

The screenwriter for the movie *GoodFellas* summed up the trend of TV and movies to display untold amounts of violence. "There are, of necessity, lots of murders, but the violence isn't too graphic." Is there such a thing as a nongraphic murder? And the director of the movie *Casualties of War* was quoted in *New York Woman* magazine saying, "When people talk about violence in cinema, it's like talking about cheese on pasta. It sorta comes with the dish and that's what makes the dish."

There is in this country an insatiable appetite for violence in films, TV, and rap and rock music. Most of that entertainment is written by men, produced by men, acted by men, sung by men, and is about men and things that are important to men. One has only to look at the list of movies playing in their town, or a list of the TV shows for the week, to see that movie and TV watching is man-watching, with a sprinkling of women thrown in in minor roles. Even the news reports are mostly about men, with women peripheral to the main action. And what are all these men doing? Committing violence.

Violence is applauded also in the huge salaries paid to actors who portray the "winners" in these violent movies. Arnold Schwarzenegger's salary for *Terminator 2: Judgment Day* was $15 million. Total costs for that movie were listed at $94 million. This is a movie where the robot, played by Schwarzenegger, is told by a child he cannot go around killing people. Because he is an obedient robot he, henceforth, only shoots people in the leg, policemen included, or anyone else who gets in his way. The audience laughs as the victims go hobbling off. *Terminator 2*, the most expensive film ever made, is said to be a movie of violence for the sake of violence.

Compare these films of men creating violence with the film *Thelma and Louise*, where women murder a rapist, blow up a truck, rob a store, and lock a policeman in the trunk of his car. This film was criticized as "toxic feminism." "Women," the critics said, "should be role models in movies. Thelma and Louise were not good role models for other women." One needs to ask why men in movies aren't being criticized as bad role models.

Authors are also doing their part to whet the appetite for violence. What are the lessons to be learned from books like James Ellroy's *The Big Nowhere*, where the victims' eyes are poked out and their genitals mutilated? Stephen King, whose novels about violence are eagerly sought by the movie industry, says he "gets off" on make-believe violence. He explains that as long as violence in the world is seen as a solution to problems, the world will enjoy make-believe violence. Interesting that he says he "gets off." Interesting, too, that Stephen King uses the word "diet," similar to the previous referral to violence as a "dish" to be served to the public. Martin Scorsese, the director of *GoodFellas,* says, "I come out of *Alien* and *The Texas Chainsaw Massacre* refreshed. Movies can provide catharsis." Like an orgasm? As mentioned before, many men tend to relate violence with sex.

Music plays its part in promoting attitudes about how to treat women. "Gangsta rap" music, which often refers to women as bitches and whores, was recently criticized by the president of the National Political Congress of Black Women, C. Delores Tucker, in the April 1994 issue of the *National NOW Times*: "Our nation will not endure as a democracy if we permit the continuation of an art form that teaches children that rape, hate and disrespect are okay, threatens the safety of our communities and ensures that this nation remains the most violent nation in the world."

The boy, having learned violence in his early years watching TV cartoons, followed by later years at the movies, is not immune to violence. By the time he is sixteen he will have seen at least 200,000 acts of violence committed by men. His sisters may have seen all this violence as well, but because the violence is committed by men, the girls do not relate to it as something they would do. The movies are telling boys, "This is the way men act." Of course the boy knows the violence is only fiction; nevertheless the brain takes it all in and gives him permission to practice what he has learned, should he later want to vent his anger for his immediate gratification.

The barrage of daily violence not only teaches boys what men do, or can do, it also teachers girls to expect that men act violently and that women might be victims of this violence. Destroying women is a general theme in the media. Consider the words from the Ghetto Boys' song "Kind of a Lunatic," which tell of a girl begging the man not to kill her. He gives her a rose and in spite of her pleading he slits her throat anyway, and then has sex with her corpse.

Just as the frequent use of pornography can lead to violent crime against women, as claimed by convicted sex criminals, so can frequent viewing of entertainment violence lead to violent actions. Entertainment violence minimizes the value of human life. The theater crowd applauds as the bad guys are gunned down, teaching that violence is the way to get rid of a bad situation. Said to be a catharsis, violence in films is preliminary to teaching that war is the solution to international problems.

What can be done? In the face of critics who would call for First Amendment rights and scream that any curtailment violates their right to free speech, the national crime crisis would indicate that some action should be taken to regulate the amount of entertainment violence. If, as the director of *Casualties of War* said, violence in cinema "makes the dish," then this country needs to find another national dish.

REDUCING GUN ACCESSIBILITY

Of the nearly 24,000 people murdered in this country in 1993 by guns, 82 percent were killed by handguns, which are easily available and difficult to trace. This is an increase of 24 percent over the five-year average as reported by the U.S. Department of Justice, May 1994. In California alone, 5,000 guns are sold each month.

Today there are approximately 214 million guns in the hands of private citizens, almost one for every man, woman, and child in the United States. If guns made us safer, the United States would be the safest country in the world, but the opposite is true. One-half of homicides occur between friends and family members, with a 43:1 chance that a gun in the home will kill a family member rather than an intruder, according to *The New England Journal of Medicine*. The gun is "the weapon of choice" to use in an argument or for any other reason.

The Saturday Night Special is the specific weapon of choice for murder because it is cheap, about $59, and easy to conceal. There are 600,000 manufactured in the United States each year.

Enacting gun-control laws has been an uphill battle against the wealthiest lobby in Washington, D.C., the National Rifle Association, which calls on the Second Amendment right to bear arms. Written during the Revolutionary era, the Amendment sought to protect citizens from what might become an overmilitarized government. Still fearful of what had happened during the colonial era, citizens wanted to guarantee that their countrymen could stand ready to defend their new hard-fought freedom.

If guns were taken from ordinary citizens, a government could reduce this new country once again to totalitarian rule. That is not the threat the NRA relies on now to sustain the proliferation of guns. Now the NRA refers to a man's right to keep a gun for hunting purposes, an argument that is not under contention.

Even when there is an outcry against the extensive use of automatic weapons by citizens, the NRA refers again to the right to keep guns for sporting reasons. But who would shoot a deer with an AK-47, or want to eat such bullet-riddled meat? Automatic weapons are made for wars against organized armies, not for wars in the streets.

The Brady Bill, so named for James Brady, who was permanently paralyzed by a bullet intended for President Reagan, requires a waiting period before a handgun could be purchased from a gun store. The bill permits, but does not require, state and local governments to obtain background checks on would-be purchasers in an attempt to keep guns out of hands of convicted felons and mentally unbalanced persons. However, in a Tulane University study it was learned that approximately 83 percent of convicted felons had purchased their guns on the black market and not through a gun dealership.

Efforts to ban handguns in Kenosha and Milwaukee, Wisconsin, during the November 1994 election were defeated, but a nonbinding referendum banning handguns passed in the city of Shorewood, Wisconsin. This is the first time such proposed legislation has been put before the voting public.

THE CRIME BILL

While people in this country consider crime a major problem, passing a crime bill in Congress took three years. Republicans and Democrats differ about where to spend fedreal money. Republicans generally want money to go toward building more prisons and putting more police on the streets, while Democrats lean more toward reducing prison sentneces for drug users, thereby getting nonviolent prisoners out of prison sooner to make room for violent offenders, and supporting crime-prevention programs, such as midnight basketball, aimed at keeping young men off the streets.

In Congress's contentious debate, preventative programs were labeled "pork," meaning they were providing money for legislators' districts and were said to be ineffectual in reducing crime.

A compromise was reached with the passage of a six-year, $30.2 billion bill signed by President Clinton in September 1994. Its main provisions include a Three Strikes element, a gun ban on twenty-nine assault weapons, more than $10 billion for hiring police, and $9.7 billion for prisons. For crime-prevention programs there is $6.9 billion.

THE CRIMINAL GENDER

The question of how responsible noncriminal men are for the horrendous amount of male violence and other crime can be equated with the question often asked after World War II, "How responsible was the rest of the world for the murder of six million Jews?"

Most men would answer the first question with, "I don't rape women, don't participate in drive-by shootings, don't

murder, don't drive drunk, don't commit arson, don't bilk people out of their life savings, and I'm not responsible for men
who do." But the response to that answer would be, "Maybe
you don't batter women, but your brothers do. Even if you
don't commit serial or mass murder, your brothers do. Maybe
you're not a drunk driver, but your brothers are. Your brothers
are murderers, stock market manipulators, gang rapists, robbers, arsonists, litterers, polluters and child abusers. Your
brothers are killing us."

Would that strike a responsive or responsible chord?
Probably not. Men are not their brothers' keepers. Except in
male-bonding groups, men are not connected to one another
emotionally in the same way women are. Women come quietly forward to protect each other from violent men. They
establish rape hot lines and support groups for traumatized
victims and set up battered women's shelters to help the
four million women battered each year, one million of whom
require hospitalization. (A battered men's shelter is not even
imaginable.)

We cannot expect men to police their own, to take responsibility for their contribution to the violence in this country,
especially at a time when the Macho Man has made his come-
back. With the Gulf War remasculinizing the country, expect-
ing men to turn from the power domain to thoughtful questioning of national priorities is wishful thinking. The sensitive
man of the 1960s is passé. And as joyful and novel as it would
be for men to say, "Yes, I'll take a fifty percent part in raising
my children from infancy," and for all the value that would be
derived from that change of attitude, it is folly to believe it
would happen. This country cannot count on its men to rectify
its violent nature. They are too much a part of it. So what is
left? Besides building prisons and increasing incarceration,
what is left? Nothing short of men paying for their own criminal gender. To ask such a thing would be a wake-up call for all
men to realize what their gender is perpetrating on society.

Gender Equity in Taxation

Half of the taxpayers in this country are women, but men commit most of the crime. Many women pay for male crime with their lives, but all women taxpayers pay for male crime with their tax dollars. True, not all men are criminals, but almost all criminals are men.

The concept of one group paying more for the services offered for a larger group is not new. Insurance companies in many states require young men sixteen to twenty-six to pay more for car insurance than women of those ages and more than other age groups because males in this age group cause most car accidents. Not all males sixteen to twenty-six cause accidents, but all men in that group pay the higher fee.

As for a fee on men for crime, it could be called a "user fee" since men are using the criminal justice system almost exclusively. Just walk the halls of any courthouse and notice who's being tried, or simply turn on the TV to see who's being arrested.

Some will say that women are committing crimes but are not being arrested because police and judges go easy on women. Not so. Many police and judges today are women, and female criminals are being sentenced today in cases where they previously received probation.

The suggestion for the tax equity would be a $100 user fee added to men's IRS returns at the time of filing a return. Of course, there will be screaming and hollering about such a fee, but one might ask, is $100 a year too much to ask to help curtail crime? What would a man pay?

And how would the money be spent? It could be used to identify boys in primary grades who are not learning to read and who come from violent homes, an often deadly combination. Every child needs school success. If he fails, he will feel unworthy and may need to develop a false bravado. Money from this "user fee" from the gender dominating the criminal justice system could be used for intensive tutoring and for family counseling.

Money could also be used to teach reading in prison. Most prisoners have not graduated from high school and return to society unable to make a living, or even to cope.

If men would recognize that crime is a male statement for which males pay more than females, there is a possibility they might help to "clean up their act." It can be said that women are expensive as well, since teenage pregnancy swells the welfare rolls, and welfare in general is paid more to women than to men. But if men would pay child support for the children they father, welfare rolls would shrink.

The best thing this country can do is to ensure that its children get medical attention and educational opportunities. The costs of paying welfare money for the good of children cannot be compared with costs of imprisoning murderers.

Men are expensive. Their crimes cost this country upward of $61 billion each year in incarceration and judicial costs alone. This figure does not include the cost of the S&L scandal nor the costs of toxic waste cleanup. In addition, millions of men do not support the children they have fathered, leaving this up to mothers or taxpayers or both. Millions of men beat their wives, creating the need for battered women's shelters. Millions sexually abuse children. Drunk drivers and arsonists kill people as surely as the murderers do. The fastest growing crime of rape terrifies half the population of this country. The greatest environmental offender in the country is the government, which is run by men. Male corporate executives and military officers who have dumped toxic waste into the ground or into the air are destroying the planet. Hate crimes are encouraged by male organizations, such as the skinheads and the Ku Klux Klan. The greatest financial scandal in U.S. history, the S&L scandal, is the province of men whose crimes will cost taxpayers at least $500 billion. Yet, where is the outrage at all this male crime?

Where are the voices of women? Are we so conciliatory that we will not speak out against this brutality? Will we permit the men to build more and more prisons so that criminals can go in and out the revolving door, gathering members and criminal skills as they go? Or will we call a halt to mother-dominated child care and require that men take their places in civilizing their sons, not in overmasculinizing them, as they have been. Can we call the legislators to attention to seek a more equitable tax structure?

Or will we choose to be forever outsiders?

The Second Question

It has been one thing to question why most crime is committed by men. It is another to question why the crime rate itself, even though currently down 3 percent except for violent crime, has accelerated over the past ten years faster than at any time in this country's history. Repetitious pointing to poverty, unemployment, substandard housing, and inadequate education does not explain the phenomenon. During the Great Depression there was no surge in the crime rate. Today, aside from maleness as a factor in crime, there is something else afoot.

During the Depression, rich and poor alike were victimized by overinvestment in the stock market, which crashed as the country expanded on credit not backed by solid assets. Investors and noninvestors suffered. The stock market failure was an equalizer. People who had lived richly, who counted their wealth by ticker-tape, sold apples in the streets and joined the janitors in the breadlines when they lost it all. Bad as it was, there was a cohesiveness in the despair.

Herbert Hoover, who promised the Depression-weary people "a chicken in every pot" in the 1932 election, was defeated by people who didn't believe him. They chose Franklin Roosevelt instead, who told us we had to face the truth, saying we had "nothing to fear but fear itself." He initiated the social security system, which gave workers confidence that they would not be penniless in their old age. By establishing the Works Progress Administration, which offered government-paid jobs to people who worked on government projects such as repairing and building roads, he "primed the pump of the economy." Wages from those jobs provided purchasing power which in turn created more jobs. And he supported the labor unions in the workers' struggle to gain a living wage.

In the 1940s there was the "good war." When attacked by Japan, we quickly summoned our strength to defend ourselves as a cohesive country. In our outrage at Hitler's rampage over Europe we bought War Bonds to finance the war that defeated him. We had determination, vigor, and self-righteousness. Without bemoaning the great cost, as a country united, we won the war and went on with our lives.

The transition to a peacetime economy initiated a period of prosperity founded on housing needs of new families and the need for automobiles, which replaced army vehicles on the General Motors assembly line. The pent-up demands for new products like dishwashers, refrigerators, and washing machines fueled a demand for blue-collar workers who could hold out for good pay. Veterans used their GI benefits to educate themselves in ways they would not have considered possible before the war. They became doctors, lawyers, and corporate executives, educated at government cost even as their housing needs were also subsidized. All things seemed possible. There was not much wanting.

In 1960 a rich, young president was elected. Possibly concerned that we were getting complacent and too self-centered as a country, John F. Kennedy said, "Ask not what your country can do for you. Ask what you can do for your country." Young people and old heard his call and joined his Peace Corps, traveling to help other people in remote countries of the world. They also joined VISTA, a similar organization, to help people in our own country. Unfortunately, in our effort to stop communism, we became involved in a war in Vietnam that became morally divisive, though not economically so. Except for that "problem over there," we felt okay about ourselves. When Lyndon Johnson took over as president and was able to carry out Kennedy's civil rights platform, minorities and women felt they were finally gathered into the mainstream of the country's operation.

In the 1970s we faced the Pentagon Papers, Watergate, and a realization that our government was not to be trusted. But, as in the Great Depression, we all faced that sense of betrayal—rich and poor alike. We extricated ourselves from the Vietnam War, some with the relief that we were getting out of an area where we had no business in the first place, and some with the humiliation that we hadn't "won." That humiliation would fester and surface in future leaders who would find ways to "win" military skirmishes in later years in Grenada, Panama, and the Persian Gulf.

Confronting the lack of ethics and honesty of the Watergate administration, we elected a morally unblemished Sunday school teacher who brought the question of human rights into the forefront of foreign policy. But Jimmy Carter was considered inept after only one term and was defeated by a perennial optimist who used the fear of communism to build up a war machine unmatched in world history, financing his arsenal by mortgaging this country to the Japanese. Ronald Reagan promised to make us unbeatable, and in that way, he told us, we would feel pride in our country again.

With one purpose in mind, the federal budget was directed toward the Pentagon. Everything else was secondary. Housing subsidies were slashed, creating a class known as "homeless." Old men died in the streets in below-freezing weather. As foreclosures on homes quadrupled in the 1980s, the financially secure absolved themselves of responsibility by saying, "The homeless choose to be homeless," ignoring the fact that the biggest segment of homeless are women and children, most escaping a battering mate. School lunch programs were cut for needy children even to the point where catsup was classified as a vegetable so that real vegetables would not have to be provided. Programs for needy pregnant women were curtailed, increasing the infant mortality rate. Affirmative action gains of the 1970s for minorities and women were cut back. From his ship of state, Reagan cut loose those who could do him no good. He talked about a "safety net" as he eliminated people from food-stamp programs and medical care. He talked about family values as he undercut programs that would help families. Then, in his fervor to "get government off the backs of the people," he deregulated industries, leaving the world of business to do as it wished and "the devil take the foremost."

The gap between the rich and the poor widened. The rich got richer and the poor got poorer and grew in numbers as people in the middle class dropped down to the lower class. The number of people living in poverty rose to a record high. But poverty is no accident. It requires a concerted lack of empathy. Reagan was applauded when inflation cooled, though it occurred because the rising number of jobless could no longer purchase consumer goods. Fearful of Reagan's surging popularity, the media and the Democrats stood by uncritically as he created the largest federal deficit and the largest disenfranchised underclass in our history.

Deregulation of industry set a tone for personal and national greed. The 1980s became known as the "Me Decade." It was everyone out to get what he could. With high-risk, high-yield junk bonds financing corporate takeovers, people who had worked for corporations for many years, executives as well as clerical help, were laid off when new corporate executives took over. Gone was a sense of belonging on the job, replaced by the fear of losing a long-held job on which home mortgage payments depended. Only a few paychecks separated families from the ranks of the homeless. In the meantime, the salaries of corporate presidents rose toward the $5 million-a-year mark, a fact not lost on the newly unemployed. In a two-term presidency, the country became divided between the haves and the growing number of have nots. Crime in every category increased in the 1980s to rates never before known. A quiet bitterness developed as millions of people recognized that they didn't matter.

We hear now that the cause of so much crime is a disregard for human life. That there is no morality anymore. Well, we had a powerful teacher.

The Third Question

The first question was to determine why crime is almost exclusively male and what can be done to change that phenomenon. The second question was to ask why there is a crime wave now. The third question is to ponder, in light of this country's level of crime and violence, what is our hope for the future?

Referred to as a crime wave, the violence is more like a mile-high tidal wave. Male criminals of all colors and stripes, including three-piece pinstripes, blow people apart, undermine financial institutions, and poison the planet. When this tidal wave has spent itself, will our country lay exhausted, its resources depleted, its people weary and spiritless? Will those who are left revitalize a nation that once believed it could control itself? In the midst of this maelstrom, it is difficult to imagine safety and security again. But maybe we could pause here and learn from history. Through the years many historians have studied the Roman Empire in an effort to learn why a civilization that was once so powerful failed, and why civilization picked up again.

The Roman Empire existed for about 700 years, with the Romans conquering most of western Europe and the northern shores of the Mediterranean, creating a prosperous civilization based on slave labor, cunning leadership, good engineering, and stolen resources, eventually overextending its military budget so that there was little money for services for its people.

In the waning years, from about A.D. 200 to 400, as anti-Roman attacks increased, the Romans realized that other people, the Norsemen and the Turks, for instance, had also grown strong. At the same time the Roman ranks in their far-reaching empire were filled with dissention and corruption. In some areas, Roman soldiers joined the locals to fight the Roman army. The superpower of the world had lost its influence in faraway lands, and because of depleted funds, its center collapsed in on itself.

Northern tribesmen nipped at the fringes of the Roman Empire, gaining ground, plundering, and inching south over a period of many years. Even as these so-called barbarian tribesmen—the Jutes, the Goths, and the Visigoths—advanced toward Rome, the Roman emperors, each in his time, kept up the appearance of optimism. They whipped up circuses and, realizing that all they had left of their empire was a show of military strength, welcomed returning soldiers with parades that lasted longer than their military skirmishes. But the people knew in their hearts that hope for the empire's future and confidence in their leaders were gone.

To camouflage their soul-sickness, the Romans wallowed in debauchery, watching the multiple slaughter of humans and exotic African wild animals in public amphitheaters. It was a long, dying gasp. The great Roman Empire, which had created a system of exemplary law codes, interconnecting stone highways and aqueducts throughout their world, was dead.

Recognizing death when they saw it and wanting to rescue at least some of the great learning of classical Egypt, Greece, and Rome from the burning and looting of the conquering tribes, a small band of scholarly monks, with a few armloads of manuscripts, slipped out of the Mediterranean and sailed to a lonely cliff-dwelling in Cork, Ireland. There, in their hovels by candlelight, they set about the business of copying and recopying the ancient writings of the playwrights, the jurists, the philosophers, and the scientists, writings they had brought with them so that learning would not also die. With the help of those scholars, knowledge secured a foothold and hung on in the fog-shrouded monasteries of Ireland as the Dark Ages descended over Europe.

For a thousand years civilization lay virtually dormant. Whole towns were decimated by armies that had crossed and recrossed their streets and were later made ghostlike by the infected fleas that brought the Black Plague. A few survivors built forts and castles to protect their own people from wandering thieves. Sometimes these "noblemen," as they called themselves, gave peasants protection within their castle walls and sometimes they did not. For most it was everyone for himself.

Without a worry about possible punishment, which hardly existed, rogues wandered the land, stealing what they wanted, and murdering if that was what it would take to get something—for instance, another man's jacket. One's life was constantly in jeopardy. There was no sense of a future. No assurance that what a peasant planted on a plot of land one week would not be trampled on by the next week. There was little hope, and no confidence that tomorrow would be better.

Yet things did get better. Hope and confidence in the future were eventually restored by the unlikely catalyst of the Crusades, which were started by one pope after another to send thousands of pilgrims across Europe to rescue the Holy Land from the Turks and Arabs. The Crusades did not achieve their purpose, but they did start a flow of commerce, new information, and artifacts from eastern to western Europe.

Most of the Crusades passed through Florence, Italy, and it was there that a new confidence emerged. Florentine men traded with returning crusaders for silks, spices, and vases. These tradesmen became wealthy, and, wanting to leave mementos of themselves for posterity, they commissioned artists to paint their portraits and to carve elaborate tombs for themselves out of Italian marble. Biblical statues were erected in town plazas for the citizens to appreciate. There was an awakening to the beauty of sculpture and, because of the exposure of many pilgrims to Oriental art and scholarship, a yearning to learn more about other lands and other ideas.

Explorers such as Columbus and Magellan set out to discover the unknown world. And with the help of the monks' copied manuscripts, which had found their way from Ireland to the far reaches of western Europe, fledgling scholars reached back a thousand years to antiquity to study those copied writings. It was the rebirth of the learning of antiquity. It was the Renaissance. A spiritual reawakening to beauty and knowledge combined with a new confidence in the future. It is what brought western Europe out of its Dark Ages and onto its feet again.

It is what is needed here and now, even before the tidal wave finishes its roll.

As the world around us erupts in a jigsaw puzzle of tribal, ethnic, and religious wars, genocide and mass slaughter in Rwanda and Bosnia, and democracies in Third World countries hanging on only by a slim thread, we can see that we are losing our influence around the world, just as we can see that we are losing control of our own country. As our jobs and money go overseas, we have little confidence in our leaders and less hope in our nation's future. We are all in harm's way, with an unprecedented violent crime wave. Our lives are not safe in our own homes or on the streets, and our money is not safe in the banks. We have a deadly medical epidemic with 50,000 new untreatable cases each year that is causing great suffering, anxiety, financial upheaval, and political wrangling. Can we wrest a Renaissance from this brink of despair, or do we need to sink into our own Dark Ages?

Can we shuck our adolescence and come of age to face the truth that our country is failing its purpose? Can we resurrect our original spirit? Cleanse our soul? Recreate the myth on which this country began? We were not founded on a principle to dominate the world, to be the most powerful. We do not need a trillion-dollar debt that impoverishes our schools, closing classes in music, art, poetry, drama, philosophy, and other so-called frills. What we need *are* those classes.

Plato said that of all the subjects a student should study, he would consider music to be the most important because it tunes the soul correctly. The Golden Age of Greece, about 500 B.C., flourished in large part because the government was totally involved in sponsoring the arts for beautification of its country and for the enrichment of its citizens.

President John F. Kennedy told us the arts were important and urged us to pay attention to them. They are, he said, interpreting for us what our country is doing. Maybe it was more his wife's doing than his, but creative artists of the Kennedy period were honored by invitations to the White House—people such as the renowned cellist, Pablo Cassals, and the great man of Southern literature, William Faulkner.

The creative arts are feared by repressive governments. In order for a military coup d'état to succeed, the dictator must silence the voices of the people. What are the voices of the people? They are the poems, the songs, the paintings, the novels. The fact that these voices must be silenced is proof that rulers recognize their power.

The arts make it possible to transcend one's condition and to aspire to limitless heights. Philosophy presents the great questions that have forever confronted humans. All children, including ghetto children, or maybe especially ghetto children, need the fine arts as much as anything else in their curriculum. We have seen that it doesn't matter if a child can read and write and do his fractions if he has no sense of morality and can't reason ethically. If one has no experience with profound questions, how does one answer such questions as, "How should a person use power?" "What does one human owe another?" "What are love, responsibility, courage?"

At this point the question might occur, "Is all that's needed to stop crime is to bring fathers into the nurturing process and to teach fine arts and philosophy?" The answer to that would be, "No, there's more. We need to do a turnaround on how we raise boys. We need to permit them to express their feelings. We need to quit rejecting their emotional needs. We need to identify those who need help and provide it. And, yes, we need to change the curriculum and we need to get started. We're runnng out of time. If we can open up our schools to a broader curriculum, we may be able to close our prisons."

But as fine arts are considered stereotypically feminine, and our society has needed to expunge that which is considered feminine from its males, there would be the criticism that we would be raising sissies. If Corregio, Titian, Brunelleschi, Michelangelo, Mozart, Verdi, or Stravinsky would be considered "sissies," then so be it. The world is better for their having been so.

If we were to raise boys who could appreciate classical music, and boys who could tour an art gallery and experience a sense of aesthetic or spiritual nourishment from the paintings, and be challenged intellectually and morally by the age-old philosophies of the right and wrong way to treat other human beings, then if these would be sissies, aren't sissies better than murderers?

We're talking here about helping boys value and develop the feminine side of their personalities. We're not talking about women, though women are more likely to project the characteristics of the feminine principle. These are the stereotypically feminine traits such as creativity, sensitivity, empathy, listening, and nurturing. The healthy, androgynous personality, male and female, encompasses these feminine characteristics as well as masculine characteristics.

Even with the above explanation, there will be those who will remind us that women have ruled countries and they will point to England and Israel. But Margaret Thatcher, known as "The Iron Lady," and Golda Meier ruled predominantly by the masculine principle. Remember, we are not talking about women. This is about the feminine principle.

The masculine world fears the feminine side of itself. It is ever fearful that one will "lose face" if mistakes, failures, or weaknesses are admitted. Though the masculine principle has good stereotypical masculine characteristics such as responsibility, courage, and competition, it often overextends its masculine side in order to "get the better of" the next person, the next corporation, the next country. It sends men steeped in the masculine principle around the world on peace missions that actually require the feminine characteristics of listening, negotiating, and compromising.

In these dangerous times of violence, of drugs and financial scandals, all threatening our governmental underpinnings, there are lessons to be learned and sides to be taken. We can either continue running and ruining our country, guided by the masculine principle, or permit the feminine principle to participate.

It is not being suggested here that men move over and women take over. As pointed out with the example of Margaret Thatcher and Golda Meier, there is no guarantee that women will run things guided by the feminine principle. Many women are very "macho," especially when they achieve power. Sensitive rulers, whether they are women or men, are guided by compassion for others, by noncompetitive methods for achieving goals, and by a desire to ensure everyone's well-being.

Men in history who have permitted the feminine side of their personality to participate along with the masculine side, have changed the world for the better. The writings of John Locke, who, in the seventeenth century, was the first person to write effectively about the rights of the common man—the peasant, the servant, the coal miner, unheard of in the era of monarchies when kings had life and death power over all their subjects—changed governments from monarchies to democracies. His words are written into our Declaration of Independence. His logical reasoning, a stereotypically masculine trait, brought him to the conclusion that even the poorest man had rights. "No one ought to harm another" represents a stereotypically feminine trait of caring about others. Yes, men, too, care about others, but typically this is considered a feminine trait.

Mahatma Gandhi used nonviolent protests against England, then the most powerful country in the world. He combined determination and responsibility, which are known as masculine characteristics, with the feminine characteristics of negotiation and patience, to lead his people to their own freedom. Jesus of Nazareth led his people with courage and righteousness, combined with verbal persuasion and by appealing to love. It is ironic that when our militant leaders embark on war, they pray to this Prince of Peace.

The pages of this book tell the story of a country losing its sense of self. Nothing the government is doing is working. Even as law enforcement tightens the screws on criminals, crime increases. In a country sick from crime, deficit spending, and lack of empathy at the top, the prognosis is negative. The crime wave is a massive temper tantrum, like a child crying for help. We know in our hearts our country's future is at stake and we have lost confidence in our leaders, who overextend military and prison budgets as they cut funds for education and research.

Education is our lifeline to the future. But the wave rolls on:

Two youths and two men were apprehended June 10, 1994, for theft of computer parts in Fremont, California. Accused of loading $100,000 worth of parts onto a rented truck, Sambath Sam Van and Khamtanh Inboya, each twenty years old, and two seventeen-year-olds were arrested after a police highway chase.

A gunman opened fire with an AK-47 in an army hospital in Spokane, Washington, killing four and injuring nineteen on June 10, 1994, before he was shot dead by a military policeman.

In Edison, New Jersey, John Arias was arrested for allegedly shooting his twenty-year-old ex-girlfriend and killing his ex-girlfriend's mother after barricading himself in their home and holding them hostage for twenty-four hours. The suspect eventually surrendered after police drove an armored vehicle up and down the street.

Et cetera.

Et cetera . . .